Grant Thorburn

aged 79

LIFE

AND

WRITINGS

OF

GRANT THORBURN:

PREPARED BY HIMSELF.

NEW YORK:
EDWARD WALKER,
114 FULTON-STREET.
1852.

PUBLISHER'S NOTICE.

It is with sincere pleasure I present this volume to the public, believing its perusal cannot fail of proving eminently interesting and instructive; while as an illustration of Divine Providence in human affairs, it will be regarded as strikingly peculiar and impressive. As an autobiography, it is full of incident, and its details are presented in a simple and lucid style, which invests the narrative with great attractive interest. One feature which characterizes the present work, and which is indeed its great charm, is the prevailing tendency of its author to recognize in the various vicissitudes of life, the indications of Divine Providence. The portraiture of a man's life whose aims and actions are governed by Christian principles, while it presents a noble example for imitation, enlists the sympathies, and exerts a powerful influence on the heart of the reader. It is true there is little of heroism in the simple narrative of the Life of Mr. Grant Thorburn, but there is much of moral greatness evinced in his persevering adherence to principle, and much of true nobility of character in his successful triumphs over adverse circumstances. The political prowess of the statesman, and the military renown of the chieftain, sink into comparative insignificance when once compared with the simple story of a life consecrated to the cause of truth. The life of such a man is a benison to his race, and its memorial

Smells sweet and blossoms in the dust.

CONTENTS.

CHAPTER VI.

CHAPTER VII.

CHAPTER VIII.

CHAPTER IX.

CHAPTER X.

CHAPTER XI.

CHAPTER XII.

CHAPTER XIII.

CHAPTER XIV.

CHAPTER XV.

CHAPTER XVI.

CHAPTER XVII.

CHAPTER XVIII.

CHAPTER XIX.

WORDS INTRODUCTORY.

I HAVE thought it the duty of every member of the body politic to do all in his power to promote the well-being of those among whom he lives, moves, and has his being; I have thought, too, it is the duty of the elder to hand down to the younger generation the amount of their experience, that thereby they may see and avoid the rocks on which they have split. I also think that many of the sober realities in my life are so checkered with the appearance of romance and fiction, that if put on record fifty years hence, some facts, which now speak for themselves, might then appear like fiction. For instance, if I live to see the eighteenth day of February next, I will then enter on my eightieth year. Now, my health is as good, my personal feelings as comfortable, mind, memory, and hearing as clear as when in my twenty-fifth year; and I verily believe I can walk as far and as fast as at any former period of my life. Now, if any doubt this fact, they may come and see me. Does any ask, And how do you live? I answer: I never was once drunk in my life, and I never eat over enough—eating too hearty only makes work for the doctor and the grave-digger. Besides, as I have drank so much more deep in the cup of pleasure than from the cup of pain, I think it is a debt I owe to the Giver of all Good that the world should know it; my crosses were merely sufficient to give a double relish to the pleasures which followed.

As so many extracts and mutilated parts of my history (mixed with fiction) have appeared in Galt's Laurie Todd, in magazines, reviews, and criticisms, I think I owe it to the public, and to myself, to give a plain, unvarnished statement of facts.

My long and checkered life is summed up in two or three sections. I have made two fortunes and lost them (and that is more than most men can boast of), but it was neither by speculation, gambling, laziness, nor riotous living of myself or children, but merely by the act of God (as the Coroner denominates his dead subject); therefore, it never lost me an hour's sleep. The revolving machinery which produced these results will form matter for a dozen chapters. These few remarks may suffice as a preface, or an introduction, or call it what you please, to the forthcoming story. I would merely remark, in conclusion, I am now in the full tide of successful experiment (as friend Jefferson said of our model republic fifty years ago); by the good wishes of kind friends, I have got a job in Uncle Sam's workshop. My *renovated* body is *competent* for the duties of my office, and, thank God, I can live by head and hand-work, though now nearly fourscore. Much rather would I work for nothing, and find myself, than be paid for sitting idle, and be fed sumptuously every day.

NEW YORK, *October 1st*, 1851.

LIFE AND WRITINGS

OF

GRANT THORBURN.

CHAPTER I.

WHERE AND WHEN I WAS BORN.—EARLY IMPRESSIONS.—MOTHER'S DEATH, AND MOTHER'S GRAVE.—THE HEART-BURN.—MY FALL.—MOTHER-WIT.—GIPSEY.—THE DUKE'S PARTY.

MY life has been a series of so many strange occurrences, that when I look back it seems as if I had been a mere machine, without any will of my own. I was born in Dalkeith, near Edinburgh, on the eighteenth day of February, 1773. My father was poor (some are cursed with rich fathers)—honest and industrious, and by trade a wrought-nail maker.* He was a very strict Scotch Presbyterian, a Covenanter, and, like his neighbor and prototype, Davie, the father of Jenny Deans—*an honest man!* Our cottage stood within two miles of Davie Deans' farm, and within three of the Laird of Dumbiedike's mansion. Those who have read Scott's novel, "The Heart of Mid-Lothian," one of his best productions, will understand what I mean.

The first scene impressed on my memory was the death of my mother. I was two years and six months old at the time; I remember nothing of her caresses, countenance, or person. I remember nothing of her funeral; I only remember I saw her gentle bosom *heave its last sigh.* Sixty-two years thereafter, I stood at the foot of her *undisturbed grave,* in the lonely church-yard of a solitary glen in Scotland, and there I communed with her ransomed spirit; for she lived the life of the righteous, and her latter end was like his.

I was neglected and ill-treated by my father's housekeeper, in consequence of which I lost the use of my limbs, and not having exercise, I became weak and sickly; and when in my tenth year I was not as large as most children are at five. But in this, as in all which to me seemed troubles and misfortunes at the time, they were only blessings in disguise. For instance, in my father's family for generations past, was an hereditary disease, termed, in Scotland, the *heart-burn*—a sore evil under the sun. I, only, of all the family, never felt its effects. I have thought that the extraordinary cures employed to keep my feeble frame and soul together was the means of eradicating the disease. I also think it gave me, as it were, a new constitution; for, during the fifty-six years I have lived in New York, I was only *one day* confined to my house by sickness. In this period the yellow fever prevailed seventeen summers, and the cholera three, but I never left the city yet. Neither I, my wife, nor any of my children, were ever visited by any of these plagues. To be sure, one day in 1798—it was on the twenty-second of September—Death on the Pale Horse stood for a moment and stopped *pawing* in front of my door, but, seeing the mark of protection on the door-posts and lintels, he *did not enter*. He in the same hour entered (the door being open) the second house from mine. Here he struck his dart in the heart of Dr. Dangly, an eminent physician, and, that night, he slept with his fathers.

Now, was I not in duty bound to observe the Thanksgiving day on the 12th of December? I was; and to keep a Thanksgiving in my heart all the days of my life.

I return to my seventh year. Being unable to walk, I sat on a low bench by the chimney-corner—a small, insignificant remnant of mortality: here I saw and learned much of human nature, and somewhat of *Mother-Wit*—a commodity which I have found useful on many occasions. My elders never thought that the mind grows faster in the dwarf than in the giant; and these children of a larger growth (thinking I had lost my eyes and my ears as well as my feet) played "such fantastic tricks before high heaven as made the angels weep." People are apt to forget that children can see and reason before they can speak. Suffice it to say, that long before I knew my A B C, I had learned the whole mystery of "*nipping and scarting*"—*Scotch folk's wooing*. (Anglais: pinching and scratching, a Scotch mode of courting.)

In my eighth year, the doctors having emptied their boxes of pills and vials of elixirs in vain attempts to strengthen my feeble frame, a *Gipsey* one day entered our dwelling, requesting something to eat (a request never denied by even the poorest in Scotland). She was a comely matron, with a Bible in her arms, and might have seen thirty summers. Having eaten her food with a merry heart, and when about to depart, my figure drew her attention, as I sat by the fire. She examined my palm, predicting good luck, and advised my father to have me transported to the top of the Roman Camp—an exceedingly high mountain near by, and so called from the fact that Julius Cæsar pitched his tents there. I was lodged in a thatched cottage on the top of this hill, and was sent out every evening after sundown to gather half a pint of *small shell snails*, which abound on that hill, and who leave their caverns at sunset to feast on the dews of the night. They were cleansed with water from the spring, and next morning boiled with three pints of milk, *fresh* from the cow; this, with oatmeal porridge, was my food, morning, noon, and night. It was very palatable.

I now grew (under this Gipsey's prescription), if not in stature, in health, strength, and spirits, and what I lost in height I gained in ambition. The taunts of the *wee bodie* from my companions at play or at school, fired my soul to equal or surpass the oldest and tallest among them, and in this I generally succeeded.

I remember a trifle which occurred in my fourteenth year, on which I still look back with fear and trembling. On that day the eldest son of the Duke of Buccleugh had completed his twenty-first year, and notice was given that the gates would be opened for an hour to admit the inhabitants of the village (Dalkeith) to see the fun. I was detained, and just as I arrived the gate was shut. I thought of the five foolish virgins; soon a dozen more disappointed ones arrived; we were all in the same predicament. A council was held, and I proposed to scale the walls—some hundred feet from the gate—it being the most accessible point, and it was some ten feet high, with a stone fence plastered outside, and as smooth as glass. Arriving at the spot, the hearts of my companions failed; none would take the dangerous leap. (Most of them were ten years older, and some were two feet taller.) I said I would go alone. Two of the strongest raised me on the shoulders of two of the tallest; I clutched the top-stone, and drew myself up. I now bethought me of the dangers which beset my path—spring-guns and man-traps for poachers, were strewed as thick as leaves in autumn—to advance might be death; to retreat and be laughed at, I thought (for a moment) would be as bad; so I dropped at once, and lit on a mountain of dry leaves which the winter winds had blown in the ditch, inside of the stone dyke. Being light, I bounced up like a cork, and, guided by the light of the fire-works, I ran through trees, spring-guns and man-traps, reaching the goal in safety.

Thank God, who, despite my *mad-folly*, preserved my thoughtless steps. The present Duke is the eldest son of him who that day came of age. On a visit to my father in 1834, he sent me a note, wishing to see me at the palace next day, at eleven o'clock, A. M. The Duke, Duchess, and myself, spent a pleasant hour together, reviewing "*The days o' auld lang syne.*"

CHAPTER II.

OCEAN VOYAGE.—ARRIVAL IN NEW YORK.—FIRST NIGHT ON SHORE.—MY BIBLE.—GOING TO WORK.—I SEE A MAIDEN.

WHEN contemplating a voyage across the Atlantic, the thought of being three months idle was a terror to my mind. However, I soon found employment enough. Having been four days out, and got over the sea-sickness, we began to think about something to eat. The captain, with the list of steerage passengers in his hand, called over the roll, and every seventh man was selected as head of the mess. His duties were, to receive from the mate, on Monday morning, the biscuit for the week, and divide it in seven equal shares, giving to every man his due; and to receive daily from the cook the boiled beef and potatoes for dinner, for himself and mess. I was a seventh on the list, and thus I had something to do, besides assisting the cook in the caboose and the steward in the cabin, by which I lived sumptuously every day, dining on roast pig and fowls with these two worthy subordinates, while my fellow-passengers in the steerage were chewing junk beef and hard biscuit. Thus time passed pleasantly.

On the 16th of June, we came to anchor in the East River. New York made a sorry appearance in those days: the stores were all frame buildings, covered with shingles, one only excepted; it was owned by Governeur and Kimble, and was built of brick. The city contained about sixty thousand inhabitants. Three steeples were all that could be seen from the water, viz., Old Trinity, the Middle Dutch (now the Post-Office), and St. George's Chapel, in Beekman street: St. Paul's was just being erected, that summer. They gave him a new outside coat, lately, but his inner man, or heavy timbers, were set up in 1794. The old City Hotel was building at the same time, and was the first roof covered with slates in America.

My first night on shore was passed at No. 8 Dutch street (now Colgate's factory). It was a small frame building, with a miserable, low-roofed garret, covered with shingles. It was a hot night (17th of June), the garret was alive with fleas, flies, bugs, and musquitoes, and I could not sleep. Midnight commenced with a tremendous storm; the thunder rolled, the winds blew, and the rain beat on that roof; and as my head lay within eighteen inches of the shingles, and it was the first time I had heard rain fall on a shingle roof, I knew not what it meant. Such blazing of lightning, such rattling of thunder, as I had never heard in Scotland! I thought heaven and earth were contending, and I lay there in great bodily fear, and wished myself at home again.

In fifty minutes this war of the elements had ceased; but fear had driven sleep from mine eyes. I arose at daylight, sore in person and depressed in spirits, with a headache to crown the whole. Not liking to disturb the family at an hour so early, and to pass away the time, I unpacked my box of books, not with the intention of reading, but to see their condition and give them the air; for they had been thirteen weeks in the hold of the vessel, and I opened them merely to see if the paper was mildewed by long and damp confinement. I happened to take a small pocket Bible which had been placed on the top by the hand of my pious father. I was thinking of him who placed this best of books where it must draw my first attention, when mine eye lit on the words, "My son." I fancied my father spoke. I read on, more and more interested by every verse, till I came to the end. On looking up, I found I had been reading the third chapter of Proverbs.

Now, reader, take up your Bible, and imagine yourself in my situation, a boy of twenty, yet a child in appearance, and, as regards men and manners, a babe; for never, till our ship weighed anchor, had I been twenty miles from the cottage of my birth, without a friend to counsel or direct, and here I was, with funds reduced to three English coppers; but happily, I was engaged to work. I presume you have read the chapter. I know not what you think, but I thought, had a scroll, written within and without, been blown from the clouds, through the open garret bedroom, containing the words of that chapter, I could not more have looked on it as an immediate message from heaven. Be this as it may, it revived my sinking soul, drove pain from my bones, and the aching from my head. I grasped my hammer and went forth with a light heart to commence a new career, resolving to take the Bible for my pilot, and this chapter for my chart. My hand now rests on this self-same little Bible from whence I read this my first chapter in America. On the second day after landing, I went to work. Blowing up the fire with the bellows, and hammering red-hot iron, during that hot weather, I thought was more than flesh and blood could endure. I therefore resolved that, as soon as I could save money enough to pay my passage, I would return to Scotland. You will see, in the sequel, that the plan I was following to take me out of the country was the means which Providence employed to keep me in it.

One morning, about four o'clock (as I was paid by the hour, I rose thus early that I might the sooner earn my passage-money), while crossing Broadway at a quick pace, on my way to the workshop, I perceived a young woman coming along in the opposite direction. We met at the corner of Liberty-street and Broadway. She turned the corner, and pursued her course towards the Battery. I stood looking after her a few minutes, and wondering in my heart what should occasion a young woman so well dressed to be abroad so early.

At this period the dress of a young woman consisted of a long, flowing robe, drawn together and tied around the neck with a silk cord, and also around the waist with a ribbon, terminating in a long trail, or train, such as you have seen in paintings of the Goddess of Liberty. I thought then, and I think so now, that that costume was more becoming the female form than any other fashion for the last fifty years. On a tall, slender person, it looked elegant. In those days there were no straight jackets of whalebone, buckram, steel springs and hickory splinters, to distort, torment, and deform their handsome persons.

My early favorite was tall, as straight as an arrow,

and walked with a slow and measured step, like a sentry before the tent of his general; her hair was flaxen, her countenance pale, sedate, and thoughtful; on her cheek was a faint blush. In short, I thought she was the most perfect specimen of female grandeur I had ever beheld. We met on the same spot, and at the same early hour, three mornings in succession—she turning her steady steps towards the Battery, and I gazing after her, wondering what could arouse the gentle maiden so early. I shortly after met her in company.

CHAPTER III.

AN EMBARGO.—MORE ABOUT THE MAIDEN.—A FUNERAL LEADING TOWARDS A WEDDING.—NEW BOARDING-PLACE.—I TURN TEACHER.—NICE SCHOLAR.

I REMARKED, that the means I was pursuing—viz., rising early—to earn money to take me out of the country, were the means which Providence employed to keep me in it. Had I not risen at halfpast three A.M., I would not have met the young woman in Broadway at four. She laid an embargo on me, which has not been removed, though fifty-six summers are [illegible] and fifty-six harvests are ended, since her person first met my admiring eyes. Seeing her approach on the second morning, at the same minute, I thought it was like witchcraft. On the third morning I looked for her, and behold she was there. She had yet a hundred feet to tread before turning the corner. I quickened my pace, and, on passing, gave her as sharp a look as I could, without infringing on common decency. I read care, delicate health, and a tinge of melancholy in her meek eyes. Retracing my steps, I took my stand at the corner. As I watched her figure receding from my view, I communed with my heart as follows: "Poor girl! something wrong disturbs thy sweet repose, and sends thee forth to sweep the morning dew. I wish I were a brother, or a *cousin*, that I might know and share thy trouble. From thy countenance it is evident thy health is delicate; and from thy dress, I presume thou must be one of those sewing-girls, with no home, about whom I hear the young men converse; and, no doubt, thou art going to walk an hour on the Battery for the benefit of thy health, before commencing the labors of the day." Some months thereafter, when we met on speaking terms, I found every word of my conjectures true to the letter. I missed her on the fourth morning. She appeared on the fifth. So we met and passed alternately for a month.

One afternoon, about this period, I saw a hearse in front of the house next to my workshop. Not having seen a funeral in this country, I stopped to see how it was conducted. In a few minutes the coffin was brought forth, followed by a comely matron, who might have seen forty summers; behind her stood this s[illegible] same flaxen-haired maiden whom I had met so often in Broadway. I gave a start at the sight of her countenance, for, by her sable robe and falling tears, I saw she was deeply interested in that funeral, and therefore an inmate of that house. But how it came to pass that I had never seen her going out nor coming in, was a mystery too deep for my comprehension, for I had been at work three months in the house adjoining.

"Whose funeral is it?" I asked of a neighbor.

"It is the husband of that matron, and the father of that young woman."

"What sort of people are they?" I inquired.

"Poor, but respectable," says he. "The father has been long sick from the effects of exposure in the camp with Washington, and their chief support for twelve months past has been the poor daughter, who sews for families, for which she receives thirty-one cents per day." A hard lot, thinks I.

Some two weeks after this period, the people with whom my brother and myself boarded were removing to the country, and we found some difficulty in procuring board to our liking. Our landlady was to remove at ten o'clock on Saturday morning, and at four o'clock on Friday afternoon I knew not where I might pillow my head on Saturday night. While my hand was on the anvil, my thoughts were traversing the dwellings in our neighborhood, viewing them in rotation. The late funeral stood prominent. Says I to myself, "Here, next door, dwell the new-made widow and her daughter. Fame says they are respectable, though poor. Poor folks must shift for a living: perhaps the widow will board my brother and myself, to help pay house-rent, etc. The daughter is of age; the father is just gone; one pillow may serve for mother and daughter; so a couch will remain whereon we may stretch our weary limbs."

While thus ruminating, James Powell stepped into our shop. His family occupied the basement, and the widow and daughter the attic. I told him my surmises about the widow, and asked him if he thought she would board us. He said he would mention it to her that night, and inform us the next morning. I told him to say that we would pay five dollars per week, and split wood and bring water for her. He returned with a favorable answer, and the next day we dined with the mother, and took tea with the daughter in the evening.

After tea her mother went to meeting, and my

brother to see a friend. I was unwilling to leave the daughter alone. While clearing the tea-table, in the act of wiping the outside of a platter, a sigh, from the depths of the soul, escaped through her lips.

"What means that sigh, Rebecca?" I asked.

"I sigh," she replied, "when I think of my ignorance. I was born on the day Lord Howe entered New York. My parents followed Washington. We were seven years in camp. I never was baptized, nor do I know my letters."

Says I, "Rebecca, I'll teach you to read."

"Agreed!" she replied.

She was anxious to learn, and I was anxious that she should do so; no wonder, therefore, that she progressed wonderfully. But I must here digress a little.

Fifty-six years ago, when I crossed the Atlantic, aft[illegible] fourteen weeks constant sailing, during many days of which time we made twelve knots an hour, I verily believe we almost circumnavigated the globe. Be this as it may, we got among the whales in Greenland. Some score of our passengers had their feet frostbitten—I being one of the unfortunate number, so that I was obliged to land in New York in bare soles—being unable to wear shoes on my sore and wounded feet.

On the Sabbath, wishing to attend a house of prayer, I followed an apparently church-going multitude, and with them entered that venerable pile, the old Methodist Chapel in John street, the first place of public worship erected by the Methodists in America. Seeing a young woman enter a pew, the second from the door, I sat down by the side of her. Her head was reclined on the book-board, and she was apparently sending her aspirations to Him who "heareth the cry of the humble." Her devout posture made me anxious to catch a glimpse of her face; but ere she raised her head, the sexton, tapping me on the shoulder, whispered, "You're in the wrong box, sir." "It's not the first time," said I; "but be good enough to show me the right one." He then gave me a seat among the gentlemen, where I found I had committed a blunder in sitting among the ladies; but it was a natural instinct, perhaps. Fifty-six years ago, the Methodists held this regulation as a matter of conscience: now, they are not so shy of the ladies—nor need they be; for I verily believe, that when the roll of the blessed is called in heaven, seven women will muster there to one man.

But, to what tends this long digression? you may ask. Simply to this—that among those ladies, where, in my ignorance, I intruded my small carcass, sat this same pale-faced maiden to whom I had the pleasant task of teaching her A B C. Oft since that day, in my waking dreams, have I indulged the thought that it was she by whose side I sat when I first entered the house of prayer in America. Certain it is, we both sang the same hymn of praise, and knelt at the same altar; for when, six months thereafter, we met on speaking terms, we both remembered the name of the preacher, the number of the hymn, and the text. Now, I know not whether it was galvanism, Mesmerism, or magnetic sympathy; but of this I feel confident—that my guardian angel led me in a way I knew not, and by paths I had not trod, till he brought me under her humble roof, and into the chamber of those who had nursed her.

But to return to our spelling-book—a pleasant, but dangerous experiment. Sometimes, while bending over the task, our heads almost in contact, she would lift her gentle, dove-like eyes to mine, and ask a question which, from its simplicity, might have come from lips of five years' growth; but the *look* was too much for my equanimity.

CHAPTER IV.

GOING TO CHURCH.—BAPTISM OF REBECCA.—THE DECLARATION.—MORNING WALK.—ALL BUT.—A RIVAL IN THE WAY.—THAT SIGH.—THE FIRST KISS.—MEETING THE RIVAL.—RICHES AGAINST LOVE.—LOVE WINS THE FAIR.—SHOOTING OR DROWNING.

I OFTEN accompanied her to the chapel; and, when asked, she would go with me to the Scotch kirk in Cedar street, of which Dr. J. M. Mason was pastor. He was the most eloquent public speaker, at that time, in America, and my pupil having frequently accompanied me to his church, became a constant attendant, and finally resolved to join the church. Not having been baptized, it was necessary, before joining in the communion, that she should submit to that initiatory rite. On the Friday night prior to the communion Sabbath, therefore, after the preparatory lecture, she was baptized. That scene decided my fate.

I felt anxious to observe her conduct on that solemn occasion; and, in order that I might note her every movement, I entered the pew nearest the pulpit, on the right hand of the minister. I watched her coming at every opening of the church door; and at length she entered. She was dressed in half-mourning—her frock of the purest white; a black beaver hat (the fashion at that time); her neck encircled with a necklace of black; her waist was bound with a black ribbon; and, the night being wet, the train of her garment was hanging on her arm. With a measured step she walked up the middle aisle, and sat down in the fourth pew from the pulpit. The thought that, in one hour, the eyes of the whole congregation would be fixed on her alone, had brought a faint blush to her cheek; and, altogether, I thought she had never looked so beautiful.

At the conclusion of the lecture, the preacher said, in a loud voice, "Let the person who is to be baptized present herself." She rose from her seat, and stood before the altar; the forty burners of the brazen candlestick suspended over her head (no gas in those days) threw a halo of light around her person, and one might almost have imagined her to be an immortal from the spheres, too refined to breathe our earthly air. While the eyes of a thousand witnesses were upon her, and the minister binding the vows about her heart, she made the responses with the same sedate, collected, and appropriate deportment, as if none but the eye of Omnipotence was upon her.

While the minister was descending the stairs from the pulpit (at that time fifteen steps from the floor), she was untying the ribbon that fastened her bonnet. There she stood, her hat in one hand, and a white muslin handkerchief in the other, and her neatly arranged locks exposed to full view. As the minister dipped his fingers in the silver vessel of the sanctuary, she closed her eyes, and turned her face to heaven, while the water streamed from her brow, and over her blushing cheeks. Her face, to me, shone as the face of an angel, and I vowed in my heart that, if Heaven so willed, nothing but death should part us.

We walked together on our way home (a short distance), her thoughts so occupied by the scene just past, that she spoke not; and mine so filled with her image, that my tongue clave to the roof of my mouth. We entered our humble dwelling; a candle was burning on a small pine table, and a looking-glass, twelve by sixteen, suspended on the wall. She laid her hat on the table, and stood before the glass, arranging her head-gear.

Either by accident or design, I stood a few feet behind, and, looking over her shoulders, feasted my eyes on her lovely countenance. She read my soul in that *over-shoulder look*, and, suspending operations, turned round.

At this moment, the extreme point of her long hair was twisted among the slender fingers of the right hand, while the same arm was extended to its full length, with a comb in the left hand, stationary on the head—a more interesting posture was never assumed by woman. Without changing her position, she remarked:

"Grant, under God, I have to thank you, as the instrument, for what I am this night. I now rank among his followers."

I stated where I first saw her, and the ways and means that brought me under the roof where she dwelt, and added, "Where thou dwellest, I will dwell; where thou lodgest, I will lodge; thy people shall be my people, and thy God my God; nothing but death shall part us, if it so wills Heaven."

While I spoke, she bent forward with a look of surprise, and when I ceased, she turned away with a sigh. Ere I could ask what it meant, the door was opened, and her mother entered. I had no opportunity to speak with her that night, but the sigh still sounded in my ears, and I am sure I would have slept better had I never heard it. Next morning, I asked if she would walk with me on the Battery that night.

She said, "I will go."

New York, at this period (1794), was like a village, compared with its present appearance. You could walk from the City Hotel to the Battery, at nine o'clock in the evening, and not meet a passer-by.

After supper we walked out together; as we reached the first picket in the Trinity Church fence, I said:

"Rebecca, what caused that sigh, when I laid bare my heart before thee last night?"

She replied, "It was caused by the thought of the pain you would feel, when informed that I am courted, and *all but* engaged."

"*All but!*" Had the "engaged" been there alone, without the "all but," it would have been a knock-down argument; but in this "all but" I found a hook whereon to hang my hopes. We walked on for a minute without speaking. I was confounded. I had now been months under the same roof, and had never seen her receive the least attention from any young man. At last I said:

"Rebecca, who is the young man? I never saw you in company with him, nor does he visit you at your mother's house."

She replied, "I sometimes sew for a week in one family, and he waits upon me home, but never comes up stairs; his name is Mr. Casteel, and he keeps a jewelry store on the corner of Liberty street and Broadway."

"Does your mother know that you are *all but* engaged?"

"She does."

"Does she approve it?"

"She does."

Here I felt like giving up the ghost. I said:

"Rebecca, Mr. C. is a rich man, and owns two houses and stores in Broadway, besides a well-filled store of jewels, etc. How long have you been courted?"

"Nearly two years," she replied.

"And why are you not married?"

"I can't tell," she said.

I thought it would be easy to knock the bottom from these slow and easy two-year courtships, and I resolved to try. We now stood by the gate of Trinity Church. Reflecting for a moment, I again broke silence.

"Rebecca, did the thought of giving me pain cause you to sigh?"

"It did."

Pity, thought I, is akin to love; so I raised my arm, she bent her swan-like neck, and on *that spot* received my first kiss. A full-orbed moon and the eye of Omnipotence alone witnessed that kiss.

On the following evening, while taking sweet counsel together on the Battery, we were met by Mr. Casteel. He must have taken the alarm, for next day he waited upon the mother of my pupil, and said:

"Mrs. Sickles, I have courted your daughter nearly two years, with your consent and hers. I wish to get married next week. Moreover, if you will help me in this, on the day of our marriage I will give you a bond for three hundred dollars per annum, to be paid out of my estate, as long as you live. I will give your daughter any house in Broadway she may choose to live in, and servants to wait on her."

The old lady replied, thanking him for his kind intentions, but added, "She is my only child. Money will never tempt me to influence her in a matter of that sort. Make your offer to her: if she accepts, well; but if she prefers Grant and poverty to you and riches, I have nothing to say."

The same evening, at tea, the mother, daughter, my brother and myself only were present. The mother was a sprightly widow of forty-one, and knew more about the amalgamation of hearts than either the daughter or myself. She used to tease the daughter about procuring a *kissing-bench*, seeing her beau lacked two inches to complete five feet, etc. While filling the cups and platters, she related (with some improvements, perhaps), the visit, the exordium, and the ultimatum, of Mr. Casteel. My brother laughed, the mother smiled, the daughter blushed, and I felt like a fish thrown on shore. After gathering my scattered senses, I said:

"Rebecca, I can't give your mother three hundred dollars per annum from my estate, seeing I have only an estate of sin and misery to boast of; I can't give you a house in Broadway; but, provided you enter into partnership for life with me, I will find a nest for you, and if it is rather small, we'll e'en sit the closer together; I can't hire servants, but I will wait on you myself; you shall neither hew wood nor draw water; and there is an arm that shall work till it drops from the shoulder, ere you shall suffer from lack of any comfort which money can command. This, with the heart of a true Scotchman, who never loved another, is all I can offer you."

I must digress a little, to make plain the narrative. I was born and reared in a secluded village. Except at the kirk, I scarcely ever saw a young woman. In my twenty-first year, when I left Scotland, I would have been as much ashamed to be seen walking with a girl of my own age, as if I had been detected in stealing a sheep. Rebecca was the only young woman with whom I had spent ten minutes in private. This gave a zest to her company and conversation few can appreciate.

Mr. Casteel was a rich merchant. At that time there were not six men in New York of equal wealth. He was a bachelor of thirty, and in personal appearance fifty per cent. my superior. Rebecca was nineteen, and I in my twenty-second. What was I, a stranger, forging nails at one dollar per day, that I should contend for the hand of her who was sought for by the man of seventy thousand? With me it mattered not; it was a contest for life. Had he been emperor of all the Russias, I could not have given her up without a struggle. I thought I must die, should I see her the wife of another. Certain it is, I could not have remained in New York. And now, having saved money enough to pay my passage, I resolved to do my best; but, if she became the wife of another, on that day I would sail for Scotland, there to murmur my regrets in my native air.

Next day, Mr. C. made a tender of himself, his purse, person, and property, to my pupil. She had not *made up her mind.* The offer was frequently repeated, but with no better success. Had he done this twelve months before, the prize would have been his own. Now, fearing that his day of grace had passed, he became partially deranged. I couldn't help that. As an instance of his madness, he once threatened to shoot himself or me. I can't say that I had any very particular objection to his shooting himself, but I must confess that I had no wish for him to shoot me. He declared he could not live, except she became his wife. I thought I could not live except she became my wife. Here was a dilemma. I considered the matter as coolly as the nature of the subject would admit, and finally came to the conclusion that it was more reasonable, more equitable, and more in accordance with the spirit of the times, for him to shoot himself, than that I should drown myself.

CHAPTER V.

BIRDS WITHOUT A NEST.—A BACHELOR CONVERTED.—THE DISAPPOINTED.—MY REBECCA BECOMES MY WIFE.—A QUIET WEDDING.—HOUSEKEEPING BEGUN.

My objections to being drowned were somewhat strengthened on the following night, as Rebecca and myself, in committee of the whole, resolved to get married at once. We had no nest, to be sure; neither have the little birds. They select a branch, on which they sit and twitter their tales of love through the silent watches of the night. At the rising of the sun, the male comes laden with sticks and straws, which he lays at the feet of his mistress. Of these she constructs the nest wherein to nurse her young.

Here, then, is the rock whereon thousands of unhappy bachelors founder and are lost. They are ever placing the cart before the horse, and are always holding on by the wrong end of the string. A few days ago I encountered one of that unfortunate class. In *all other respects*, he is an excellent member of the Church and of the State. It is years since last we met. I asked, "Are you married?"

"No," says he; "but I expect to be, before the year is out."

"How old are you?"

"Forty-six."

Said I, "Man, my second crop said 'Grandfather' before I was fifty."

"Ah," says he, "furniture was cheap in your young days."

I replied, "Furniture has nothing to do with the choice of a wife. Go and catch the bird first, and you will soon find a nest to roost in."

He took my advice, and soon after was enjoying the happiness of a wedded life.

Having digressed inadvertently, I now return to my narrative. Mr. Casteel, in the derangement of his ideas, consulted Mr. (afterwards Chancellor) Kent and Doctor Pilemore, at that time a popular preacher in the Episcopal Church in Ann street. From their firesides, the report spread through the city (then nearly bounded by the Park). A poor seamstress had refused the hand of a rich merchant, and was going to wed a poor nail-maker. The excitement was equal to that in Strasburg, on the Rhine, when the man with the long nose rode through the city. Some said it was a paper nose; some said it was a wooden nose; and still the wonder grew. Some cried one thing, and some another; but the greater part said it was right; that we ought to come together. I thought so, too. New York, at that period, numbered but about fifty or sixty thousand inhabitants. Consequently, almost every one knew his neighbor. My pupil was almost a prisoner in her mother's house. At the church, in the market, in the highways and by-ways, she was the observed of all observers. I also came in for a share of the notoriety. We postponed our marriage from day to day, hoping Mr. C. would become reconciled, and the nine days' wonder cease. Finding no *lull* in the *squall*, my pupil took counsel of Mrs. Lindsey, the wife of George, a worthy Scotchman, a master stone-cutter, and an elder in our kirk. His wife was an American, and a mother in Israel. Mrs. Blake was also taken into their counsel. (Three women will sooner unravel a matrimonial puzzle than twenty men.) It was resolved in counsel that we should be married on the following night. To this arrangement I made no objection. Doctor Mason (father of the late worthy scion) and his lady, Mr. Lownds (long remembered as the head engineer of the City Prison), two young ladies, two young men, Rebecca and her mother, were invited to drink tea; and, as there would be no fun till I came, I also was among the prophets.

Supper being ended, Mrs. Lindsey announced a wedding! This was news to all but the parties concerned. The young ones looked round, *somebody*, blushed, and I felt as well as I ever did in all my life. In two minutes, a groom and bridesmaid were selected; in five more, we two were made one, according to the canons of the Kirk of Scotland, in like case made and provided; wine and cake passed, and nuts and jokes were cracked. At ten the assemblage broke up, when Rebecca and I accompanied the mother to her own dwelling. She gave us her blessing, with a dew-drop on her cheek.

"Grant," says she, "take care of my jewel."

"Mother," said I, "I will take care of *my own jewel*."

We entered our own room in peace. In this room I nourished and cherished her for three years and six months, when her Father called, "Come up hither."

He gave me her likeness, however, in her only child, my oldest son.

Here, then, you will say, was a Scotch Covenanter's wedding. It was so, and, as I think, it is the best way in the world to make a wedding. Here was no boisterous laughter, like the crackling of thorns under a pot, and which maketh the heart sad. Our hearts knew their own happiness. The stranger intermeddled not with our joys. Here we sat in our humble dwelling, with the peace which the world can neither give nor take away.

For the benefit of those who hesitate to consummate their happiness, because furniture is dear, I will give an inventory of what I commenced housekeeping with: One white-pine table, cost fifty cents; three rush-bottom chairs, cost twenty-five cents each; three knives and forks; three cups and saucers, a rag-carpet, and other utensils in the same proportion. Though plain, they were all new. Ten dollars closed the concern. The old lady supplied the upholstery, gratis. We had enough, and a chair to spare; in fact, we often had two chairs to spare, for it not unfrequently happened that one chair held both of us—and there was no harm in that. Of what use are your four dozen of chairs? You can only sit on one at a time, and the rest are only vanity and vexation of spirit. You gain nothing by rising from one chair and sitting down on another. With my three chairs and pine table, a companion who had spurned a palace to sit by me in a cottage, I was content, and would not have exchanged them for all the honors of a dukedom.

CHAPTER VI.

THE DISAPPOINTED RIVAL LOADS HIS PISTOLS.—PREFERS MARRYING THE FIRST GIRL HE MEETS.—DOES SO.—DIES.—HIS WIDOW, DAUGHTER, AND MY BOYS.—NOT TO BE.

BEFORE we had been married an hour, some officious neighbor informed Mr. Casteel of the fact. Mr. C., being a bachelor, boarded out; but, as guardian of his valuable stock of goods, he slept in a room adjoining his store. Next morning at eight o'clock, the neighbors seeing the store unopened, and knowing the state of Mr. C.'s mind, burst open the door, and found him loading his pistols. The men in the neighborhood met, and agreed to watch him, two at a time, relieving one another every two hours. In this they continued ten successive days and nights; at the end of which time he settled down to his right mind. One day, after ruminating three whole hours without speaking (so one of his watchers told me), he sprang to his feet, and swore he would marry the first girl he could catch. Before a week, he married a girl who had seen thirty summers, and whom he had never known till the day when he started in search of a wife. She was as poor as a church mouse, and as ugly as a stone fence. His temper was soured. Hers was never sweet. Consequently, they got on about as comfortably as two cats tied together by the tails and thrown across a clothes-line. He died about five years after marriage, leaving her with a son and daughter to count the *siller*.

Now, friend reader, this story looks so much like the romance-books of the present day, that some may set it down as a mere fiction. It is no fiction, but a plain, unvarnished tale of truth. My manner of life, from my youth up, is known to all the inhabitants of New York. If Mr. Unbeliever will stake a thousand dollars (to pay expenses), I'll cover it, and prove every item by one hundred witnesses who yet live, and who saw and were cognizant of the facts. A Mr. James A——n, a respectable millionaire, dwelt next door to Mr. C. The sons and grandsons of Mr. A. yet live in this city. The former bore witness, and also the latter, to their having heard their grandsire repeat the tale.

Twenty-five years from the date of these occurrences, a well-dressed lady, who probably might have seen fifty-five summers, visited me. With her was a handsome young woman, who appeared to be about twenty-two years of age. At that time I kept store in Liberty street, in a large building, formerly the Friends' Meeting-house. They walked up into the gallery, where I kept an aviary for birds. The old lady soon came down, leaving the young one to await her return, and listen to the singing of the birds. She came near where I stood, and asked,

"Do you know me?"

"I do not."

"I am Mrs. Casteel," said she, "and the young woman in the gallery is my daughter. After the death of my husband I removed to the country. There my son died. Our property has increased very much in value since Mr. C.'s death; and that girl is heir, at my death, to the whole. I have not a relation that I know of on the face of the earth. I came into this world without the benefit of clergy; was laid at the rich man's door; was brought up in the almshouse, and bound out until I was of age. Now," she continued, "it was through you that I became possessed of this property. It is my wish, if Providence so orders, that one of your sons, as the husband of my daughter, may possess this property when my head is laid in the grave."

I was astonished. At this moment we were sitting within twenty feet of the counter, behind which my three sons were waiting on customers.

"Are these your three sons?" she inquired. "They are good-looking young men. How old are they?"

"The eldest is twenty-nine, has a wife and three children; the next, twenty-four; the other, twenty-two—both, very much against my wishes, are bachelors."

"What is the name of the oldest bachelor?" inquired Mrs. Casteel.

"William," said I.

"A suitable age for my Mary," she replied; "for she entered her twenty-third year only last week."

Here, then, was an under-tow, or romance of love, from a quarter I never dreamed of. I entered fully into the old lady's plans, and liked the thing very much, resolving to gather fun, should I reap nothing else from the concern. Mrs. Casteel continued:

"In prosecution of this plan I have come to spend the winter in town, and have engaged lodgings over the way. Your store and green-house are places of public resort; my daughter and myself will visit here daily, and should an attachment spring up between the young ones, my wish will be gratified."

I cheerfully seconded the motion; but remarked, that her daughter and my sons must know nothing of the matter.

The long talk with the mother, and the long stay of the daughter in the gallery, induced my sons to inquire who they were. I told them. "Now," said I, "one of you make a prize of the daughter; you will get a handsome wife, and a hundred thousand dollars to buy pap-spoons with."

She was often in the green-house. I always sent one of my sons to wait upon her, and often gave him a hint as broad as a Spanish *sombri*. They all said she was pretty—and she *was* pretty; but the engine wouldn't work. That marriage, not being registered in heaven, never could be consummated on earth. In the spring, the old lady flew away with her young chicken to another roost. She was married within a twelvemonth, I hope and believe, very comfortably.

Now, my young bachelor friends—you who are halting between two opinions—you may gather instruction from the fate of Mr. Casteel. He embittered his after-life by procrastination. He could have been married to my pupil six months before I saw America. There is nothing to be gained in dangling for a twelvemonth after a sensible woman, talking unmeaning stuff—words without wisdom. Tell her your wish *like a man*, and not like a blubbering school-boy. She will never trifle with your affections; and if there are three grains of common sense in your *muckle* carcass, she will be your own before a month has passed. See the history of Rebecca, in Genesis, 24th chapter, 57th verse: When Abraham's servant had concluded the preliminary contract with Mrs. Laban, on the part of her daughter, to become the wife of Isaac, the old man was anxious to get home, to show his young master the *bonny lass* he had brought him; the mother wished him to remain a few days to recruit himself and his camels. He persisting, it was finally referred to the daughter. "We will call the damsel, and inquire at her mouth," said the mother. When Rebecca appeared, her mother asked, "Wilt thou go with this man?" Rebecca replied, "I will go."

There was a noble girl for you. No tear starting from her black eyes; no whining, nor simpering, make-believe, nor mock-modesty; but what her heart wished her lips uttered. Like an honest maiden, she replied, "I will go." Now, young ladies, go thou and do likewise. When the man whom you prefer before all others in the world says, "Will you go with me?" answer, "I will go."

By-the-bye, ladies, when you wish to read a true, simple, and unsophisticated love-story, just read over the twenty-fourth chapter of Genesis.

CHAPTER VII.

OPENING A STORE.—REBECCA SEWS AND I SELL.—EVENINGS AT HOME.—YELLOW FEVER.—MOTHER OF REBECCA FLIES.—OUR FIRST-BORN.—PALE HORSE.—SCENES IN THE FEVER SUMMER.—DR. DINGLEY.—ROBERT HOE.

We will now return to our own fireside. We had been twelve months married, the experience of every day knitting us closer and closer in the bonds of love. I rented a small store, and with the money I had saved to carry me home, in case of a certain emergency, I purchased tape, bobbins, thimbles, thread, scissors, and Oxbery's needles. Mr. Oxbery was an Englishman. I think he kept a genuine Whitechapel needle-store, corner of Liberty and William streets; and so high were the needles in repute, that neither lady, miss, nor waiting-maid would enter a stitch (without a frown) unless the needles came from Oxbery's. Ask your wife, mother, or grandmother, and they will confirm the fact. Now he sleeps with his fathers.

This small mercantile concern was quite an amusement to my pupil, and we watched its profits and increase with as much interest and pleasure as ever did John Jacob Astor his ship-load of bear and otter skins. The store was in Nassau, near Liberty street. My workshop was in Liberty, opposite Green street. When any thing occurred, in a trade or speculation, too perplexing for her young ideas, I was called, when, putting our heads together, the mystery was soon solved.

A board partition separated the store from our parlor, which latter served for kitchen and all. A glass door opened opposite the fireplace, where she rolled the dumpling or broiled the steak with one eye, and kept a squint on the store with the other. At noon I came in, the pot boiling over the fire on the trammel-hook (no coal-ranges or cooking-stoves in those days). After a few minutes' domestic consultation, I stood in the Fly Market, at the foot of Maiden Lane, where (the "upper ten" and the boarding-houses being already supplied) I could buy a steak, fish, or cutlet, for a twelve-penny paper bill of the Corporation of New York, sufficient to satisfy the wants of Rebecca and myself for twenty-four hours.

"Ah, mother," exclaims a little miss who has seen seven summers, "they must have lived on love." "They did, my dear," replies the mother. The old lady spoke from experience.

In the afternoon, sitting behind the counter, Rebecca measured tape, made my shirts, or mended my stockings. She was my storekeeper, housekeeper, bookkeeper, and cash-keeper. In short, she was to me, intrinsically, more than all the world besides.

While a bachelor, I paid three dollars per week for board and washing. Now this sum more than covered our expenses, and the profits of the store paid the rent (only fifty dollars per annum). I came home at seven in the evening, and always found the table set, the kettle singing, a hickory fire burning, and Rebecca smiling. I had not another wish.

Tea over, while smoothing my linen or crimping her collar, I read to her from an instructive and amusing book, or from *Harrison's Weekly Museum*, published at No. 3 Peck Slip, or sang to her a love-song from the clifty rocks of Scotland—and none speak more pathetically the tender feelings of the heart. This lightened the cares of my partner, and brought a smile on the face I so fondly admired.

At nine in the evening (if fine weather), we put the key in our pocket, walked the circuit of the Battery, and sat down under our *trysting-tree*—our feelings, though less anxious, yet infinitely more sublime than they were fourteen months previous. This oak yet stands, full of sap, and flourishing, and long may the "*woodman spare that tree.*"

We had been just twelve months married when the yellow fever commenced its ravages. Its progress was more like a Turkish plague than any yellow fever I have ever seen. Our neighbors all fled to the country, among their friends; but we had no friends to flee to, nor any money to support us in idleness. So, after some consultation, we thought we might as well die of the plague in the city, as to die of famine in the village. The heart of Rebecca was fixed where fear never enters. Her slender foot was firmly placed on the Rock of Ages, and with her hand she took a grasp upon the skies, and bid troubles roll, nor feared their idle whirl. Now, with every morning service, our prayers went up, that if one of us was to be taken, the other might not be left. On retiring at night, we sang the 121st Psalm, P. M.:

No burning heat by day, nor blast of evening air,
Can take my life away, if God be with me there.

I'll go and come,
Nor fear to die,
Till from on high,
Thou call'st me home, &c.

Thus we lived, as it were, in an ideal world of our own creating, while all was death and solemn reality around us. With a firm reliance on a kind Providence, our hearts were kept in perfect peace. On the 25th of August my brother, twenty months my senior, and residing in Front street, was attacked. I nursed him, and he recovered. From this date to the 22d of September I attended night and day among the sick. At the door of the Methodist church in John street I met a poor widow (a mother in Israel), whom I engaged as a companion and comfort to Rebecca while I ministered to those who were ready to perish. The fear of death had driven the mother of Rebecca into the country.

When all had fled who were able, and the Board of Health had removed the poor to temporary buildings out of town (viz., Harlem Heights, then styled), the census was taken, and it appeared that only fifteen thousand men, women, and children remained. Out of this number sixty-three died on the 22d of September, 1789, which is the highest number of deaths recorded during the prevalence of the yellow fever in New York.

On this fatal day my first-born, for the first time, beheld the light of the sun. Without was heard the voice of weeping, wailing, lamentation, and woe; but in my house was joy and peace that day, for it was well with the mother, it was well with her child, and well with all under my roof. To be sure, Death on the Pale Horse, in going the rounds, stopped in front of my dwelling; he reconnoitered the premises for a moment, while the horse stood pawing at the door; but, seeing that the posts and lintels were *marked* by the angel of protection, he dared not enter; but, slowly descending to Maiden Lane (I lived at the corner of Nassau and Liberty streets), he stopped at my second-door neighbor's, where he left a dart in the heart of Doctor Dingley. At ten that same night he was laid in the Potter's Field.

It is a remarkable instance of providential preservation, that, during all the fevers, I never left the city, and, though more or less engaged in nursing the sick every season of its prevalence, neither myself, my wife, nor any of my children, were ever attacked by that malignant disease. During the fever in 1822, my porter, an intemperate, aged man, went out on a Saturday evening, in spite of my earnest remonstrance. During the evening a thunder-storm broke upon the city, and at midnight he came home, *drunk*, and wet to the skin. I stripped him to nudity, and put on him a large red-flannel shirt, and then put his feet in warm water. I afterwards put him in bed, and covered his body with two blankets, hoping to promote perspiration. In five minutes he was fast asleep. Fearing an emergency, I slept in the room adjoining. His groans awoke me at four o'clock in the morning. Doctor Kissam felt his pulse in thirty minutes thereafter. I nursed him myself. At six o'clock on the following Saturday afternoon he slept with his fathers, in Potter's Field.

This was the only death by yellow fever that ever occurred under my roof. No other of my family were affected, though he died in our midst. *The total absence of all fear*, I yet think, was the means which Providence employed for our preservation. We neither took preventive pills nor powders; but, with a firm reliance on our Maker and Preserver, kept on the even tenor of our way, with moderation in all things, shunning heat by day and chills by night. To be sure, in my visitations among the sick, I walked the streets during all the silent watches of the night; but this was imperious duty, and I felt confident that death could not and would not touch one hair of my head while I was engaged in so necessary and meritorious an act.

During the prevalence of the yellow fever, when not in attendance on the sick, I was busily employed in making nails for the coffin-makers. A carpenter in Warren street kept twelve men constantly employed in making white-wood coffins, not painted, which he sold for five dollars each. Two stout lads, with a hand-cart load, went daily through the streets, stopping at every corner, and crying out, " Coffins, coffins, all sizes, only five dollars." In many instances, the coffin stood under the bed of the patient for days and weeks, waiting for him. Some recovered, and paid the carpenter for their own coffin. Undertakers, as a profession, were not known in New York at that period (1798.)

My dwelling was on the corner of Nassau and Liberty streets, where Suydam, Nixon and Co.'s dry-goods store now stands. In Liberty street, nearly opposite the post-office a house was closed, the family having fled. The cellar was occupied by a man and woman. I saw them daily for some time; at length I missed them for two days. The door being open all this time, I began to suspect that something was wrong. On the third day I stood at the door, and knocked; no one opened. I called; no one gave answer. I stepped in upon the cold, damp floor. The room was very dark. After a few seconds I could discern objects, but saw no living creature. I listened, and heard the sound of heavy breathing, like a strong man in a sound sleep. I followed the sound, and, in a remote corner, on a miserable bed, lay a man and woman, their eyes fast closing in the sleep of death. Between them lay a child, *fast asleep*, which, from its appearance, might have seen ten months. The child must have been in that state of happy unconsciousness for at least twenty-four hours, for, from the appearance of the mother, she could not have ministered to its wants in all that time. It is a beautiful idea, which prevails in Switzerland, that when a child is born, God appoints its guardian angel. And why not? History records many cases where the mother has been struck dead by lightning, and found with the child on her lap, asleep, without even the smell of fire on its garments.

But to return. I looked around, and saw nothing either to nourish or to cherish life. I procured, however, a cup of cold water, and, with a towel, washed their parched lips. I could do no more. "Lord, receive their spirits," I mentally prayed, and left them. Returning in two hours thereafter, their spirits had winged their flight to that God who giveth and who taketh away; and the child was striving to draw sustenance from the cold breast of its mother. I reported the case to the Board of Health, which sat (in fever times) day and night, in the old almshouse in the Park. The parents were laid in the Potter's Field, and the babe placed under the care of a nurse.

Thousands of valuable lives were lost during the fever periods, for want of proper attention. For instance: fifty years ago, many of the master-mechanics boarded all their apprentices, and part of their journeymen, in their own families. It often happened that a son, an apprentice, and one or two of the journeymen (shoemakers, perhaps, for at that period most of the in-door work was done in the house of the employer) would, when the family was about to leave, propose to stay, work, and keep house. The consequence was, when those bachelors were taken sick, there was no one to nurse them. Thus, on an average, eight bachelors died to five married men. Mark this, neighbor bachelor; and if you mean to live all your days, get married as soon as you can. In 1708, from the fifteenth to the twenty-second of September, I had seven of those useless mortals on my sick-list, viz.: one in Liberty street, three on the corner of Front and Pine streets, and three on the corner of Dover and Water streets—three Americans, and four Scotchmen. There was no one to give them a cup of water, myself alone excepted. Two Americans and one Scot died. With the exception of two or three hours' sleep out of every twenty-four, I was with them, night and day, the whole week. They were all seized on the fifteenth; two died on the twentieth, and the other on the twenty-second, aged twenty-one, twenty-five, and twenty-six.

Returning, on the twenty-first of September, at eleven o'clock in the evening, from visiting my three patients at the corner of Dover and Water streets, the night was dark, a thick, wetting mist was falling, and the street lamps twinkled just enough to make darkness visible (no gas in those days). Descending the hill in Franklin Square, from Dover street, I met two hearses, both filled to overflowing with dead mortality, each containing fourteen coffins. One of the hearses was issuing out of Peck Slip, and the other out of Ferry street. They turned up Pearl street, on their way to the Potter's Field. The wheels of these chariots of death rolled heavily up the hill, the springs and timbers screeching and groaning as if chanting the requiem of friends departed. Each hearse had a driver and assistant, sitting in front, with a lantern between their feet. They sat as dumb as mutes. The pale light from their lanterns flickered across their stupid, unmeaning countenances, which looked as white as the face of Samuel, just peering out of the grave, when called by the witch of Endor from the mansions of the dead.

Dr. Dingley came from London to this city a few months previous to the commencement of the fever, furnished with diplomas from the Magdalen and other hospitals. By the opportune setting-in of the yellow fever, he soon got into a large practice, and it is said that he was very successful. He left a wife and family in London. He kept his head-quarters in a boarding-house in Nassau street, the second door from my dwelling, near Maiden Lane. About the 1st of September, the boarders and landlady fled, leaving the doctor, and his man who had charge of the horse and chariot, to keep bachelor's hall as they pleased. On the evening of the 16th, the doctor came into my house to light his candle.

"How is the fever to-day, doctor?" said I.

"Worse and worse," he replied; "fifty deaths and sixty-five new cases. I do not feel very well myself."

Next day he was reported among the new cases; this was on Monday, the 17th. He was visited daily by almost every doctor who remained in the city (for the eminent physicians and rich citizens fled, leaving the poor and destitute to battle the fever as best they could). From Monday, till sundown on Friday, three or four chariots were constantly in front of his dwelling. None appearing on Saturday at mid-day, I concluded that the doctor must be either dead or better, and thought I would go and see. The front door standing wide open, I struck the knocker, but got no answer; I repeated the sound, but no one came forth; I stood on the first platform of the stair, and struck the board with the heel of my boot—still no man regarded. I ascended to the second platform, and, on listening, I heard a heavy breathing. I followed the sound till, on a cot in the centre of a large room—the three windows wide open, the day being hot—I found the body of the doctor, his spacious chest heaving like a bellows with every respiration, his eyes set, fixed on the ceiling, and glazed with the films of death; a swarm of house-flies formed a black circle round his mouth. I spoke—he heard me not. On the sideboard stood a decanter of wine. I swept the flies from his face, wiped his parched lips with a wet cloth. I poured a few drops of wine into a silver spoon, and, gently raising his head, poured the wine into his mouth. The moment the spoon touched his lips, he extended his jaw and clutched it firmly with his teeth. The stillness of death which pervaded the street and the room caused the clang from the silver spoon to reverberate loudly through the silent room. It was the knell of his departing spirit; for, ere the clock had struck another note of time, his soul had crossed that great gulf which separates time from eternity. As I held the spoon in my hands, when he clutched it with his teeth, it sent a thrill through every nerve in my system, like a stroke from an electric machine. It required some exertion to draw the spoon from between his clenched teeth. That night, at ten o'clock, he filled a stranger's grave in the Potter's Field. As I stated above, the doctor was seized on the 16th; on the 21st he was pronounced by six physicians a dying man. His English man-servant mounted the horse and fled, fearing the fever might catch him also. He left the house open to admit the grave-diggers, as he told me some months afterwards—a bright thought.

At this time the Board of Health hired men, to whom they gave money to seek out and relieve the necessities of the poor at discretion. They offered to put my name on their list, and give me my hire. I thanked them, but told them that money could not hire me, but that, while God spared my life and health, I would do my duty, and He would see to my wages. "Doth Job serve God for naught?" is the only truth that Satan ever uttered.

In September, 1805, the yellow fever prevailed to a fearful extent in this city. As I never left town while it was raging, I was sitting in my tent door in the cool of the day, and lifting up my eyes I beheld a stranger, a rare sight in fever times. He was moving from Cedar street along Nassau, having his face set towards Maiden Lane. He walked in the middle of the street, and was reading the sign-boards on the right and left. He paused in front of my open door, and mine was the only store open in the block. As he stepped in, he said, "Mr. Thorburn."

"Where did you learn my name?" I inquired.

"I saw it over the door," said he. "I have just come on shore from the ship Draper, from Liverpool. I am a carpenter by trade, my name is Robert Hoe; I am now in my eighteenth year."

Says I, "Robert, were your indentures fulfilled before you left England?"

Says he, "I never was bound, I learned my trade with my father; I can't find work, I have no money; can you recommend to me a house in a healthy part of the city, where I may board till I get employment, when I will pay them honestly?"

I knew the heart of a stranger, having been a stranger myself, and there was so much of honest simplicity in his speech and deportment, my heart warmed towards him; I gave him a chair, and ran up stairs; says I, "Gude wife, a stranger standeth at our door; shall we take him in?" "If thee pleases," she replied. "If he takes the fever, will thee help me to nurse him?" "I will," she answered. "Thank you, dear, for this; God will bless you." Now, says I, "Come and look on his honest English face." The impression was favorable. Says I, "Robert, this neighborhood is accounted the most healthful in the city; you will lodge here; if you take the fever, my wife and I will nurse you, you shan't go to the stranger's hospital." His eyes spoke thanks more eloquent than words. As he had no business abroad, I advised him to stay at home.

The fever seized him, however, in less than a week. I procured an eminent physician; my wife and I nursed him. In seventeen summers that I've nursed among the sick, I do not think that I ever saw a case so violent but it terminated in death, his only excepted. On the fourth day, generally the crisis, the burning fever was coursing through his veins, and drinking up his English blood. His skin burning, dry, and yellow, heart-sick, home-sick, all-round-sick; and his spirits sunk down to his heels. I sat by his bedside, he fastened his restless eyes on mine: "O Mr. T., Mr. T., I shall die, I shall die—I never can stand this;" and he threw his brawny arms across the bed, as if going to grapple with death. "Die," says I, "Robert, to be sure, we must all die, but you are not going to die this week." In this I spoke unadvisedly with my lips, but I thought of Pope Pius and his Bull, to wit, that the end would sanctify the means. He was under the influence of powerful medicine at this moment; I knew there would be a lull, as the sailors say, soon; and I meant to take advantage of the circumstance to persuade him to live, if possible. *Fancy kills, and fancy cures.* I left him for fifteen minutes. On my return, I felt his pulse; said I, "Robert, you are fifty per cent. better already; I hope to see you walk from the bed, and sit by the window to-morrow." I sat by his bed conversing to cheer his spirits. I continued, "Death is nigh at hand at all times and in all places; but my impression is, that you will not die with this attack. I hope to see you a thriving master-builder, married to one of the bonny Yankee lassies, *and to hold your grandchild in my arms.*"

From this hour the fever left him. Shortly after this, the fever disappeared from the city. He became a master-builder, and died in 1843, aged 56. But his name will never die, while types are set, and printers breathe. *Hoe's Printing Press* is probably the most useful discovery that has blessed the world, since the first sheet was struck from the press. Formerly, we paid one hundred and fifty cents for a Bible, now we buy one as good for *twenty-five cents.* It may be said of his sons (a rare occurrence in this country), that they are better men than their father, inasmuch as they have added many improvements to their father's plans. Mr. Hoe dwelt in New York thirty-eight years. After his recovery from the fever in 1805, we met times without number; his never-failing salutation was, "Grant, as the instrument under God, I have to thank you for my recovery from that fever." I have received many tokens of kindness from his worthy family of sons and daughters. And nothing in my past life affords such pleasing reflections as this act of duty and humanity to a stranger. When his aching head lay on my breast, as I held the cooling draught to his parched lips, I little thought that in his head lay the germ of a machine destined to revolutionize the world of literature, and shed light on the dark places of the earth, whose habitations are full of horrid cruelty.

About seven years ago, I stepped from the cars in a country town. Among them who were looking on, stood a man of genteel appearance; said I, "Sir, I wish to stop here for a week, I don't like to put up in a hotel; can you direct me where I may lodge in a private family?" He said he could. We entered the next street, he stopped in front of a respectable two-story brick tenement; on the front stoop sat a comely matron. She might have seen twenty-eight summers; on her lap sat a babe. Said my friend to the matron, "Gude wife, this is Mr. Thorburn, from New York; he wishes private board for a week, can you accommodate him?" "Yes," says she, "for a year, or a lifetime, if it is his wish. Oft has my father told me, when he was sick, and a stranger, that Mr. T. took him in, and administered to his wants." "What was your father's name?" I inquired. "Robert Hoe," she replied. "And is this your child?" "It is." I held the babe in my arms, it smiled on my face. "Now," says I, "madam, this day my prophecy is fulfilled in your eyes; it's just forty years, at a critical moment in your father's life, when I told him that I hoped to hold his grandchild in my arms."

CHAPTER VIII.

DEATH OF MY WIFE.—SECOND MARRIAGE.—ANECDOTE OF MR. VAN HOOK.—GROCERY BUSINESS.—SEEDS AND PLANTS.—NARROW ESCAPE BY FIRE.—ANOTHER CHANGE.

My wife recovered soon, and enjoyed good health till the month of August, 1800, when she was seized with the symptoms of a rapid consumption; and, though every means was resorted to, she died, in the peace and hope of the Gospel, on the 28th of November of the same year. On her death-bed she was often visited by the elders and praying members of our church. Often she told me how thankful she was that God had made her to be acquainted with me, which was the means of introducing her into such society. Had I married that man of the world, she would say, what now would have been all his riches to me? Not one of his acquaintances is able to speak a word of comfort to my soul. On the morning of her death the sun rose in all his rich effulgence, so strikingly mild and beautiful at that season of the year: his beams fell on the end of a brick building, in such a position that it reflected its light in her face. I asked her if I should close the shutters. She answered, No; it did not hurt her eyes; it made her think of the glories of heaven, where they have no need of the sun, neither of the moon, the Lamb being the light thereof. Her mother and I sat by her bedside: she turned her face towards the wall, and in five minutes, without speaking a word or heaving a groan, her spirit escaped from its cage.

As much as I valued this precious gift of Heaven, I dared not repine. He gave her to me as by a miracle, and He had a right to his own when he pleased. A few hours before she died, I sat by the side of her bed, with her son on my knee. She fastened her expressive eyes on him for some minutes. I said, "Rebecca, have you any regret in leaving this child?" "None!" she firmly replied: "I have given him over to the care of his heavenly Father, who will never leave him nor forsake him; and his earthly father I know will be kind to him, for my sake." The hope that supports nature in such extremities must be from above.

Being thus left with a child two years and two months old, with a care of a house and store, and thinking it more creditable and wise to marry a wife than to hire a housekeeper, I again entered into that state in 1801. Shortly after this, the introduction of cut-nails cut me off from making a living by my hammer. I now kept a grocery, and had a good run of customers: I still resided at No. 22 Nassau street.

On the east corner of Nassau and Liberty streets there lived the venerable old gentleman, Mr. Isaac Van Hook, so well known as the sexton of the New Dutch church opposite his house, for nearly fifty years. James Laing and William Smith, both cabinet-makers, and carrying on a respectable business, having in their employment ten or twelve journeymen and apprentices; these men took a mad resolution, gave up the business, sold their stock, hired the corner house over the head of poor old Van Hook,* turned him and his tobacco-pipes out of doors, and commenced the grocery business. Theirs being a corner, took away the most of my customers; insomuch that I was obliged to look round for some other mode to support my family. This, you may be sure, I considered a great misfortune; but, in the sequel, you will see that Providence was thus preparing the way to put me into a more agreeable and profitable business; and what we may often think is a great misfortune at the time, is only making the way for a greater blessing.

About this time the ladies in New York were beginning to show their taste for flowers; and it was customary to sell the empty flower-pots in the grocery stores; these articles also comprised part of my stock.

In the fall of the year, when the plants wanted shifting, preparatory to their being placed in the parlor, I was often asked for pots of a handsomer quality, or better make. As I stated above, I was looking round for some other means to support my family. All at once it came into my mind to take and paint some of my common flower-pots with green varnish paint, thinking it would better suit the taste of the ladies than the common brick-bat colored ones. I painted two

* This Mr. Van Hook was so great a smoker, that the pipe was not out of his mouth perhaps one hour in the twenty-four: he used the longest kind of Liverpool pipes. In the house, in the street, in the church, and in his bed, have I seen him with the pipe in his mouth. One day, a wag sent a countryman to ask if he sold any *smoked tongues?* The old man took the hint, said he had none to sell, but directed him across the street to old Mr. Watkey's, another noted smoker; between them they *smoked* the man, and, after drinking some good old Hollands, parted good friends.

pair, and exposed them in front of my window. I remember, just as I had placed the two pair of pots in front of my window on the outside, I was standing on the sidewalk, admiring their appearance, a carriage came along, having the glasses let down, and one lady only in the carriage. As the carriage passed my shop, her eye lit on the pots; she put her head out at the window, and looked back, as far as she could see, on the pots. Thinks I, this will take; and it did take—for these two pots were the links of a chain by means of which Providence was leading me into my extensive seed establishment. They soon drew attention, and were sold. I painted six pair; they soon went the same way. Being thus encouraged, I continued painting and selling to good advantage: this was in the fall of 1802.

One day, in the month of April following, I observed a man, for the first time, selling flower-plants in the Fly Market, which then stood at the foot of Maiden Lane. As I carelessly passed along, I took a leaf, and rubbing it between my fingers and thumb, asked him what was the name of it. He answered, a rose-geranium. This, as far as I can recollect, was the first time that I ever heard that there was a geranium in the world; as, before this, I had no taste for, nor paid any attention to, plants. I looked a few minutes at the plant, thought it had a pleasant smell, and thought it would look well if removed into one of my green flower-pots, to stand on my counter to draw attention. I remember, after smelling the first leaf of the rose-geranium, and also when I received additions to my stock, how I was struck with wonder and amazement, at the power, wisdom, and goodness of God, in imparting to the *green leaf* of one plant the fragrance of another, such as the balm, musk, pennyroyal, &c. How condescending to our senses, how indulgent, as it were, even to our childish and playful fancies! It was thus my mind was struck when I smelt the first leaf. Thought I, it is strange that a *green leaf* plucked from a plant no way similar, should possess all the flavor of the *flower* plucked from another.

Observe, I did not purchase this plant with the intention of selling it again, but merely to draw attention to my green pots, and let the people see how well the pots looked when the plant was in them. Next day, some one fancied and purchased plant and pot. Next day I went when the market was nearly over, judging the man would sell cheaper, rather than have the trouble of carrying them over the river, as he lived at Brooklyn,—and in those days there was neither steam nor horse-boats. Accordingly I purchased two plants; and having sold them, I began to think that something might be done this way; and so I continued to go at the close of the market, and always bargained for the unsold plants. And the man finding me a useful customer, would assist me to carry them home, and show me how to shift the plants out of his pots and put them into green pots, if my customers wished it. So I soon found by his tongue that he was a Scotchman, and being countrymen, we wrought to one another's hands: thus, from having one plant, in a short time I had fifty. The thing being a novelty, began to draw attention; people carrying their country friends to see the curiosities of the city, would step in to see my plants.

In some of these visits the strangers would express a wish to have some of these plants, but having so far to go, could not carry them. Then they would ask if I had no seed of such plants; then, again, others would ask for cabbage, turnip, or radish seed, &c.

These frequent inquiries at length set me to thinking, that if I could get seeds I would be able to sell them; but here lay the difficulty, as no one sold seed in New York, no one of the farmers or gardeners saved more than what they wanted for their own use; there being no market for an overplus. In this dilemma I told my situation to George Inglis, the man from whom I had always bought the plants in the Fly Market. He said he was now raising seeds, with the intention of selling them next spring, along with his plants, in the market; but if I would take his seeds he would quit the market, and stay at home and raise plants and seeds for me to sell. A bargain was immediately struck; I purchased his stock of seeds, amounting to *fifteen dollars;* and thus commenced a business on the 17th of September, 1805, that became the most extensive of the sort in the United States.

It is worth while to look back on the steps by which Providence led me into this business, without my ever planning or intending to become a seedsman.

1. By the introduction of cut-nail machines cutting me off from making a living by my own trade of nail-making.

2. By shutting me up, so that I could not make a living by keeping grocery.

3. By directing my mind to the painting of green pots, which induced me to purchase the first plant that

ever drew my attention; and this merely with a view of ornamenting my store, and not for the purpose of sale.

4. In being led, by the sale of this plant, to keep a quantity of them for the same purpose, which induced people to ask for the seed of the plants, and also for vegetable seeds, long before I ever thought of selling seeds.

I now advertised in the papers of the day garden-seeds. In a short time my small stock was all sold out; I knew not where to replace them. In this difficulty a friend stepped into the store, and introduced me to his friend, Mr. Morgan, just arrived from London, having a small invoice of garden-seeds, which he was willing to sell at a small advance. A bargain was soon struck, for the invoice contained the very articles I was daily asked for, and knew not where to obtain. Next day, on opening the casks, I found a catalogue of seeds for sale by William Malcolm & Co., London; this was at that time a prize to me, for never before this had I seen a seed-catalogue. This catalogue had noted on the margin the time of sowing—a thing I was totally ignorant of. Having now a plan, I published a catalogue of my own, and, with the assistance of my friend the gardener, at Brooklyn, adapted the time to suit our own climate; so that now, when my customers asked when such and such seeds ought to be sown, I was able to give the necessary information. Next fall, I sent a small remittance with an order to Mr. M. The seeds arrived in good season, and, with the seeds raised by my friend at Brooklyn, composed a good assortment to commence business in the spring. The seeds I had imported and got raised here, proving very good, my sales increased beyond what my friend could supply; and some of the market-gardeners, supposing they might be able to sell me seeds, had this year raised seeds for that purpose. Having no other resource, I was fain to purchase such as were offered; and, being a mechanic by profession, and alike ignorant of seeds and gardening, I had long to struggle with the impositions of unprincipled seed-raisers, they often selling me spurious seeds, and asserting they were of the most genuine quality.

Having at length brought the business to a pretty respectable footing, it narrowly escaped total destruction in 1808, by a great fire, which commenced in a soap and candle manufactory adjoining the store. This fire broke out at midnight, the 25th of August, and was so rapid that five of the inmates of the house where it commenced, perished in the flames. Several circumstances occurred in connection with this fire in which I could discern the kind hand of Providence, and are in themselves so remarkable that they deserve never to be forgotten. It was impressed on my mind, long before it took place, that the factory would be burned. For many months previous, when the fire company belonging to engine No. 16 came to the pump, corner of Liberty and Nassau streets, on the first Monday in every month (according to law), to wash and clean the engine, I used to tell them, in a jocose manner, how I wished them to act when the candle-box (as I termed the building) should take fire. I got my property insured a short time before the fire took place; it was in time of the long embargo. I had on hand a large stock of early York cabbage and other seeds, which I was obliged to import, but which could not then be imported, on account of the restrictions existing. At dinner, the day previous to the fire, I told my wife I was going to pack my most valuable seeds, and head them up in flour barrels, that they might be safely removed when the fire broke out next door. I came from my store between nine and ten o'clock that evening. My wife was much fatigued with nursing our youngest child, who was sick at the time; I told her to lie down, and I would nurse till she got some sleep. She arose about five minutes before twelve. As I laid my head on the pillow, the clock in the corner of my room struck twelve. I must have dropped to sleep immediately; for the next day I found my clock in the New Dutch Church, with the hands stopped at fifteen minutes past twelve; it having been seized and carried into the church at that minute, to save it from the fire. I was awoke by a loud scream from my wife, who was then rocking the cradle; I sprung on the floor before my eyes were opened, and asked what was the matter. She said we were all on fire. I opened the back window, and was saluted by a column of smoke and fire, issuing from the back of the soap-works. Having for many months previous resolved in my mind how I would act when the thing took place, I was in nowise alarmed; she being dressed, I told her to take herself and child to a place of safety, and I would wake up and take care of the other children and servants. I afterwards dressed, and put on a pair of double-soled boots, fearing that in the confusion I should tread on a rusty nail in some of the boards that might be pulled down. I then went in my store, which was by this time on fire, and secured my valuable papers and money, by pinning them in my jacket-pocket; I wet my night-cap and put it on, to preserve my hair from being singed. As the engines came up, I directed them to the place where their services would be most useful, and then ran from place to place, saving and preserving such property as I could.

The buildings where the fire originated stood on the south side of my premises, my back store, a wooden building two stories high. The wind blew fresh from the south, which covered this building with flame; but, notwithstanding, there was so little damage done this building, that ten dollars put it in as good repair as it was before the fire began. There was only an inch-board between the factory and my back building. The day previous, I had been painting pots with green varnish. The shelf on which the painted pots stood was next to the factory; one pot contained about four pounds of verdigris, mixed with spirits of turpentine and varnish; a pitcher also contained half a gallon of rosin, varnish, &c., with a jug containing half a gallon of spirits of turpentine. The fire burned through the boards directly opposite where these inflammable articles stood; the end of the shelf burned through, and dropping about twelve inches, rested on the floor, and then was extinguished; but by what means no one could tell, as no engine, person, or water, could reach that spot during the fire. The heat melted the paint that was on the outside of the pots and jug, running down the sides; when the fire subsided, they were found glued fast to the board. The jug with spirits of turpentine was corked; the pots containing paint and varnish were without covering, but completely filled up with black coals, which must have fallen in while burning. Yet for all this, these inflammable articles did not take fire; had they taken fire, my whole premises must have been consumed.

Next day, when the carpenter and his men came to repair what little damage was done, they were the first to observe this circumstance; and being struck with surprise, not only called me, but several of the neighbors, besides others, to see it, before they removed the articles. One of the neighbors observed, it was impossible that they could have stood there during the fire without being burned; when one of the carpenters told them to lift up the pots and jugs. They found them glued fast to the board, and were then convinced that, however strange, it was true. For my own part, I saw in it the power of Him whose hand is in every thing, whether it is the fall of an empire or a sparrow. In short, the small damage that was done to my premises surprised many; and many came from a distance to view the buildings for months after. Eight or nine houses were burned on the rear and on the windward side of the factory where the fire commenced; while my store, which was joined by nails and boards, had scarcely the smell of fire on its roof.

In 1808, when all intercourse between America and Britain was suspended, and we were therefore prevented from importing such seeds as were necessary in our business, I was advised by my friends to attempt the raising of them myself. I was drawn into this business much against my own inclination and better judgment, as you will see in the sequel.

A few years previous, a gardener from England, by

the name of Thornly, purchased about seven acres of land near Newark Bridge, which he improved as a kitchen-garden, and for raising a few seeds; but failing of success, and getting in debt, he absconded. He owed me a hundred dollars at the time; so, when he got to Philadelphia he executed a deed, whereby he constituted me owner of the soil, the first intimation of which was my receiving said deed per mail. As there was a considerable crop of seeds on the ground at the time, I resolved to gather the seeds as part payment; and as there was a mortgage for two hundred dollars on the premises, to let the land go to whomsoever had the best claim. The seeds were gathered, and the crop hardly paid the men's wages; but still I was persuaded to pay the mortgage and keep the place, as my well-intending friends all said it would do wonders under the management of an active man. It did wonders with a witness; for, after striving and toiling by sunlight and moonlight, in wet weather and dry weather, I found, at the end of five years, I had spent the whole earnings of my life, and was several thousands worse than nothing. I now gave up my all to my creditors; and, that I might be enabled to commence business anew, I applied, with an empty pocket and a clear conscience, for the benefit of the insolvent act. For this end it was necessary, as a first step, that I should either go to jail or the limits. I preferred the former, as I could board for half the expense. So, in December, 1813, I left my wife with one dollar and sixty-two cents, and four young children to support, without any certainty where the next dollar was to come from, in a solitary house, the nearest neighbor being one-fourth of a mile distant, and on a stormy day. You may suppose my feelings at this moment were not of the most pleasant kind.

The following circumstance took place, which struck me forcibly at the time, and on which I often reflect with wonder and gratitude. As I was walking down the main street in Newark, on my way to jail, the sheriff's officer politely going some distance either before or behind me, it matters not which, I was accosted by a man whom I had not seen for two years previous. Says he, "Mr. Thorburn, I have owed you fifteen dollars for a long time, but it never was in my power to pay you till now; just step in this store and I will pay you," pointing to one close by. I received the money with as much wonder and thankfulness as if I had seen it drop from the clouds in my path. I had not seen this man for so long a time, that I never expected the money. This circumstance inspired me with so much confidence in a superintending Providence, that I went into jail with a light heart, and *slept*—yes, my mind was so composed, after witnessing this signal proof of the goodness of God as a *Provider*, that all my anxieties on account of my family fled, and I *slept*. I knew that He who hangs creation on his arm, and feeds her at his board, would not suffer my children to starve. This man told me, some months after, that at the time he paid me that money he knew nothing of my difficulties. Well, having stayed the time appointed in jail, and gone through the forms by law prescribed, I came out whitewashed from all claims as far as the *law* could go; but I thought I was as much bound in *justice* as ever I was to pay my honest debts, should

Providence put it in my power, by prospering my future exertions. He did prosper my future exertions, and I can now show receipts for thousands of dollars which were by law cancelled.

In the course of my life I have experienced at times the depths of sorrow and the heights of delight; but just enough of the former to give a relish to the latter. When I failed, and gave up my property to my creditors, as usual, it was sold by the sheriff. At the public sale of my furniture, a cradle, in which lay one of my children asleep, then about two months old, was sold among the rest. This was more than my philosophy could stand. A gentleman among the company had it knocked down to him; he observed, with a smile, he supposed the child now was his property, as well as the cradle. Being answered in the affirmative, he called the mother of the child, and made her a present of both. Such seasonable acts of kindness, in times of trouble, give a double relish to the deed. While I was filled with gratitude to the instrument, I was also thankful to Him who has the hearts of all in his hands, believing that all men are to me what he makes them to be. He who gave Joseph favor in the eyes of his fellow-men is the same yesterday, to-day, and forever.

In 1815 I returned to New York with my family, and only about twelve dollars in my pocket. Being out of employment, I hired myself as porter to the store of Mr. D. Durham. He always treated me with kindness, though the other servants about his office complained of him as being a hard master. In January, 1816, a friend advanced me five hundred dollars, with which I commenced business in the cellar of a house corner of Nassau street and Liberty. For seven years previous, in spite of all my exertions, every thing went backwards,—now every thing seemed to thrive of itself.

Previous to my removal to New Jersey, my seed establishment was kept at No. 20 Nassau street. After my failure it was occupied by Mr. Grundy as a seed shop; and he, being in possession of the original stand, nearly engrossed all my former custom. He, however, neglected his business, took to habits of dissipation, was sold out by the sheriff in turn, when I purchased part of the stock and all the fixtures, and continued the business in my old stand.

On the day of my discharge under the insolvent act, Mr. Grundy was the only person who brought forward any opposition. It was not founded on the plea of fraud, but in trying to make out some sort of a flaw in the papers, as not having got the full two-thirds of my creditors to sign off, or something to that purpose: and had it not been that the recorder saw through the motive, and withal being a man proverbial for leaning to the side of mercy, he would have frustrated my discharge at that time.

When Mr. Grundy arrived in America he lodged first in my house, and continued under my roof several years, where he was always treated with kind attention; yet, when I was surrounded with difficulties and trouble, he proved my most determined enemy.

Again I had an opportunity of returning good for evil. When he got low I gave him employment: the last shilling he received in the world was from my hand. The streets were glazed with ice: I urged him to go home before night; he stopped on the way with a friend; it was very dark; he fell backwards, and was dead before morning.

Finding my business again in a prosperous state, I left New York the 8th of July, on a visit to my friends in Scotland.

CHAPTER IX.

A SCENE AT SEA.—JOURNEY TO THE BAY STATE IN JUNE, 1829.

On the 8th September, 1818, I sailed from Greenock in the Iris, Captain S., of New York. One morning, at sunrise, having been out near four weeks, we discovered a vessel far astern, seemingly following our track. The captain, after looking some time with his glass, observed, "That fellow wants to speak us." I requested him to slacken sail, as perhaps they were in distress. Having now a fair wind and a good breeze, he was loth to comply: again applying his glass, and laying it down, says he, "They want to speak us." I again renewed my entreaties; the captain ordered to take in sail. When the vessel came up, she proved to be a small schooner from Nova Scotia, bound to Liverpool, laden with rum; had encountered a storm three days previous; her decks were swept, and almost a wreck, with only five gallons of water on board. "Now, captain," says I, "had you known their situation you would have lain by all day for them." Says he, "I would." "Well, sir," says I, "I hope you will remember this." (At this time we were about the middle of the Atlantic.) Our captain told them to launch their boat, and he would give them a cask of water. They replied, their boat was stove, and would not live in the water. We then lowered our small boat, rolled a hogshead of water overboard; three of our men in the boat dragged it to the schooner, where it was hoisted on board. They gave the three men as much rum as they would drink, besides a quart-bottle full to each. They also sent a demijohn, containing five gallons, with a quantity of onions and lemons, for the captain. As our men came on board, I observed the bottles under their jackets; I followed them below to ascertain what they had got, and found it as above stated (observe, I was the only cabin passenger—there were twenty-two in the steerage). It was now eleven o'clock, A. M.; the heavens began to gather blackness, and, as I thought, threatened a storm. I told the captain the situation of the three men; the liquor they had drank on board the schooner already made them unfit for duty. "Now," says I, "when the others go down to dinner they will drink the three bottles, which will make them all drunk; and as the sky looks threatening, it may be attended with serious consequences." I therefore advised that he would go in the forecastle and get from them two of the bottles, which afterwards he might divide among them when necessary. He shrugged his shoulders, and said there was no danger.

Twelve o'clock, P. M., it blew fresh. While the captain and I were at dinner I heard considerable noise on deck between the mate and men, but said nothing. As was my custom after dinner, I was sitting on the forecastle smoking my pipe. A woman from the steerage, with a child in her arms, came flying along and screaming with all her might, "O! Mr. Thorburn, Mr. Thorburn, come, come, the captain is murdering the men!" I made for midships as fast as possible, when I beheld the captain with a broadsword, swinging away among the crew like a man thrashing oats.

In about an hour after, when the uproar had nearly ceased, I learned that the men had drunk up all the rum, as I predicted. The gale had increased almost to a storm, as I predicted. The sails wanted handling, but the crew were top-heavy and bottom-heavy, and when ordered, first by the mate and then by the captain, they were unable to go aloft. He ordered one of them to be tied up and flogged; the others resisted; he ran for his sword, and was flourishing away like a sans-culotte in the streets of Paris, when I arrived at the scene of action. Among our hands was a strong, active fellow by the name of Tom: he was with Commander Porter, in the Little Essex, when she fought the *two British sloops* of war till the blood of the whole crew had nearly run out at the scuppers. This man seized the captain's arm, wrenched the sword from his hand, and next moment it skimmed the waves like a sea-gull. The captain sprung into the cabin at three steps, returned with both hands full of pistols, and began firing away like one of our Pearl street Invincibles, in the Park, on the 4th of July. Finally, the crew laid hold of the captain, pistols and all, pushed him down the cabin stairs, and shut the door. During all this affray, the mate stood holding on by the fore-chains, and trembling like a dog on a sand-heap. He was a poor milk-and-water-looking son of a woman: he looked more like a psalm-singer from Danbury, than a mate on the quarter-deck of a ship. Having sailed from New York with this captain and crew, I knew the trim of all of them. I was on very good terms with the men, having lent them books to read when they had leisure. With the help of the mate, passengers, and such of the crew as were able to work, we got the ship in safe trim. I then went down to the captain. He was as mad as a *March hare.* I told him there was a ship to leeward: he took his glass, and after a minute's observation, said she was bound to the States, and added, he would run down, go on board of her, and leave the ship to the mate. I used every argument to dissuade him from this, without effect. I then went and got two of the women passengers out of the steerage, each having a child in her arms. I hastily told them how they should play their part. (You will here observe, he had a wife and children in New York, of whom he appeared very fond, as nothing pleased him so much as conversing about them.) We now descended into the cabin, renewed the attack on the side of domestic economy, spoke to him of his own wife and children, &c. The tears of the mothers, and smiles of the babes, at length prevailed: he consented to stay by the ship. (Perhaps it may be well to remark, by the way, that if this man had been a *bachelor*, we might have all gone to the bottom, for in this case he could have had no fellow-feeling for either wives or children.) By this time we had neared the vessel, and was preparing to speak, she lying-to for us. I requested the captain to say nothing about our situation, as by her sailing it was likely she would make New York a week before us (we got in first by two days, however), and the news would give his family and mine much uneasiness: to this he assented. The ship was the Comet, from Havre to New York.

But here our troubles were only commencing. He told me next morning he was resolved to make for Halifax, and deliver over to the British authorities his mutineers. I told him, as soon as the men got knowledge of his intention they would throw him overboard (as they knew the British government made short work with such characters), then make the first land, and run off. So by this means we passengers may all go to *Davy's locker*. He finally proposed, that if the passengers would divide themselves into watches (there were seventeen men, nine to go with him, and I with eight others on the mate's watch), he would keep on his course. I then dived into the steerage, and had a vast deal of trouble to get the men to comply; they all said the captain was to blame for not taking the liquor from the men. I said it mattered nothing to us now who was to blame; but if he steered for Halifax, and we went to the bottom, they would never see New York. With many more frightful words I labored to persuade them. At length the women and children began to cry, and the men were compelled to give in. I then told them the captain had another request, which was, that every man who had either a gun or a fowling-piece should loan them to him till our arrival at New York; with this they also refused to comply: at length they offered me their guns to carry into the cabin; I told them I cared no more for the captain than for the crew, only in as far as our own safety was concerned, and provided we once had our foot in New York, he and they might go to *Hackensack*, in the Jerseys, for any thing I cared: but says I, gentlemen, half measures won't do now; don't behave like children, but act like men; every one of you shoulder his musket, walk down in the cabin; the men will thus see you are determined to support the captain's authority, right or wrong; if he has injured them, they can get redress by the laws of their own country; but let us look to ourselves. This had the desired effect; they up with their pieces (seven in number), went off into the cabin, while I remained behind. The crew eyed them askant, but I saw their insolent looks had fled, and were replaced with something like fear. The captain then ordered two of the men to be confined in the forecastle, to be fed on bread and water till we arrived at New York, and threatened to shoot them if he caught them abaft the windlass. One of the confined was Tom aforesaid, a desperate mad fellow; he swore he would not be so treated, and threatened to come on deck. I advised him to submit, and if he sued the captain when we arrived, I would assist him as far as was right. He was fond of reading, and I supplied him and his fellow-prisoner with books, which made the time pass more easily. But between them and the captain I had my hands full; the latter was very passionate, and when in this state was not to be controlled; however, he was passionately fond of music and Scotch songs. We had a few Paisley weavers among the passengers who could sing and play well; I gave them the hint, and whenever the evil spirit was upon him, I stepped into the steerage. J. M'Farlain and his bass mate straightway were on deck, exerting their powers, vocal and instrumental; the sounds never failed to absorb all his attention, and in this way we kept down the evil spirit, just as David of old played the devil out of Saul. From this night till our arrival in New York (three weeks) the other passengers and I stood our regular watches with the captain, mate, and crew,—no very pleasant affair, you may be sure, to mount watch at eight, turn in at twelve, rise again at four, and stand till eight; but the thought of home, and hopes of meeting them I held most dear, still kept my spirits up. Were life's voyage never clouded in tempests, we could not sò sweetly relish the sunshine of prosperity. These events took place in the cold dark stormy nights of October. Often in the beginning of my watch have we shipped a sea, been drenched to the skin, walked the deck four solitary hours; yet I was not sick for an hour, nor ever caught the slightest cold. On the 3d of November we arrived, after fifty-six days' passage. Finding all well more than repaid me for all my past troubles. As soon as the ship struck the wharf, the hands jumped on shore and run off, the captain offering no hindrance. Next day the following appeared in the "New York Gazette," 4th November, 1818.

"A Card.—We, the passengers on board the ship Iris, from Greenock, return our thanks to Captain J. S. for his care and attention to our health and safety during the voyage; also to Mr. Grant Thorburn, of New York, cabin passenger, for his mild and conciliatory exertions in suppressing and averting the consequences of an alarming dispute among the crew, whereby our lives and the safety of the vessel were for some time in imminent danger.

(Signed) James Anderson,
John Lawrence,
In behalf of the other passengers."

It's of no use for a man to write his journal, except he can get it printed, otherwise nobody will know that he has been travelling at all; and as I kept one when journeying to the Bay State, in June, 1829, I will here occupy a few pages in giving it publicity.

I heard much of a country peopled by the daughters of Puritans and sons of the Pilgrims; and, besides, that of late years they had made such rapid advances in what they termed *rational religion*, that I thought it was there and then that the millennium, so much spoken of in the "Progress of the Pilgrim," was about to commence. I was anxious to see this people, not to take the height of their cornstalks, nor the diameter of their pumpkins; but among them I thought was to be found the perfection of the church militant, and I longed to see a sight so imposing. You will see in the sequel how sadly I was disappointed. But I'll begin with Fulton slip, from which we started, in the steamboat Franklin. After we passed the Gates of Hell, and got over the Hog's Back, two dangerous rocks in the Sound, on the eastern shore of Manhattan Island, the captain, knowing from former experience that his goodly boat knew the road well enough to go by herself, turned his attention to more important matters. He sent forth a little boy, his face as black as Lehigh coal; a bell, white as silver, in his hand, went tinkle, tinkle, round the deck. "Passengers will go to the captain's office and pay their fare." (Thinks I, these Yankees have their office of deposits everywhere.) I was carried along with the crowd, and came to a stand with my head right under the port-hole, or office-window, as they called it; when up came squeezing a long-legged fellow, and shoved me aside like a thing of naught. Says I, "Sir, in New York he who comes first with his pail to the pump gets it first filled." He *looked down* on me—that was all; he held between his finger and thumb, while it floated with the breeze, a fifty-dollar bill,—as much as to say, you see I have more money in my purse than wit in my head. Captain Bunker, with one eye observed the manœuvre, while with the other he was giving change from a ten-dollar bill. Says he, "Mr. T., it's your turn next (I wondered where he got my name); you are getting squeezed among these big men; "I'll let you go." Mr. Long-legs looked as flat as a pancake without yeast. This wee bit of civility from the captain gave me a good opinion of his heart and head. Having nothing else to do, I observed him through the passage, up-stairs and down-stairs, sunlight and moonlight; he was always doing the thing as it ought to be; always good-natured and laughing. I believe if he stood in a storm on the last plank of his boat he would smile; though he looks like one that would never give up the ship while two of her timbers hung together.

Next morning we saw Newport. I wondered to see a great heap of men, I dare say near a hundred of them, bigging up something like a great stone dyke, with windows in it. I asked the captain what it was for. He said they were making a battery of one hundred and fifty guns for the *protection* of Newport. I thought their poverty would be a good protection for them. I asked if the men wrought by the day or the job. He said, by the day, he believed. I thought so; for from the time the boat came near enough to see the white of their eyes, till we had passed them so far that we could not tell the color of their coat, they stood gaping and looking; and from a hundred men, with each a hammer in his hand, you could not hear a stroke in a minute.

I asked if the town or state paid them? He answered, it was *Uncle Sam* paid them. Oho! thinks I, this solves the whole mystery; these men will never finish this till another job as good comes to hand. Poor *Uncle Sam* has not only to pay his stewards high wages for collecting his rents, but some of them share off twenty-five or thirty per cent. for commissions; and others, knowing that their reign will be short (as the next man who comes into power will kick them out of doors), make the most of their time, and so become defaulters for the whole. I really wonder how *Uncle Sam* gets along so well as he does.

At Providence, coaches were ready; we flew through the dust and sweat of the day like Jehu. At the tavern of ——, the dinner was ready, but there was no contract for time to eat; after grace from Dr. Cox (which I thought was too long for the occasion), we began to eat. Scarcely had I swallowed half of my first course, when in came the driver hallooing, "All ready!" I thought there was something like a stable-yard understanding between him and the landlord; for, while we were brushing the dust from our clothes, mustering, and saying grace, he was eating and drinking as fast as he could, and I did not observe that he paid any thing. Having a fine stern breeze, we flew along at the rate of ten knots an hour, amidst clouds of smoke and dust. All along I could see houses, and doors, and windows, and folks looking out of them; but I had no time to inquire either into their principles or practice: so I wisely resolved (as I thought) to suspend all further inquiries till I got to Boston, setting down in my mind, that if I found the fountain pure, the streams would be pure also. We arrived at the Eagle Tavern about sundown; the ladies' hats and frocks, which in the steamboat showed colors enough to have decked fifteen rainbows, were now one, viz., ashes on ashes, and dust on dust.

Next day being Saturday, as I could not prosecute my main inquiry, I went to Bunker's Hill. By the monument I stood with feelings all my own: the history of that battle brought to my mind the first of my newspaper recollections; but a tale hangs there, which I have not time to repeat, nor a wish to tell to every ear—but the monument—I wish it were finished. The young ladies of Boston can do it alone. Let them with one consent place a neat little box on every sideboard; when their young friend presents them with a box-ticket, receive it with thanks, and add, "Now we are going to finish the monument—for one year from this date we will suspend this pleasure." Let the price of the tickets be placed in that box, and our monument of *gratitude* will *rise*. The Boston Elm, a monument of antiquity—I stood under its shadows with great delight, and thought of former days. Were a neat stone fence two feet high; and an iron railing three feet more, placed round this tree, it would protect its bark from the knife of idle boys, and its roots from the foot of the ox; six wagon-loads of good fresh mould laid on the surface would help to invigorate its old age; one dollar from each of the owners of those princely mansions round the mall would accomplish this.

I rose about five on Sabbath morning, resolving to examine the exterior and interior of the churches. Whenever I could spy a steeple for a guide, into most of them I found access, as the sextons were either dusting inside or sweeping outside. I thought this was hardly consistent with *purity*, for they might give the man a dollar a week more, and he would do this work on Saturday afternoon. I was struck with the grandeur of all of them (they beat our New York churches hollow). I was pleased that they did not let the house of God lie in ruins, while they themselves were living in palaces. But there was such a wonderful profusion of scarlet curtains and scarlet cushions behind the pews and before the pews, behind the pulpit and before the pulpit, I thought it had an *awful* squinting at the mother of harlots riding on the scarlet beast, whereof you may see a more particular account in the 17th chapter of the Revelations, from the first verse to the end. In another church, where the back of the pulpit was near as broad as the east end of the City Hotel, in Broadway, was an anchor hung up, large enough for the Washington 74; and, in place of tarred ropes, it was bound round the stock with fine scarlet cords; the wall was covered with scarlet cloth. I should think there was a hundred yards of it, which hung in beautiful festoons over the flukes of the anchor. The sexton told me the cloth and anchor was made a present to the church by a *single* gentleman, and that it cost a thousand dollars. Presuming the man was a bachelor, as the words *single gentleman* seemed to imply, I thought he had better have bought furniture with the one thousand dollars, and gone to housekeeping with one of those bonny lasses I saw playing under the elm-tree; and he had better have painted the back of the pulpit a good sky-blue color, and given the balance to the poor missionaries, or even to one of the Female Auxiliary Temperance Societies, whereby these kind-hearted creatures would have been enabled to feed and clothe a few score of these poor starving brats, whose fathers drink up all their money in rum, because the bread is so dear. But I don't mean to enter into the merits of this case. I only tell you what I thought: this was a rational church, and I dare say the man thought he was acting on rational principles, and that is enough for me, especially as I found the puritan churches decked out pretty much in the same manner—nothing but the eternal red scarlet everywhere, like the hats of the fat cardinals at Rome.

At ten the bell rang, as it does in New York: the minister told the folks to *join with him* in singing to the praise and glory of God. Had you seen me at this moment, with mouth open, and eyes staring with surprise, when, instead of joining with him in singing to the praise and glory of God, up starts a long string of young lads and lasses, who sung out most lustily to the praise and glory of *themselves*, and behind them was an organ, roaring as loud as the arms of the man and the wind of the bellows could make it: I thought, if this be worship, a pair of Scotch bag-pipes might do as well. I turned to see how the minister brooked the affront, as no one joined with him; when lo! there he stood as mute as a mummy, his psalm-book shut, a hand on each side of the pulpit, supporting his noble frame; his face, instead of displaying anger (as I expected), was almost mantling with a complacent smile, as he looked under the broad brims of the lasses' hats, and seemed absorbed in contemplating the sweetness of their warbling throats. His ruddy cheek and glistening brow told me in accents louder than the organ's roar, that, however satisfied he might be to worship God by *proxy*, he did not carry the principle into the ordinary walks of life—at least in as far as eating and drinking was concerned. By the time they had sung a verse, I found it was a good old Scotch tune, by the name of *French*, they were at; and as I had joined with a thousand voices in the old Grayfriars' Kirk, Edinburgh, forty years ago, in singing "David's Psalms" to this same tune, I up with my book, turned my back to the minister, like the rest, and sung away as loud as I could, keeping time with the lads up stairs. The folks stared: one said, "He is a Yorker"—others that I was daft; but, thinks I, they may laugh that win; I am doing my duty in joining with the lasses (if the minister won't) in singing praise, and at any rate, am leaving testimony against this anti-puritan mode of worship; so I sung on to the end of the hymn. Thinks I to myself, these folks' religion may be rational enough for aught that I know; but they appear to me to have a queer way of showing it. I thought how much better this thing is done in Scotland. Professor Silliman, in his journey through that country, takes notice of being in the Tron Kirk of Edinburgh, where generally about a thousand people assemble for worship on Sabbath days. He says they all joined, men, women, and children, in singing the Scotch version of the Psalms: it made him feel as if standing on the outside of heaven's walls, and hearing the sound as the sound of many waters, &c., and it thrilled his very soul. These are not the exact words (as I have not his book by me), but they are the substance.

In the afternoon I went to another church, to see if I could find any thing more pure. The minister, after inviting the people to join with him, &c., having read a hymn, and the organ played a solo, a woman, dressed pretty enough, and her cheeks I thought rather more ruddy than nature commonly paints them in the month of June, got up and sang most sweetly all alone by herself, praise and glory in the name of the whole congregation, as I could neither see man nor minister that joined her: nothing was heard but her sweet pipes, and the tin pipes of the organ. After I got out, I asked a decent-looking man who she was that sung? He said she belonged to the play-actor folk; and, if he was rightly informed, had been singing at twelve o'clock the night previous, in one of the theatres, to the *praise* and *glory* of the *devil*. The puritan church paid her three hundred dollars, and the devil's church six hundred dollars per annum; so, between the *two*, she cuts a bright figure. I said to myself, if one of those stern old pilgrims who landed on Plymouth rock that cold stormy day, with their noses as red as a northwest moon, were to enter now, how these pigmy degenerates would sneak into mice-holes! To return—(but I must observe, that all the ministers I heard in this eastern country are readers, not preachers of the Gospel). After the woman had finished her song the minister made a very decent prayer. In it he besought the Lord to lay plentifully to his *hands* of the *food* of *souls*, &c. Now, thinks I, we will have a preaching. Well, his prayer finished, without a blush on his face, he pulls from his pocket a roll of black leather, in form of a tobacco-pouch; from this he unrolls about a sheet of paper, and, without ever opening the Bible, reads a text from the head of the sheet, and so reads on till he comes to Amen, at the end of the sheet. I wondered at the indecency (to call it no worse) of the man. Did he think he was addressing a stock or a stone, that did not hear him? Did he suppose his Maker did not know that all the food he was about to deal out to the hungry souls before him was in his pocket? I have heard this same mode of prayer used by reading ministers in New York. I hope hereafter they will pray for the blessing of light, and eyesight, and the use of their tongue; for, by this system of reading, I had almost said they put it out of the power of God Almighty to help them. I have been to Guilford and Stonington, to Bambury and Danbury—everywhere they read their sermons, and sing praise by proxy.

It was harvest, and very warm. Saturday was fine for getting in the grain: it was full moon. Many of the farmers kept their men-servants and maid-servants, their oxen and their jackasses, at work till one o'clock on Sunday morning. At half-past ten they got all to church. The minister began to read off his task; but scarcely had he got to *thirdly*, when I looked round and found they were all asleep except a few old women (and they would have been asleep also, but having *dozed* for the last forty years under the droppings of this drowsy preaching, for the life of them they could not sleep an hour longer), and about two dozen of Sunday scholars in the gallery, who were cutting sticks to make windmills. I observed that the teachers, male and female, were asleep, and the minister was reading the dead languages: To keep myself awake, my thoughts run ahead in the following strain:—Before this I never could comprehend what was the employment of those chaps in Yale College who are called professors of the dead languages. I now felt satisfied that it must be they who teach the young Yankees to read sermons; but what a pity the old farmers, their fathers, should squeeze and starve all the rest of the family to raise forty dollars per month, to pay board and fees, and fire and candles, and pens and paper, to teach a boy to read sermons in New Haven. Only send them to New York, and we will teach them for *ten shillings* per month to read nearer to the points than many whom I heard; and they can buy for one hundred as many sermons as they can read in fifty years: this, too, would save a great deal of paper, for a sermon reads just as well when printed as written. We have heard much of the march of intellect since the days of the pilgrims; but with regard to pulpit life, oratory, and eloquence, it has been in an awful *retrograde* line. Cotton Mather, and his contemporary champions of truth, would preach hours on a stretch without a paper within a mile of them except their Bible. The Edwardses and Witherspoons, the Rogerses and Lins, the Livingstons and Masons, made the souls of their hearers, as well as the walls of their churches, tremble, with their extempore pulpit eloquence. Now we have boys fresh from the college; their beards as soft as the down on a mushroom-top; green spectacles to hide their conscious shame, reading from a dead paper to a company of dead souls, and with a manner, too, as dead as the devil (who always attends church) could wish it. Why, if these men were to go into congress, the bench, or even the theatre so, they would be kicked from the hall, or hissed from the stage. Is it not a shame, to say the least of it, that a man in congress, or in a court of justice, will speak hours to the purpose, and often in support of a doubtful point, without paper, and yet a minister of the Gospel, who has the range of three worlds—heaven, earth, and hell—with all the sublime doctrines of the Bible at his finger-ends, can't speak forty minutes without a quire of paper held up as an extinguisher of truth between his eyes and the eyes of his hearers? If you want to convince men in argument, they must see the fire of truth flash from your eyes. When Paul stood before Felix, and reasoned of righteousness, temperance, and a future judgment, his eyes kindled with the mighty theme, darting conviction through the eyes of the tyrant into the dark corners of his guilty, black, iron-bound soul-case, which made him tremble on his throne,—yes, on his throne, and before a prisoner in chains, too. Truth, when well spoken (not read), will make any tyrant tremble.

There is no excuse for this *banisher* of pulpit eloquence—laziness is the cause. Forty years ago, you would rarely have seen a paper in any pulpit in New York. The abilities of our young men are as good now as they were then; memory, like all faculties of the mind, will improve by using; ministers only, of all public speakers, take neither pride nor pains to excel. Were I a minister, I would throw my paper in the fire, and say, I will be second to none, were it only for the *honor* of the *profession.* The ministers in the devil's church, the theatre, deal out their fictions and lies in such a solemn strain of eloquent pathos, that they can chain the attention of their audience, and bathe them in tears for hours; but many of the ministers of the Most High deal out their solemn realities as if they were mere fictions, and they can barely keep the people from going to sleep. The "thoughts that breathe and words that burn" never flowed from off a paper. One Sabbath evening, about seventeen years ago, I went into the brick meeting to hear Dr. W., from Connecticut, preach. There he stood, with all the insignia of office—white bands, silk cloak, and tassels enough to bedeck a modern hearse—a tall, fine-looking man. I thought he was Boanerges personified. Out came his paper: he read along pretty well for fifteen minutes. The thunder began to roll over Snake Hill, in the Jerseys; the heavens were clothed in darkness, his spectacles failed, and he was obliged to sit down, till the sexton procured lighted candles. I thought this spoke more than volumes against the pernicious practice of reading. However, next day I learned he had been a professor of theology for seven years previous, and being a man of a very charitable turn of mind, I thought it was probable he might have given away whatever little stock of divinity he once possessed, for the benefit of those young students whose heads he had been polishing, and thereby left nothing to himself. I also learned he had been a preacher for twenty years, ten of which he had passed away under the title of doctor of divinity; but there he sat, and could not speak one word for his Master, without the help of paper, ink, and candle-light. Such were my reflections returning home in the steamboat Washington, Captain Comstock.

But I have said nothing of the town. The men were kind, sociable, and sober. I heard it said that their temperance societies existed long before the Revolution. The merchants are not quite so bustling as in New York, but I think they do it more *cannily*. You meet very few by two o'clock who have five hundred dollars short painted on their countenance. Their markets are fine, neat, and clean—all shut up as tight as a store at night. No drunken, dirty rascal sleeps there at night, as in our markets, on the stalls, till aroused in the morning by the butcher throwing down his quarters of beef. Their provision-shops are well supplied, and are a great convenience to the inhabitants—a blessing we are deprived of in New York by law. The ladies are handsome, intelligent, and good-natured.

CHAPTER X.

PURCHASE THE FRIENDS' MEETING-HOUSE AND GROUNDS.—INSTANCE OF SPECIAL PROVIDENCE.—THOMAS PAINE.—ANECDOTE OF HIM.—HIS NARROW ESCAPE FROM EXECUTION IN FRANCE.—EFFECTS OF INFIDELITY IN FRANCE.—GENERAL MOREAU.

During the time I was gardening in New Jersey, I sunk twelve thousand dollars and upwards; but when, in 1825, I made the purchase of the Friends' Meeting-House, this loss was *providentially* made up to me in one day, inasmuch as I paid twenty thousand five hundred dollars for the Meeting-House and ground, and in a few days thereafter was offered forty thousand, and again was offered fifty thousand and upwards. The house was situated in Liberty street, and had been occupied by the Society as a place of burial, school, and meeting-house,* for upwards of 140 years.

For the following reasons I think I see the kind hand of Providence in this matter. As it was a transaction of great importance, I earnestly prayed for direction from Him who has said, "Acknowledge me in all your

* It is another curious incident in my life, that I was making nails on the opposite side of the street at the time the Meeting-House (afterwards my store) was building—part of the nails used were made by myself. Little thought my good friends (the Quakers), while they were paying me for nails to assist in rearing the Meeting-House, that, at the same time, they were preparing for me a shop, wherein to sell seeds—but so Providence orders our lot.

ways, and I will direct your steps." I did so, and I think he directed me in that important matter; for, 1st, Every step I took towards furthering my views succeeded beyond my expectations. 2d, Every time I went to see any of the persons concerned in the sale, I always found them at home, and did the business I went about without once going on what we call a *needless errand*. 3d, I bought it at *private sale*—a circumstance which had not happened, in the sale of so much valuable property in the lower part of the city, for very many years. The circumstance is more remarkable, as several individuals had also applied to make a purchase; also the New York Athenæum, and other public bodies; besides several gentlemen, who wished to have it for building lots. Likewise, a company of gentlemen in the lower part of the city had a plan laid out, and a company organized to purchase it at any rate, for the purpose of converting it into a select school for their daughters. In this state of things each party was preparing for the contest of public sale. One broker since told me that he was authorized to bid as high as $32,000. I purchased six lots for $26,000, Mr. Tilletson paying $5200: so our four lots on Liberty street, with the building, cost us only $20,800. Every one who knew the circumstance was surprised, and unable to conceive a reason for its being sold at private sale. Under the above circumstances, for my own part, I can only say that so Providence ordered it should come to our hands; for, had it come to public sale, it would have gone far higher than our business would afford to pay the interest for the purchase money.

Our expenses in erecting a green-house, and other

necessary fixtures for carrying on our business to advantage, were great; however, our sales so increased, that we were able to meet the demands.

The following is one out of many instances in which Providence directed me, almost by miracle, in the furtherance of the seed establishment. In April, 1803, I commenced the selling of seeds. One evening, in the fall of the year, a merchant gave me an order for a quantity of spring-wheat: at that time I knew not there was such an article in use. However, I promised to get it if possible. At the same time there lived, at the corner of Stone and Mill streets, a grain-broker, by the name of Reynolds. Next morning I started with the intention of making my first inquiry of him. Having a small bill against Mr. Henry Coster, whose office was situated in William street, directly opposite the post-office, I took it along with me, as it lay in my way. When I entered the office, Mr. Coster was conversing with a gentleman; Mr. Coster inquired my business, and insisted that I should stop: their conversation continuing, I again offered to retire, but was prevented by Mr. Coster, who observed he should be at leisure presently. In a few minutes the gentleman went out; I finished my business, and, just as I crossed over to the post-office, I met J. Patrick coming out with a handful of letters. As we were going the same way, his office being on the west side of Old Slip, we kept company, talking about the weather, &c., till we came to the corner of Stone street. Just as I was turning to pursue my original intention of calling on Reynolds, at the corner of Mill street, says Mr. Patrick, "Mr. Thorburn, as you are a seedsman, do you know of any one who wants a quantity of *spring-wheat*, which was sent me yesterday from Hudson?" Surprise prevented me from answering for a few moments: I did not tell him I was in pursuit of the article, but we walked to his store, when I made an easy purchase of the whole. Returning and ruminating on the circumstances and occurrences of the last half hour, I thought I would still call on Reynolds. He had no spring-wheat, nor did he know where it could be found. He said very few raised it, and it was seldom brought to the city.

Thus, you see, had I not met Mr. Patrick at that precise moment, I should have gone on a needless errand; and had not Mr. Coster twice detained me, against my wishes, I should not have met Mr. Patrick coming out of the post-office.

I could relate many such instances, in which I could see the directing hand of Providence, and abundant proofs that not a sparrow falls to the ground without the notice of our heavenly Father:

In each event of life how clear
  Thy ruling hand I see!
Each blessing to my soul more dear,
  Because conferred by Thee.

When I look back I remember some ludicrous and curious scenes in which I have been part actor. I have come in contact with several of the men whose names have borne a conspicuous part in the history of the last forty years: such as Thomas Paine, General Moreau, &c. When Thomas Paine escaped from the dungeon of the Committee of Safety, men whom the writings of

Paine, and such as Paine, had turned into monsters, he put up at the City Hotel in this city. One morning, about nine o'clock, a person came in my store and stated that he was standing on the steps in front. As I lived in the next street, and being anxious to see him, I, with two gentlemen who happened to be in the store at the time, went round to have a look at him; but before we got there, he stepped in. While I stood considering how to get a sight of him, I observed Samuel Loudon, the printer, enter the hotel. As I knew Samuel and he were copatriots through the whole of the American Revolution, I presumed he was going to see his old friend. I proposed to my companions to go in; and as I was acquainted with Mr. Loudon, we would thus get introduced. They declined going. As I went alone, I asked the waiter—

"Is Mr. Paine at home?" "Yes."

"In his own room?" "Yes."

"Alone?" "Yes."

"Can I see him?" "Follow me."

He ushered me into a spacious room, where the table was set for breakfast—a gentleman at the table writing, another reading the paper. At the further end of the room a long, lank, coarse-looking figure stood with his back to the fire. From the resemblance to portraits I had seen in his *Rights of Man* I knew it was Paine. While I followed the waiter, presuming Paine was alone, I was preparing an exordium to introduce myself to a plain republican alone; but when I thus found myself in company with the great author of "Common Sense," for a moment I was at a stand. Says I, "Gentlemen, is Mr. Paine in this room?" He stepped towards me and answered, "My name is Paine." I held out my hand, and while I held his, says I, "Mr. Paine, and you, gentlemen, will please excuse my abrupt entry; I came out of mere curiosity to see the man whose writings have made so much noise in the world." Paine answered, "I am very glad your curiosity is so easily satisfied." Says I, "Good morning, gentlemen;" walked out, and shut the door behind me. I heard them all burst out into a loud laugh. Thinks I, they may laugh that win; I have seen Paine, and, all things considered, have made a good retreat. The gentlemen called the waiter, and inquired who that was. "It is Thorburn, the seedsman." They reported the matter at the coffee-house, and among their acquaintances. As the story travelled, it was told with all manner of additions. One was, that I told Paine he was a rascal; had it not been for his books I would never have left my native country, &c., &c. In short, there was nothing heard for many days but Thorburn's visit to Mr. Paine.

At that time I was clerk, or psalm-singer, in the Scotch Presbyterian church in Cedar street, of which the famous Dr. John M. Mason was the minister. The church-session caught the alarm; an extra meeting was called. To be sure I was not noticed to attend—perhaps they were afraid of contamination from one who had shaken hands with Mr. Paine. Be that as it may, I was suspended from office for some months.

A few years after this, when Paine had fallen into disrepute, and his company shunned by the more respectable of his friends, on account of his unpopular writings and hard drinking, he boarded in the house of one William Carver, a blacksmith and horse-doctor. This Carver and I had wrought journeywork together in the same shop ten years before that period; so, having free access to the house, I frequently called to converse with Mr. Paine. One evening he related the following anecdote:—He said it was in the reign of Robespierre, when every republican that the monster could get in his power was cut down by the axe of the guillotine, Paine was in the dungeon, and his name on the list, with twenty more, ordered for execution next morning. It was customary for the clerk of the tribunal to go through the cells at night, and put a cross with chalk on the back of the door of such as were to be guillotined in the morning. When the executioner came round with his guard, wherever they found a chalk the victim was brought forth. There was a long passage in the cellar, or dungeon, of this bastile, having a row of cells on each side, containing the prisoners. The passage was secured at each end, but the doors of the cells were chiefly left open, and sometimes the prisoners stepped into one another's room to converse. Paine had gone into the next cell, and left his door open, back to the wall; thus having the inside out. Just then came the chalkers, and, probably, being drunk, crossed the inside of Paine's door. Next morning, when the guard came with an order to bring out twenty, and finding only nineteen chalks (Paine being in bed, and his door shut), they took a prisoner from the further end of the passage, and thus made up the number. So Mr. Paine escaped; and, before the mistake was discovered (about forty-eight hours after), a stronger party than Spirie's cut off his head, and about thirty of his associates; and so Paine was set at liberty. But being afraid to trust his head any longer among these good democrats, for whom he had written so much, he made the best of his way for this country.

I asked him what he thought of his almost miraculous escape. He said, "The *Fates* had ordained he was not to die at that time." Says I, "Mr. Paine, I will tell you exactly what I think: you know you have written and spoken much against what we call the religion of the Bible; you have highly extolled the perfectibility of human reason when left to its own guidance, unshackled by priestcraft and superstition; the God in whom you live, move, and have your being, has spared your life that you might give to the world a living comment on your own doctrines. You now show to the world what human nature is when left to itself, to wander in its own counsels; here you sit, in an obscure, uncomfortable dwelling, powdered with snuff, and stupefied with brandy; you, who were once the companion of Washington, Jay, and Hamilton, are now deserted by every good man; and even respectable deists cross the streets to avoid you." He said, "He cared not a straw for the opinions of the world." Says I, "I envy not your feelings." So we parted. In short, he was the most disgusting human being you could meet in the street. Through the effect of intemperance his countenance was bloated beyond description—he looked as if God had stamped his face with the mark of Cain. A few of his disciples, who stuck to him through good and through bad report, to hide him from the gaze of men, had him conveyed to Greenwich, where they supplied him with brandy till he died.

One evening, shortly after he gave me the history of his escape from the guillotine, I found him in company with a number of his disciples, as usual abusing the Bible for being the cause of every thing that is bad in the world. As soon as I got an opportunity to edge in a word, says I, "Mr. Paine, you have been in Ireland, and other Roman Catholic countries, where the common people are not allowed to read the Bible; you have been in Scotland, where every man, woman, and child has the Bible in their hands; now, if the Bible were so bad a book, they who used it most would be the worst people. In Scotland, the peasantry are intelligent, comfortable, sober, and industrious; in Ireland, they are ignorant, drunken, and live but little better than the brutes. In New York, the watch-house, bridewell, alms-house, penitentiary, and states-prison, are filled with Irish; but you won't find a Scotchman in these places." This being an historical fact which he could not deny, and the clock having just struck ten, he took a candle from the table and walked up stairs, leaving his friends and myself to draw our own conclusions.

Mr. Paine was very fond of company; but his habits being intemperate, his chief associates were mostly among the second orders in society. From my acquaintance with William Carver, the blacksmith, at the corner of Cedar and Temple streets, I often used to spend the evening conversing with Mr. Paine. He had seen much of men and their manners; had a clear, strong head, but (as I thought) a very unsound heart. Politics and religion were the chief topics of our discourse. We agreed on the former; on the latter we differed, but always in a friendly way. One evening he was describing, in his usual strong manner, the mischiefs (as he termed it) produced in society by the Bible and its followers. Says I, "Mr. Paine, the first night I slept in America was on a hard mattress, laid on the floor of a close garret, in a hot night in the warm month of June—the place swarmed with musquitoes and other *domestic animals*, and whenever sweet sleep approached, they drove her from my pillow: sore feverish, and sunk in spirit, I rose by break of day to while away the time till the family got up. I com menced unpacking my box of books; I opened the first book that came to hand, merely to see if it had received any injury by confinement in the hold of the vessel for so many weeks; my eye lit on the words, '*My son*'"—(this book was in two small volumes: often when I went to see Mr. Paine I put it in my pocket, to set him right when he misquoted a passage). Having the book by me, I asked, and he assented, to hear it read—it was the third chapter of Proverbs; we sat with the table between us, his eyes fixed on my face till I had done. "Now," says I, "Mr. Paine, put yourself in my situation—a poor, sick stranger, just entering on the untried scenes of life without a pilot, and conceive, if you can, a set of instructions more suitable: why, sir, it drove away my fever and my fears—I went forth, to commence my new career, with a heart as light as a feather, trusting in Him who hangs creation on his arm, and feeds her at his board." He heard without interruption, when, patting me on the head, with a good-natured smile, "Ah," says he, "but thou art a young *enthusiast*." So we parted for the night.

I will now, to give Mr. Paine his due, mention one good action he performed. The man who suffered death instead of Paine left a widow, with two young children, in poor circumstances. Paine brought them all with him to this country, supported them while he lived, and, it is said, left most of his property to them when he died. The widow and children lived in apartments up town, by themselves; I saw them often, but never saw Paine in their company: he then boarded with Carver. I believe his conduct was disinterested and honorable to the widow. She appeared to be about thirty years of age, and was very far from being handsome.

The friends of Mr. Paine, merely in attempting to contradict my statement, have lately asserted that this woman was not the widow of the man guillotined, and, from what I lately learned, I believe she was not. One thing I know, when he first brought her out, he and his friends passed her off as such; and it's a pity they should have taken from him the credit of the only good action he was ever thought to have performed.

There are some who have read little, and thought less, on the events that have passed before our eyes within the last forty years, who may honestly wish to see the experiment tried, whether society can exist in any thing like a state of order, without the religion of the Bible: but the experiment has been tried and found wanting. The Governor of the world, as if to leave men without excuse, gave the management of the affairs of France, for several years of her late revolution, into the hands of men who were freethinkers in principle, and enemies to religion by profession.

Having the power, they put their principles into practice: they abolished the Sabbath, and substituted every tenth as a day of rest or amusement—they shut up the churches, and banished the ministers, except a few, whom they styled priests of the religion of nature—they dressed up a female (the Fanny Wright of Paris, no doubt), according to their notion of some heathen deity, whose costume was any thing but modest—they placed her on a pedestal in one of their public squares or temples—they bowed the knee and paid her divine homage, under the style and title of the *Goddess of Reason!* Yes, gentle reader, these men were the philosophers of the day, the Timothy Jenkinses of France, who shouted in the ears of the simple, We are the men—we are the men! and wisdom will die with us! It was enough to make the *devil blush.* The gutters of Paris were turned into a scarlet dye, so mighty was the devastation and murders of these philanthropists—these friends of man! Bonaparte, and a few other men of strong mind, seeing the nation was rolling fast towards the dark gulf of worse than savage barbarism, took the reins from the hands of these unskilful drivers; they scattered the council of five hundred into thin air, restored to the people their weekly Sabbath, their altar, and their priests—and again were the people happy. Now, my good friends, look out for the rocks on which others have split. We have as much, and more, liberty to carry, than we can fairly stagger under; no religious denomination can lord it over another in America, as the Constitution has placed these, as they ought to be, *all on a level;* and while we have neither lords temporal nor spiritual in our country, you will never be hurt by priestcraft. If it is a craft, I think it is the poorest craft I know of in America; for, except in New York, and two or three of the largest cities, they scarcely are paid enough to keep soul and body together. Were we, as in England, obliged to pay tenths to a man whose church we never enter, we might complain of priestcraft; but here we have free churches, and in every church are free pews for those who are unable to pay: so, in America, above any other spot in the world, it may emphatically be said, "the poor have the Gospel preached unto them."

When General Moreau fled from Bonaparte's persecution, he took up his abode in New York—he and his lady, the beautiful Madame ———, daughter of a banker in Paris. She was said, at that time, to be the richest and handsomest woman in Europe. Be that as it may, she was a very pretty little woman, and fond of flowers. The general condescended to all her whims and notions about plants; and very well he might, for he was rather ugly, and old enough to be her father. When any thing was to be arranged among the plants, she was not pleased except the general and I had the fixing of them. One day as I was placing some pretty little modest Scotch daisies in his study, I cast my eyes on his hat, coat, sword, and other accoutrements, hanging on one side. Thinks I to myself, it is but a few months since, with that sword in hand, he was arranging the ranks, and directing the most masterly retreat, perhaps, on military record; and here he is seemingly exerting all his mind in *ranking* up flower-pots. He observed the direction of my eyes, and spoke in French to his servants, who told me the general wished to know what I thought. I said I wished to know if that sword and hat were with him on the field of battle. He said they were. I told him what I thought; he explained to the general, who laughed as loud as Frenchmen generally do.

It was a pity he ever left New York: he was a pleasant, unassuming man, and was much liked. He had plenty of money, and might have been very happy here, had he been only contented. I would rather live in America on an annuity of two thousand pounds sterling, than mount the throne of any monarch in Christendom.

CHAPTER XI.

JOURNEY TO ALBANY.—THE GENESEE GIRL AND HER LITTLE RED BOOK ON HER JOURNEY OVERLAND TO ALBANY: A STORY NOT FOUNDED ON, BUT ALL FACT.

On a very cold morning in February, 1831, we left Hoboken, fifteen of us, well packed, in a stage with wheels, besides a very neat coach which held only four. I was very politely asked to step into this coach, and, so foolish was I, and ignorant, I thought this same fine close carriage would carry me all the way, through thick and through thin, whither I was bound, even to the gates of the State House in Albany. In two short hours mine eyes were opened on the deceitfulness of *first* appearances.

We stopped at Hackensack, a tavern, grocery, grogshop, and post-office, all under one roof. Here we changed horses. Our rum-selling post-master began to bluster and swear he had no carriage, covered or uncovered, wherein to stow so many passengers; he said the *Jockey Club* in New York kept all the money, and gave him all the trouble. In short, said he, except you remain here till 4 P.M., you must go on with such conveyance as I have got. We applied to our Hoboken driver; he said his orders were to *drop* us at Hackensack, and bring back the carriages. As he went back on his way rejoicing, a passenger remarked, these carriages are kept as decoy-ducks. I thought in our case they had decoyed geese. Here we were detained nearly an hour. I stepped into the bar-room, a large place; in the centre stood an old-fashioned ten-plate stove, surrounded by a dozen of large, lazy-looking fellows; on the stove (which was very hot) stood a number of pots, pitchers, mugs, jars, and glasses of beer, brandy, ale, and cider; some running over with the heat with a hissing noise, and the fumes which rose to the ceiling and intermixed with pipe and cigar smoke, rebounding again on the heads of the smokers, nearly shutting out the light of day, and carrying back the mind to the midnight revels of Macbeth's witches dancing round the infernal fire, with Satan standing on the edge of the caldron, stirring the ingredients of their incantations. As the bar-keeper went round, filling the cups of these thirsty souls with liquid fire, I thought of Lucifer in hell as walking his daily rounds, when feeding condemned spirits with fire and brimstone from an iron ladle, yet seven times more hot. Oh how I wished for the powers, pencil, and canvas of Hogarth; I would have daubed these fellows into eternal SHAME.

We now set forward in a chair, sulky, and Jersey wagon. It began to rain, and when we reached the next stage to change horses, we looked like moving pillars of salt, our hats, cloaks, and storm-clothes being covered an eighth of an inch with ice transparent. Here we were placed in a *covered box* with runners, the cover being white-wood boards, placed an eighth of an inch apart, without *paint*, *leather*, or *canvas*. Seventy-five cents in canvas, twenty-five cents in paint, and half an hour in time, would have made this machine both air and water tight; but in this district, time, talents, cents, and every comfort, seemed all swallowed up with the rum-jugs and the ten-plate stoves. The rain descended, and snow came, our hats were frozen to our capes, and our cloaks to one another. I saw by the wayside delicate women hewing wood and drawing water; children in the snow, without shoes or stockings; while the lazy, drunken husband and father was stewing the *cider-mug* on the ten-plate stove in some pandemonium rum-shop.

Among our passengers was a young woman who, from her appearance, might have seen seventeen summers. Having finished her education in New York, she was returning to her friends in the West, and was under the protection of a young man who, from his polite, but cool attentions, I thought must be nearer related to her than a *cousin*. Had she been a witness in the hall, the reporters would have said she was a very interesting young lady; but, as I don't quite understand the phrase in this connection, it may be as well to say at once, in plain Scotch, she was a bonny lass. Most of the day there sat on her right hand a respectable farmer from Ohio; a man of sound principles, and who, by his observations, must have seen much of men and their manners. On her left sat a young man about 22, in the vigor of life and health, and whiskered to the mouth and eyes (observe, this was not her protector). Our farmer, in answer to a question by a passenger, when speaking of the inhabitants in the new settlements, remarked, that wherever there was a church, and a stated minister, the people for five or six miles around were more orderly, sober, and circumspect than were those who did not enjoy this privilege. This remark drew forth the tongue, the learning, and the eloquence of our young hero of the whiskers. He had been to college, and was studying law in New York; he spoke long and loud about priestcraft and witchcraft; said the laws of Lycurgus were better than the laws of Moses, and the Bible of Mahomet than the acts of the Apostles. He said the story about hell and the devil was invented by priests to scare the ignorant, and that death at the worst was only a *leap in the dark.* But ah, this leap in the dark! We little thought we were so near the precipice, and that our courage, in a few minutes, would be put to the test. It had rained all day, the sleighing got bad, and the driver swore he would take to the river; the passengers, one and all, remonstrated, to no effect. At every stopping-place, while the horses drank water, the driver drank rum. He was now at that point of high-pressure that he declared he feared neither death nor devil. We knew the ice in the river was strong enough to bear a hundred sleighs; our fears arose from the danger of getting into air-holes, which could not be seen, as the ice was covered two feet with water. Fear was now on every countenance. I looked on our farmer; his eye was uneasy, startled and twinkling with fear. I asked what he thought? He said it was very unsafe and very imprudent. I looked on the young woman; she was pale, thoughtful, and serious, but spoke not. On her lap she carried a small willow basket. While I watched the effect of fear on her countenance, she took from her basket a *little red book;* she opened it, turned a few leaves, fixed her eyes, and read about a minute. As she shut the book and replaced it in her basket, she turned her face towards the heavens; she closed her eyes, and her lips moved. Now, reader, if you ever stood on the corner of Broadway and Liberty street, you may have seen in the window a painting of a beautiful Italian nun at her devotions. Thus looked the countenance of this young woman in this trying moment. As she opened her fine black eyes, the hue of fear, which for a moment had blanched her rosy cheek, passed away like a showery-cloud on the side of a green hill on an April morning. I looked on the whiskered young man; he trembled in every limb. He was like one without hope; this *leap in the dark* had taken him by surprise; he was dumb, he opened not his mouth—while she, placing her slender foot firmly on the Rock of Ages, with her hand she took a grasp upon the skies, bid the waves roll, nor feared their idle whirl.

We arrived at Albany by sundown. She, her protector, and I, put up at the same hotel. Supper being ended, we took sweet counsel together till ten P. M. I asked to see the little red book. Its title was "Daily Food for Christians;" being a portion of Scripture and a hymn for every day in the year, &c. I asked what portion pleased her so much when we were sleighing in the water? She pointed to the text for that day in February—it read: "As the mountains are round about Jerusalem, so the Lord is round about his people," &c. The hymn,

"Ye fearful saints, fresh courage take,
The storm you so much dread
Is big with mercy, and will break
With blessings on your head."

Returning the book, I said, Miss, there be many who say this book is all delusion; and what if it is? it is, at least, a cheap, a comfortable, and a very innocent delusion. They may call it what they please, she replied, but I intend to make it my companion through all my journeys in life.

I now learned that this young lady was the adopted daughter of the Hon. William Campbell, Surveyor-General to the State, a man of great wealth. She was married in April, 1835, to Dr. Grant, of Utica; a few weeks thereafter they sailed from Boston for Constantinople, as missionaries to the Nestorians in Persia; and there she died, 4th of January, 1839, aged twenty-five years.

Next day was clear and fine sleighing; at two P. M. we stopped at Bement's; the sun shone full down on State street, the sleighs and the bells danced merrily along, and every thing bore the appearance of life and comfort. In our company was a lady who a few days before had arrived in one of the Liverpool packets, and was on her way to join her husband in the West. Fear on the river stopped not her utterance, but had quite a contrary effect. She was a small body, and when her little English tongue broke loose, it went like the hammer of a mill-clack: if the fellow was in her country, he would be prosecuted and mightily punished for such presumptuous behavior to passengers; and declared, if she lived to see Albany, she would have satisfaction, if there were any laws in this country, &c. While the driver was untying our baggage, says I, "Ma'am, that big house on the top of the hill is the place where the king, lords, and commons are now sitting, and making laws as fast as you would pitch half-pennies: over the way is Mr. Van Blarcum's office, the lawyer. Now, if you are willing to spend a sovereign or two, and board ten or twelve days in this hotel, you will find as much law and justice to punish that driver for putting you in bodily fear in this as in your own country." She looked in my face for a moment. "Dogs take the fellow!" says she; "I would not stay another week from my husband for all the coachmen in America." "Good-by, ma'am," says I. So she jumped into the Schenectady, or some other stage: I saw no more of her.

CHAPTER XII.

REFLECTIONS ON BOARD A STEAMBOAT.—DR. GRAHAM'S ADDRESS.—BLACK HAWK'S REPLY.—ARRIVAL AT BOSTON.—DIGRESSION.—NEW YORK FORTY YEARS AGO.—OLD TIMES.

MAY 25th, 1833, I left New York per steamboat Franklin, Mr. Bunker, the old commodore himself, commander. Intending this as a voyage of discovery, that I might learn something more of men and of their manners, I took no encumbrance, save only a small trunk, and left all my live lumber at home. The history of one steamboat voyage on our northern or eastern waters may answer for the history of one hundred at the same season of the year, it being the season when men, as well as the bird creation, make choice of a mate. You may always observe a reasonable proportion of these twos made one. On board, you may easily distinguish them from those who have been buckled together in this holy alliance for the past three years; for, provided you are a keen observer of nature, you will see the fair *new-made one* cling fast to the arm of her natural support up stairs and down stairs, to the table, or to the promenade, always linked together as close as the bands of matrimony can tie them. Even in a crowd, where they can't go abreast, you may see her pressing sideways along, still grasping the arm, as if she were afraid he might drop into oblivion. After supper, and when most of the passengers have retired, you may see them pacing the deck, or sitting, in a lonely corner, like the turtle-dove on a solitary tree, repeating their tales of love. There they sit till midnight. But now the cold northeast wind comes pouring down from St. Anthony's Nose (a high rock on the Hudson River so named, but, alas! the Railroad has broken the nose off), or round the bleak corners of Point Judith (a point in the Sound, so named, where it sometimes freezes in the month of June, and the waters are proverbially turbulent). These winds are more like to form icicles than to fan the flames of love, and admonish them to retire. They now walk to the door of the ladies' cabin; but hitherto they may go, but no farther. Here the imperious law of the boat, in direct contradiction to the words of the *ceremony*, part those asunder whom God has joined together: no more dares he to set a foot there, than to enter the harem of a Turk. There, with the pearl dancing in her eye, they shake hands, and part as if it were forever—she, to sleep if she can, and he, to the bar to drown his sorrow in a glass of champagne.

I now saw a few pairs of them whom I had observed on my former voyage three years ago. Then they were newly *linked*—now they were settled down in all the sober realities of life. No squeezing sideways arm and arm in a crowd; no leading down stairs or pulling up stairs by the hand, or tip of the fingers, like the hauling of a drowning man from a mill-pond; no snatching at a fan, a glove, or a handkerchief, before it had reached the deck; but merely a very sedate ejaculation of "My dear, you have dropped your fan," when very quietly raising it up, to be sure. I thought how much easier they now got along, the one before and the other behind, in all the composure of true Indian style.

If any of my thinking readers should suppose that the picture is too high colored, they have only to visit Albany and Boston by steam, between the month of June and the month of January, and they will see the same comedy and the same tragedy acted over some scores of times.

Next morning I arose at five A. M.: having washed, shaved, and dressed, I sat down with my pipe in a snug corner, forward, to smoke, and ruminate on what I had seen and heard the day previous. Says I to myself, I have been young and now am old, yet have I never seen an unhappy marriage but where the improper conduct of the husband lay at the root of the evil. The temper of a woman must be very bad indeed if a man of sense can't lead her along. It is contrary to a woman's nature to be driven; but by kindness and persuasion you may lead her anywhere.

Mrs. Socrates, if history speaks true, was a woman of a violent temper, and a tremendous scold; yet her husband, who was a man of sense, could get along with her very comfortably. It is written of her, that one day having scolded near half an hour without being able to draw an angry word from his tongue, or to discompose a single idea in his contemplative brain, thus finding the powers of wind had no effect, she thought she would try the powers of water; seizing a vessel that usually stands in the corner of the room, she made for the front window, where seeing he still sat composedly on the stoop, solving some problems among the stars, she emptied the whole contents on the bald head of her husband. He then mildly observed to a friend who sat by, "After thunder we may always expect a shower." No doubt this sensible remark of the husband made the old lady draw in her head and smile; and, I dare say, when they met again on the stairs, they were as good friends as ever they had been since the first day they were linked together. Now, had Mr. Socrates been as hot-headed as some fiery fools of husbands that I have known, he would have run up stairs and broken her favorite china tea and milk pots, and may be driven his hand through the looking-glass. She, in revenge, would then have torn his portrait in pieces, and may be have cut the throat of his favorite cat. Then there would have been a time of it in the house; but instead of this, he only poured the soothing oil of forbearance on her stormy temper, and soon the waves were still.

Those pests of society—the bachelors of forty—as an apology for their sins of omission, and their sins of commission, in transgressing alike against the laws of nature and of nature's God, will assert that they are afraid of being caught in the matrimonial trap, seeing so many promising young ladies have made very indifferent wives, and very bad housekeepers. This, I say again, is a mere excuse; besides, it is a downright slander. I can say, from thirty-seven years' experience and observation in these matters, that I never saw a bad wife except there was first a BAD husband. When two are yoked together, they must calculate to draw equal if they expect to get along easy. In the higher walks of life (for there I believe the daughters of Eve suffer more keenly for the sins of their grandmother than they do in the lower) I have seen the young, accomplished wife, before twenty moons had waned since she changed her name, sitting lone and solitary as the sparrow on the house-top. Perhaps her health was now delicate; the nourishing and cherishing care of her partner was almost necessary to her existence; but he was gone—gone to some political, literary, or may be some jockey-club. Perhaps he returns at midnight, breathing the fumes of wine, and steaming with the smoke of cigars—a pretty sort of a fellow, to be sure! how unequal the yoke to a young lady of twenty! and yet he has the confidence to account himself a suitable companion to a sensible, delicate, well-educated female. Such usage, and worse, when often repeated, will sour the temper of any woman, though naturally as sweet as the dew-drop appending to the mountain-rose. I have heard the eloquent Dr. Mason assert from the pulpit that there were more ways of breaking the heart of a woman besides breaking her head.

Again, in the lower walks of life have I seen a delicate little woman—she was clean and neat about her house, her person, and her dress, but very unequally yoked to a great lump of a fellow, with an arm as thick as the leg, and a hand as heavy as the foot of an ox. He was by trade a currier of hides, a profound politician, a thorough reformer, and a warm friend of the people; and so completely was he filled with a *disinterested* love for all mankind, that he had not one particle left to bestow on his wife and children; for every night, as the sun went down, would he, after scrubbing his own hide, and drinking his tea, adjourn himself off to the Indian Wigwam, or Tammany Hall, and there would he harangue, cajole, rebuke, and debate, till the going down of the moon; and having made the science of political economy and national government his study from his youth up, he was positively never able to spare a moment of his time to think how he should govern *himself* or his *own house.*

In these long, lone winter nights, there sat his pretty little wife, her pale and interesting face yet more pale from the flickering light of the lamp—there she sat, one child asleep in her lap, her foot on the cradle rocking the babe, and at the same time mending his coat or darning his stockings. About twelve A. M. his heavy foot is heard on the stairs; his head buoyant as the balloon, from the fumes of ale and the smoke of cigars. Rough and uncouth as her portion of animated clay appeared, she yet welcomes him with a smile. "Han," said he (her name was Hannah), "have you got any thing to eat?" Softly raising the child from her lap, and depositing it on the bed, she went quietly about placing something on the table to fill his capacious jaws. As the cradle stood still, the babe began to stir. "John," said she, "please to turn the cradle a little." "Rock the cradle yourself, and be hanged to you!" and strutting across the floor in all the swell of strong stimulance and self-importance, "Rock the cradle yourself, I am one of the *lords of creation!*" A *lord of the creation*, indeed; it is enough to make the *evil one blush.*

This thing took place in 1798, when the federal and democratic parties divided the country, or when, to the shame of America, Who is for France, or Who is for

England, was the watch-word—not a solitary voice for their country—Washington, Hamilton, Jay, Adams, and a few others who had bled for independence, excepted. I think Louis Philippe served those chaps right, when they went as a deputation from our *meddling, officious*, would-be *conspicuous* wise men of *Gotham*. They went to congratulate him on the revolution of July, 1830, which placed him on the throne, and made him a *king*. *Very consistent with republicanism!*

Having heard their flat address, "Gentlemen," said he (in plain Scotch), "hereafter learn to mind your own business, and never burn your own noses in other people's *kail;* right about face, march!" These are not the exact words, to be sure, but certainly the substance.

The New York republican procession, with the *French cockade* on their hats, and the New York republican committee's address to King Philippe of Paris, in 1830, are two of the most beautiful specimens of *republican simplicity* I was ever witness to, except it may be the following, from the "New York Commercial Advertiser" of June, 1833.

"*The Address of John A. Graham, LL.D., of the City of New York, to Black Hawk and his Companions, on the* 17*th inst.*

"Brothers! open your ears; you are brave men; you have fought like tigers, but in a bad cause. We have conquered you. We were sorry, last year, that you took up the tomahawk against us; but we believe that you did not know us then as you do now. We think, in time to come, that you will be wise, and that we shall be friends forever. You see that we are a great people, numerous as the flowers of the field, as the shells on the sea-shore, or the fish in the sea. We put one hand on the eastern, and at the same time the other on the western ocean. We all act together—if sometimes our great men talk loud and long at our council-fires; but shed one drop of the white men's blood, our young warriors, as thick as the stars of the night, will leap on board our great boats, which fly on the waves and over the lakes swift as the eagle in the air—then penetrate the woods, make the big guns thunder, and the whole heavens red with the flames of the dwellings of their enemies.

"Brothers! the President has made you a great talk. He has but one mouth, but that one has sounded the sentiments of all the people. Listen to what he has said to you—write it on your memories. It is good—very good.

"Brothers! Black Hawk, take these jewels—a pair of topaz earrings beautifully set in gold, for your wife or daughter, as a token of friendship; keeping always in mind that women and children are the favorites of the Great Spirit. These jewels are from an old man whose head is whitened with the snows of seventy winters—an old man who has thrown down his bow, put off his sword, and now stands leaning on his staff, waiting the commands of the Great Spirit.

"Brothers! look around you, see all the mighty people, then go to your homes, open your arms to receive your families; tell them to bury the hatchet, to make bright the chain of friendship; to love the white men, and live in peace with them, as long as the rivers run into the sea, and the sun rises and sets. If you do so you will be happy. You will then insure the prosperity of unborn generations of your tribes, who will go hand in hand with the sons of the white men, and all shall be blessed by the Great Spirit. Peace and happiness, by the blessing of the Great Spirit, attend you.

"Farewell! JOHN A. GRAHAM."

Black Hawk's Reply.

"Brother, we like your talk. We will be friends. We like the white people; they are very kind to us. We shall not forget it. Your counsel is good, and we shall attend to it. Your valuable present shall go to my squaw. It pleases me very much, and we shall always be friends."

But, to return to the gentlemen in high life, and the mechanics in low life. Had the former stayed at home when his partner was indisposed and unable to accompany him abroad,—had he with his own hand held the medicine-cup to her lips,—had he sat by her bed and conversed, or read to her from some entertaining book (as he was in duty bound), he never would have cause to complain of a sour-tempered wife. And had the latter kept at home at night, and assisted his true yoke-fellow to nurse the child, while she was washing the clothes (for the bird creation will assist his mate to rear their young), he never would have broken the heart and soured the temper of his delicate wife. So I think I have shown, beyond all controversy, that if a man only bears his share in the troubles of life, a woman will never flinch from bearing hers.

Those consummate blockheads, the *bachelors*, they too must join the hue and cry to deface and to defame the most beautiful part of the creation. Conscious that they are running *contrary* to all laws, human and divine, they come forth with hard words in place of arguments; they are not able, say they, to support a wife; why, it costs many of you more money in six months to pay for the soda-water you drink, and the cigars you smoke and give away (two articles that you can well dispense with, and articles, too, that your fathers never saw), than it would take to support a sensible woman for a twelvemonth. You are afraid of the expense of a family. He that hangs creation on his arm, and feeds her at his board,—He that hears the young ravens when they cry, will never suffer the young Yankees to starve. When you have got money enough to buy furniture, you will then go to housekeeping and marry. Here the fowls of the air will teach you: in the spring he looks out for his mate; he has not got a stick nor a straw towards housekeeping; together they gather the sticks and the straws; in a few days a dwelling is prepared for the little family. But the bachelors in every thing put the cart before the horse—always wrong end foremost with them. They say, as soon as they get a nest they will then look out for a bird—thus running quite cross-grained in the teeth of nature.

When I was not worth one hundred and fifty dollars I married. My wife earned thirty-one and a half cents per day with her needle, I earned seventy-five cents per day with my hammer; yet I never until this day was without a loaf of bread and a shilling. You have read how "Laurie Todd" began housekeeping; the inventory is true: we had but three chairs—it was one more than our need; you may have a hundred, but you can only sit on one at a time.. Had I my life to begin anew, and in the same circumstances, I would do just as I did then; at the age of twenty-two I would rather lodge by the bush with the woman of my choice, than to strut over a Turkey carpet, gape on the sofa, yawn by the piano, and dream over the sideboard, in all the dark, gloomy, and horrible forebodings of a bachelor of forty; for they know the time is past—twenty-five is never to be recalled.

By the time I got through these ruminations, Providence came in sight. My ticket for the stage was No. 2; whether it was what people call *chance*, or whether it was a plan of the captain's, I know not: be that as it may, I found myself seated with my back to the driver, comfortably stowed away with eight well-dressed females—I being the only male creature on board. I soon learned they were two mothers with their four daughters and two young waiting-maids. I knew none of them, but soon found out they had been to Philadelphia, had visited my store, and were now on their way home to Boston. Having so precious a cargo in charge, I thought myself in duty bound to do what in me lay for their comfort: at every watering-place, such as were thirsty I got abundantly refreshed with lemonade, milk-punch, or spring-water: when we stopped to dine, while the other passengers were feasting on beef and brandy, we quietly sipped our tea and cake in a neat little room by ourselves. To shorten the time on the road, I amused them with Hogg's Tales and Scott's Stories; you may be assured there was not a heavy eye in the coach. About 7 P.M. we were quietly set down at the Tremont. Since my former visit, three years ago, I received many invitations from ladies and gentlemen from Boston, who had called to look at our store. I discovered by the way that I had left most of my cards behind; reflecting on the circumstance, thinks I, should I pass the door of any of those good folks, they will think, either that I am destitute of common civility, or wanting in truth; so I inserted the following in the "Boston Transcript."

"NOTICE.—Through the progress of the two years just gone by, I received many *pressing invitations*—*beautiful cards*—and made many *fair promises* to call on Mr. and Mrs. So-and-So the first time I was in Boston; unhappily, however, in the notes of preparation, I came off forgetting most of my *cards* and part of my *wits* in New York. Not wishing to be thought guilty of a *breach of promise*, or wanting in the common civilities of life, I wish only to inform my good friends aforesaid, if they will leave their address at the seed store, No. 52 North Market street, I will endeavor to redeem my pledge.

"If spared, I intend remaining about a week."

I had another reason for publishing this notice: I knew that among some of the fashionable folks they think they are obliged to practise a great deal of hypocrisy. I remember many years ago of carrying a bill to a fashionable lady in Broadway, New York; she and another lady were just coming to the door—the former asked me to step into the parlor; she was warm in her thanks to her neighbor for calling, and *seemed earnest* in her invitations for her to call again soon. As I had never seen any thing of fashionable life, you may think I was almost confounded, when, after shutting the front door with a *loud slam*, she returned into the parlor, and, without paying any attention to me, began to harangue to her daughter most vehemently; she wished that "hateful woman would never enter her door again,.that she always gave her the headache, as her tongue was as rough as the sound of a grindstone," &c., &c. Thinks I to myself, this is another way of doing business. She paid my bill, however, that was my business; the other affair was her own. So I thought about my cards; it may be that some of those fine ladies, whose cards are so smooth and brightly polished, after all, would rather see the grave-digger coming into the house than to see me: so, thinks I, this notice will put all to rights; those that are sincere will send their cards, and on them I will call; those that are not sincere will see the advertisement, and so take the will for the deed.

I must here digress, while I state what New York was forty years ago, and what it is now, and then I will return to Boston.

At that period, most of our dry-goods stores were in Pearl and William streets—the shop in front, and generally a room behind; a glass door intervened, through which the master of the house could see while eating his dinner; and if a person entered, he immediately arose, left all, and waited on his customer. But look at it now. Half-past three P. M., yesterday, I called at the boarding-house of Mr. S., in Broadway—rang the bell—was answered by a colored waiter. "Is Mr. B. within?" "He is at dinner, and can't be disturbed when at dinner." Says I, "Go tell Mr. B. my business is urgent, and can't be delayed." However, he did not appear till after fifteen minutes, while I sat in the parlor gazing on some shabby pictures, and magnifying every minute into ten. When he appeared, says I, "Sir, I have seen your employer, near forty years ago, rise from his dinner to sell a yard of tape." This fellow is now third or fourth clerk *under*, in an auction store in Pearl street; receives about one hundred dollars per annum and board: he was just from the tail of the plough about eighteen months ago; he now wore a coat much in appearance like the wind-sail of a vessel in the tropics: it reached to the middle of his thighs, which, with his legs, were covered with a stuff called *gum-elastic*, adhering so close as to resemble in appearance the bandages around the limbs of an Egyptian mummy, and made his legs appear not much thicker than a Bologna sausage; the toes of his shoes were as broad as the heel; his neck screwed up in a black leather collar. His face was of the true Wethersfield cut, of a mixed hue, between Dutch-pink and brick-dust. His nose sharp enough to have gouged the eye of a musquito; whiskers enough to have covered his whole visage, had they only been transplanted over the surface. Such is the miserable remnant of mortality who expects to become a merchant for the next generation.

CHAPTER XIII.

A WEEK IN BOSTON.—REFLECTIONS ON PRESENT STATE OF SOCIETY

But to return to Boston and the *cards*. The day after my advertisement appeared, the second edition of cards came pouring in like hail from a thunder-cloud in the month of July. Punctual to the hour, I ascended the steps of the princely mansion of the handsome Mrs. Otis, just as the clock struck seven. When the door of the parlor opened, the blaze of lights, dress, youth, and beauty, was something more than my senses were prepared to receive. "Be not forgetful to entertain strangers, for some have thereby entertained angels unawares," was the first idea that struck my mind. The lady of the manor on which I stood once entered my store; she was to me a stranger; I entertained her, not knowing I was entertaining one, in many respects, so far superior to what we usually meet in the ordinary walks of life. My thoughts on this occasion may have taken a wrong flight (as they have done many a time both before and since), but I merely state what they were. It was the first time I had met an assembly where the sights were so *imposing*. The amusements of the evening commenced with what they call handing round tea (a thing I had never seen performed in Scotland): first came a servant with tea-cup and saucer; another with bread and butter; then there came cake, rusk, tongue, and sweetmeats: here I was brought to a dead stand—my hands were full—I could neither eat nor drink. Says I, "Madam, this tea-drinking concern of yours reminds me of the man who was going to bury his wife in Scotland. They had three miles to walk, and were going pretty fast: 'Not so fast, friends,' says the husband; 'don't let us make a *toil* of a *pleasure.*' Now," says I, "Madam, your tea-concern is all very good; but the way in which you manage the business makes a real *toil* of a *pleasure*—at least to me." The lady took the hint, and very politely placed before me a small stand, when I got along very comfortably.

Among the many fine eatables placed on the board, or paraded round the room, an article came in, in size and appearance resembling a seven-pound ham, very neatly roasted. In answer to my question, the queen of the feast informed me it was a *roasted yam.* Never having seen a roasted yam, and never having tasted a yam in my life, my curiosity was awake. In a few minutes the heart of the yam was nicely scooped out with a silver spoon, placed on pretty little china plates, neatly compounded with the sweetest of butter and essence of spice. According to order, it was handed first to the ladies; all were loud in praise of the yam: then to the gentlemen; nothing was heard but the delicious yam—the famous St. Domingo yam. (I thought of the man with the long nose riding through the town of Straatsburgh.) I took one tea-spoonful of the yam, then another. Thinks I to myself, were it not for the sweet butter and odoriferous spice, the heart of a corn-stalk would taste better. The lady of the feast asked how I liked the yam. Says I, "Madam, it reminds me of the story of a young countryman, whose grandmother died and left him a fortune. He came into Edinburgh to see life. Observing that people were carried from street to street in sedan-chairs, he applied to the porters for a ride. They seeing he was a *flat*, one of the porters winked to his mate, who drew out the bottom of the chair, on one side, just as his fellow opened the door to let the young man step in on the other side. When he stepped in, the door was shut, and the young man stood on the pavement. Away they go, through mud and through mire, always crossing where the mud was deepest. At length, they stopped in front of the hotel where he lodged: being let out, and his fare paid, 'Well,' says the carriers, 'how did you like your ride?' 'Oh,' says he, 'it was very good; but, were it not for the *name* of the *thing*, a body might just as well *walk*.' Now, madam," says I, "were it not for the *name* of the *thing*, a good Scotch potato would make a better feast." I am sure that the laugh which followed did the mistress and her guests more good than all they derived by eating the yam.

By-and-by the music and the dance went round: a lively widow of forty asked if I would *waltz* with her; I told her if she would show me how it was done, and I liked it, I would try. She jumped up and threw her arm round the slender waist of a tall girl; away they flew to the sound of the tamborine; when done, she sat down by me on the sofa. "Well," says she, "how do you like it?" Says I, "Madam, I think it's coming to rather too close quarters." I never till that hour knew exactly what waltzing was; and, I must say, I tremble for the sons and fathers of the next generation, if we are to go on in imitation of those vile European customs. I asked her if the lads took hold of the lasses when they were at those pranks: she said they did. "Then," says I, "the lasses are the more fools to let them."

June 5th.—Went to Faneuil Hall to witness the proceedings of the meeting held to raise funds for completing the Bunker Hill Monument. As I entered, a gentleman whom I knew not spoke to me by name, and introduced me to the mayor, who directed one of his friends to provide for me a comfortable seat. I felt grateful for their kind attention. The circumstances, and the place, brought to my memory one of my earliest newspaper recollections. One evening, about the beginning of September, 1775, the Edinburgh stage-coach stopped at my father's door, and delivered the paper as usual. It contained the British account of the battle of Bunker's Hill, and concluded, of course, with the prediction of the total destruction of the American cause. My father, I remember, expressed much sorrow while reading the account to his family, and in his evening prayer remembered most fervently the poor oppressed Americans. Being then in my third year, I knew not the nature of the contest, but thought it strange that my father should be *sorry* when our side *won*—as we used to say at school.

While the speakers were depicting in eloquent language the happy results that have flowed upon mankind in consequence of that important battle, I thought perhaps there was not one in all that large assembly who could feel exactly as I did at that moment. I beheld the ground on which scores in each contending rank had dropped into eternity, with each repeating *charge:* I thought of my father's principles with regard to that contest, and how they grew with my mind, and strengthened with my years, and the influence they held on my after-life. His principles made me set up as a reformer of the world, before I scarcely could tell my right hand from my left. These principles made me a prisoner in chains before I completed my nineteenth year; these principles procured me the privilege to banish myself, when, by the directing care of Providence, and the help of the good ship Providence, belonging to my worthy friend Mr. Samuel Campbell, of New York, I was landed in America; thus placing me in the best country in the world—the best State in that country—the best city in that State—the best street in that city—and, *as I think*, the best spot in that street: so, you see, had it not been for the principles so successfully contended for on that hill, on that day, it is not probable I ever should have seen America, and this book and its author would never have seen the light of the sun in Boston. Such were my ruminations after the meeting broke up, as I was plodding my way through Washington street, to spend the evening with a select party at the house of Mr. ——; but as the history of one steamboat trip will answer for one hundred on the same waters, so the description of one evening party will answer for six in the same city. The next day I visited many of the gardens in and around Boston. Nothing I have seen in America will bear the least comparison with the houses and gardens of the Messrs. Perkins. The vegetable and flower gardens, the green-houses and hot-houses, the grape, peach, apricot, and nectarine houses, particularly those of

Thomas Perkins, are superior to most, and inferior to none, of the same sort I have ever seen in Britain. And why should they not? These men are as rich as princes, and more hospitable than kings. Such men are the true nobility of any country: the majority of what are styled nobles, and noble bloods, all over Europe, were nothing originally but royal robbers. When no law but the law of might prevailed, some mighty robber associated with himself a set of lewd and lawless fellows of the common sort, and robbed, plundered, and destroyed their weak neighbors: the sons, approving of their fathers' sins, kept possession of the stolen goods from one generation to another. In process of time they styled themselves *noblemen:* and at this day you may find fellows in Europe boasting of their blood and pedigree, whose fathers, had there been either law or justice in the country, would have been hanged. But such princely merchants as are to be met with in every quarter of Massachusetts—men who have made their own fortunes (not made by the father)—these are the true nobility.

Next morning, at half-past six, I called at the country-seat of General Dearborn; walked round the premises some time, thinking the family might not be up: a few minutes before seven I knocked—the door was opened by the general himself—found breakfast on the table—his lady and daughter present, in a very becoming morning-dress: ate a comfortable breakfast, and got so absorbed in a very interesting conversation, that time flew without our taking note, till it was lost; it was near ten before we rose from the table. I have not met a more agreeable lady than the mother, a more polite lady than the daughter, nor a more finished gentleman than the general.

In the afternoon, visited Mount Auburn. I don't think a spot more beautiful and more suitable for the long home of the weary traveller can be found in the world. As you trace the neat and solitary walks, darkly shaded by the thick foliage of the ancient trees, the very breeze seems to whisper in your ear, *there the weary are at rest.* The monuments are simplicity itself: no gorgeous robes nor war trophies there; nothing save the emblems of the solemn realities of eternity. One plain square stone denotes the names of five children, sons and daughters of T. and E. Story, once the hope of their parents. After recording the name and age of each (they all died under twenty-four months), it adds, "*of such are the kingdom of heaven.*"

The Botanic Garden at Cambridge is well enough, but the green-house is a mere *apology* for a thing; considering, too, that it forms part of a public institution. It is neither long enough nor broad enough—it is neither wide enough nor deep enough—in short, it is a mere burlesque of a house to be called a public botanic garden *green-house.* The churches and colleges, the students' houses and professors' houses, are all well enough. The students appeared to have food to eat, and raiment to put on. Some of them *looked like fools*, and some of them are fools from the foundation. The former wore coats shaped like a flour-barrel, both ends out; and they also wore strong black leather collars bound about the neck, which made them look like a snapping-turtle, sitting on the edge of a ditch in a summer day, with its mouth open to catch flies. I thought they were making those chaps doctors or lawyers, or some other sort of *necessary evil*—for I could not, for the life of me, conceive what other use they could make of them, except they were to stick them on a bean-pole to scare crows. The latter, I thought, were intended for *readers* (not preachers of the Gospel). Their heads, I thought, the professors might as well save themselves the trouble of polishing, as they had only to send them down to Cape Cod, or Stonington, where, in rummaging some old chest in the garret, they might find as many sermons, preached by their grandfathers, sixty years ago, as would serve them to read for their lifetime. Indeed, I have always thought it was time and money thrown away to teach a man to speak Greek when he had only to read English sermons in Connecticut.

The professors, too, are men of sense, and, I wish I could add, men of *feeling* also; but were they possessed of one drop of this sweet milk of human kindness, sure am I they never could look on that fine *Protia Argentia** of theirs without the most painful sensations. There he stands, or rather is compelled to sit, in the centre of the stage; and, for aught that I know, he may have sat there for half a century. Again and again has he strove to raise his silver locks towards his native heavens—again and again has he been beat down. Bowing to the earth, twisted this way, bent, coiled, and confounded the other way—like a snake with forty rattles, or like some *lang*-legged Yankee crammed in a molasses cask till his heels grew fast on

* Classical name of the Silon-tree.

his shoulders—and all these chapters of misery arose from a narrow contracted spirit, a narrow contracted purse, or a narrow contracted house. It is a pity but some old rich bachelor would die in that neighborhood, and, by way of atonement for the sin of omission, would leave some thousands to build a green-house for the college, on condition that they would call it after his own name—then, indeed, his memory would live among the orange-trees and myrtles, though his name might perish from the house of his fathers.

I knew none of the gentlemen about the place, but they knew me, and treated me as a friend. I there found a geranium I had never seen; it was named the *Davieanum.* I was very kindly presented with a plant. I carried it through flood and through field, in stage and in steamboat, bringing it safe to New York without losing a leaf. As the good people of these States in Congress assembled assume the right to alter a man's name, so when I, with much care and labor, got this exotic safely landed in my own State, thought I also had a right to give it a new name; so, instantly procuring a painted stick, had it newly labelled Quincyanium, in respect to the worthy president of the institution.

Next day I went forth with my package of cards to make my calls of ceremony—knocked at the door of Mrs. ——, in Beacon street: the door was opened by a smart-looking white waiter, who said Mrs. —— was from home. (I could read in the man's eyes he spoke not the truth.) I gave him my card, and told him to give it to Mrs. —— when she came in—(perhaps I ought to have sent in my card at first, but I wished to see how matters were managed among the quality). Walking slowly from the door, I was tapped on the shoulder by the man, who said Mrs. —— was at home, and wished to see me. I was shown into the parlor: Mrs. —— was sitting on the sofa, in a neat eleven-o'clock dress. She met me in the middle of the room, and taking both of my hands—"O! Mr. Thorburn," says she, "had I known it was you, I would have been at home." "Then," says I, "madam, you really are at home." "I am." "Well," says I, "I have often read of the witches in New England, who could be home and not home at the same time—but I never saw one of them till this moment. But," says I, "had they been all as handsome witches as thou, I don't think they would have burned so many of them." She smiled. "But," says I, "madam, are you not ashamed to hire a man by the month to tell such tough stories for you? (she blushed.) It was as easy to have said you were fixing your curls, or crimping your cap, and could not be spoke to till four o'clock P. M." She said it was true, but we can't get along without a portion of deceit. "However," says I, "madam, I am not come to scold, but to crave your help in a small difficulty. Here are two cards, Mrs. A—— and Mrs. B——, within a few doors of you; are you on visiting terms?" "We are." "Then, madam, as I can't be in three places at one time, like you *young witches*"—(*a blush*)—says I, "so you may blush—(observe here, she took it all in good part—perhaps the compliment at the beginning might gild the pill—and she really was pretty)—and as your card says seven this evening, cannot you invite them, or get them to invite you? this will be like killing three dogs with one bone." She said it was a good idea, and carried it into effect most brilliantly that same evening.

Next morning, going to Medford in the stage, and thinking on the occurrences of the day previous, says I to myself, how much happier might we live in this goodly land, where Providence is daily loading us with more benefits than falls to the lot of any other people under the sun, were we only to use them like beings possessed of common sense! The rich make themselves very unhappy by relinquishing their own liberty and independence, and tamely submitting to the caprice and folly (to call it by no worse name) of the most powerful of all tyrants, *fashion*—each striving to outdo his fellow in extravagance and show. Mrs. A—— goes to drink tea with Mrs. B——: she there finds a new and very expensive addition to the tea-equipage; she goes home in misery, and can neither eat, rest, nor sleep; she then *my dears* her husband day and night continually, till he procures for her the like, or may be something more costly. Now this is the only *speck* on the *sun* of a *woman's blaze* of *excellence;* but even this a man of sense may, in a great measure, remedy, by *kindly* and *candidly* making known to his partner his real situation and circumstances.

The second class make themselves miserable by looking up at, trying to imitate, and envying their superiors. A great majority of the laboring class make themselves miserable by getting drunk, forgetting to make hay when the sun shines, and forgetting to lay up stores in summer, that they may be able to sit by a good fire, and crack their nuts in winter, as the squirrels do—and almost every one thinks his neighbor happier than himself, and this is because he cannot see the snakes that gnaw his neighbor's heart. The only secret of happiness is in *comparison:* when you think your troubles are more than any man's, look round, and you will see thousands in a worse condition than yourself: when you break your arm, be very glad your legs are whole; when you break your leg, be very thankful it was not your neck; and when *Willie Wilson's* draft for $200 comes back *protested*, be very thankful that it was not *Jamie Jammison's* for $400. Just view every thing as coming from the directing hand of a wise particular Providence, and, my life for it, all the powers of earth and hell will never be able to rob you of your confidence.

Saturday, 8th of June, left Boston at 12 o'clock M. My feelings and impressions were of the most pleasing nature—the most polite attention and kindness was shown me everywhere by the gentlemen and the ladies.

At Providence I tarried two days, where I met with the same kindness, particularly from Mr. ——, one of the best and kindest men in Rhode Island, at whose house I lodged.

On reviewing the last ten days, I think I have seen more of what may be termed *high life* than ever I before witnessed; and from what I have seen, I am more than ever convinced, that if each knew his neighbor's troubles, he would find that what are termed the good and evils of life are pretty equally divided. I have seen the man whose riches increased, and wealth flowed in from every quarter: he was the envy of his neighbors, because they knew not the sorrows that wrung his heart;—he had no children to share in his wealth, and no babes to whom he might leave his substance; this was the worm that continually gnawed at the root of his *gourd.* I have seen the servant, while dusting the costly furniture, and cleaning the handsome grate, place the shovel on the side where the tongs used to stand. Such a trifle as this have I seen throw the wife of that rich man into a state of so much turmoil and passion, that the blood receded not from her face, nor the fire from her eyes, nor did the music of her tongue cease to play for an hour to come. I have seen the poor man, who had barely food to eat, or raiment to put on—but then he could rejoice in the strong arms of three industrious sons, while his wife could smile at the light step, the ruddy cheek, and healthy looks of her active daughters.

The rich man fares sumptuously every day; but in most cases, by abusing his mercies he turns them into a curse. I have seen the prosperous merchant return from his office to his house in Broadway, or *palace* near town. His table was furnished with every luxury—three or four courses; then nuts, fruit, and wine; perhaps half a dozen fowls of the same feather in company: they have a real set-to of eating and drinking, for four hours on a stretch. Had you seen these men in Wall street, at two P. M., their eyes sparkling with intelligence, and the whole countenance lit up with mercantile enterprise, and look on them now—they are like beings of another sphere. It is seven P. M.; the table is strewed with apple-skins and orange-skins—with nut-shells and almond-shells—cigars half-smoked and whole-smoked—bottles half-full and empty—wine, red, white, and blue, mixing with the shells, skins, and tobacco aforesaid, forming altogether a beautiful chemical, vegetable, and compound dye, which flows from the board for the benefit of trade, and the hopes of the merchant of Brussels. But look now at their keen, calculating, Wall street eyes; they are sunk, glazed, and vacant—half-shut, half-asleep—their chairs turned half round, facing one another in pairs; there they sit, staring in one another's faces, muttering half sentences of incoherent nonsense, and looking like a set of most consummate fools. No wonder that the ladies retire from such a scene, as soon as the bottles and cork-screw are called for. Next morning, at nine A. M., you may see them crawling out of bed; the weather is hot; their heads are buoyant from the fumes of wine; they stagger across the room, and are brought up at the back window by a chair or sofa; for ten minutes they sit inhaling the sweet breeze from the cooling waters of the Hudson; having shaved, washed, and dressed, they descend, holding fast to the banisters. The breakfast-table is set with every thing to tempt the appetite, but appetite they have none; a pump-bolt itself could not cram these good things down their burning throats. Again they walk slowly on to Wall street, where, in some soda-water or doctor's shop, they drown their burning thirst.

Now this is what these men call *good living;* fast living it is, in all conscience; and I think these must be the very sort of bodies mentioned in the *Auld Book*, who "live not out half their days." I know some of these men; they were boys when I was married; now they are old men at forty. You may see them of a fine afternoon crawling along by Trinity Church; you may know them by their short step of three inches; by placing the heel first on the ground—no elastic spring of the foot, that bends to the toe—no such thing with them; already are their toes twice dead—plucked up by the gout. You may see them bending on their staff, or holding with both hands to the railing of the church-yard—perhaps reading the monument of his grandmother, or the tombstone of some brother of the cup, long departed, and he himself grinning in horrid anticipation of the fast-approaching night when he, with his gouty feet and corny toes, will moulder in that clay. So much for *good living.*

Now look at the sober house-mason. At six A. M., March 10th, he goes forth to work; at eight, his pretty little daughter, with a basket of bread and butter, and may be a smoked herring, all covered with a clean, neat cloth—a small tin kettle with his pint of coffee: he sets himself down on a cold stone, where he eats his bread with a merry heart and a good appetite. Now if this man is blessed with a thankful heart, and a *trust* in a kind Providence, he is happier by far than the man who fares sumptuously every day, and has no such *trust:* no gout, cramp, or dyspepsia ever disturbs his rest.

CHAPTER XIV.

INTERVIEW WITH THE EDITOR OF THE SUBALTERN NEWSPAPER.—EFFECTS OF INFIDELITY.—HISTORY OF WILLIAM.—A VISIT FROM HIM.

I CALLED to see Mr. ——, of the *Subaltern* newspaper. This gentleman had given me some very hard names, because he and I differed about Mr. Paine's principles and practice. He had said, "I was an old bigoted Scotch dotard." I called at his printing-office. "Is Mr. —— within?" (he sat by a table examining some papers.) "My name is ——, sir." Says I, "Have you ever seen me?" "Not to my knowledge," says he. Says I, holding out my hand, "My name is Thorburn." He colored for a moment. Says I, "You and I have had a small paper war; now, if there is any bad feeling between us, I am come to make it good." We were friends immediately. "Now," says I, "Mr. ——, I do not presume to call you to an account for your opinions; that is a matter between God and your own conscience; but I claim an equal right to hold mine. You think society can exist, and be in more comfortable circumstances, without religion and the Bible than with them. I think otherwise: the experiment was fairly tried in France thirty years ago, when the Free-thinkers had the government in their hands. They abolished the Sabbath—they shut up the churches, and the country became one field of blood. The tendency of your system is to send our clerks and mechanics to the fields on Sunday, where they soon spend their money, find bad company, and contract bad habits; come home at night sorely fatigued, and may be drunk; next day are unable to enter on the necessary labors of the week. Ours leads them to the temple of Him in whom we live, move, and have our being, to thank Him for the mercies of the past week; and in this there is a luxury of pleasure that only the thankful heart can feel. There, they are not exposed to bad company; are not tempted to spend their money; they do not get drunk; they rest and recruit their frame: on Monday morning they enter on the labors of the week, refreshed in body and mind, and no horrible regret at a day misspent." In this strain we conversed in a comfortable manner near half an hour, and parted better friends than when we met.

Of late a good deal has been said about Miss Wright and her Temple of Reason. I think the plain, simple, but true history of myself and William, affords as good a practical comment on the effects of infidel principles as any thing I have met with.

In a short time it will be sixty winters since I first landed in New York; I was then in my twentieth year, without a face that I knew, or a friend to counsel or direct. On the first Sabbath morning after we landed, three young men of our passengers called and inquired where I was going to-day? I said, "To church." They answered, "We have been near ten weeks confined to the ship; let us now walk out and see the country; our health requires exercise, and we can go to church another day." I said, "As long as I can remember, I have gone to church with my father every Sabbath of my life; and when we parted, his last words were, *Remember the Sabbath-day.*" They went to the country—I went to church; they spent a few shillings of their wages—I put two one-penny corporation-bills* in the collection for the poor. Some of them were good mechanics, and got from eight to ten dollars per week; my branch was poor, and it was only by close application I earned five dollars per week. They continued going in the country, found loose company, spent most of their week's wages, came home half drunk, sometimes caught by a thunder-storm, which spoiled their fine clothes and hats; rose late on Monday morning, bones and head aching, and could work but little all that day. I went to church, saved my wages, rose early on Monday morning, my bones rested, my head sound, and started on the labors of the week with a light heart and quiet conscience. At the end of the year they could show fine clothes and powdered heads on Sunday; but I could show $100, piled in the corner of my chest. They have all been gone long ago; having lived fast, they died early; while I, as one consequence of regular living, have not been confined by sickness for one day in all that period.

Now, Mr. Deist and Mrs. Deist, you who profess to reform the world by destroying the Bible and abolishing the Sabbath—you who profess to speak and write for the good of society, I would ask you, who lived the most comfortable life, they or I? Who were the most

* Paper money then in circulation in New York, before the United States had established a mint.

useful members of society? They died, and left their wives and children beggars. One of the young men of whom I speak was a baker: in a fit of intemperance, while working dough in the trough, alone, he lost his balance, tumbled in with his head buried in dough, and in this situation was found dead. This fact is known to scores of his countrymen now in this city.

If I die to-night, my family have the tools and hands to make themselves independent of the world.

About three months after I landed, there came from England into the shop where I wrought, a man by the name of William; he had a fine little woman for a wife, and one or two young children. He was an excellent mechanic, and the first, I believe, who manufactured coach-springs in New York; he was, by religious profession, a Baptist, and went to the church in Gold street. Dr. Foster, I believe, was then the pastor. He continued a consistent professor, attending church regularly with his wife and children. But William was a warm politician—a democrat, as red hot as the iron he hammered. He was soon found out by the radicals of that day. About this time there came to the city a man by the name of Palmer, who was either born blind, or had lost his sight by disease. This blind leader of the blind used to lecture on Deism, in what was then called the Assembly Room, in William street. William was led by some of his new associates into this dungeon of despair, and drank deep in their dark and cheerless doctrine. In a short time he came out a flaming Deist; and instead of going with his wife and children to church, he led them to Long Island, or the fields in Jersey; or he went by himself to some low tavern, and harangued on Mr. Paine's "Age of Reason," to any set of blockheads who would hear him. His children, as they grew up, being left to wander as they pleased, soon associated with bad company, and turned out worse than good-for nothing. He had commenced business for himself, and for some time was in a very thriving way. But now every thing was forgotten in his zeal for propagating his new principles. You might find him in every street and corner, pouring out his new light; and so vulgar and brutish was the language in which he blasphemed every thing which society in general holds sacred, that moderate men of any principles got disgusted, shunned his company and shop, and his worldly circumstances began to fall into decay. As old shopmates, he and I have ever been, and now are, on the most friendly terms when we meet; and from the beginning have I expostulated and warned him of the ruin he was bringing on himself and family in this world, laying the next aside. Though he could not deny the truth of what I said, yet he seemed like one who had gone so far that he was ashamed to recede.

One morning, about ten o'clock, he called on me and asked for something to buy his breakfast, as he had not tasted any thing that day. I looked on him with sorrow, almost to crying; says I, "William, has it really come to this with you?" He said he had not a cent, a friend, or child to help him in the world. I asked for his sons and daughters by name—they had all gone to ruin, or were dead. The few old friends of the William street *Illuminati*, now that he was poor, knew him not. I gave him a small sum, and told him to call on me in his extremity. Says I, "William, there are my sons and daughters; they are an honor to their parents, being all useful members of society. Your children and mine were brought up neighbors to one another—what should make them to differ?" He was silent. Says I, "I told you, thirty-four years ago, your mad principles would beggar yourself and ruin your family. While you carried your children to the fields, or left them to wander in the road to destruction, I carried mine to the church, where they were not exposed to bad company; and now they walk in the ways of wisdom, which are pleasantness and peace." I added, "You must now be convinced that religion is the best thing for this world; and in the next, they who profess it will be as well off as you. But if the Bible is true, you may say with the miser, 'I was starved in this, and damned in that which is to come.'" He confessed I had the best of the argument, and said he might have been a rich man if he had stuck to the principles he brought with him from England. He said he thought of going into the alms-house—it was a good last retreat. "And for this," says I to William, "you have to thank Christianity; for where the Bible is not known, they have neither alms-house nor hospital." I have only to add, that this story is no fiction, nor combination of characters that may have existed; but it is literally true. My friend William now lives; he is a man of truth, though a Deist, and will vouch for what I have said, were he asked. If any one doubts, I can point them to some of the men, still alive.

August 2, 1833, I had a visit from my friend William; he calls as usual when his funds run low; gave him something of the needful. Being a hot day, and not many customers, we sat and conversed about *old times*. Says I, "William, it is now thirty-nine years since the first week that you and I wrought together. Now," says I, "William, there is no use of disguise about principles, or any thing else, between you and me. You *must* be in the grave soon, and I, though nearly twenty years younger, may be there first; but would you do as you have done, could you recall the last forty years of your life?" He answered firmly, he would not. Says I, "In what would you improve?" Says he, "I never again would deny my religion, or forsake my church;" and added, "he believed he would have been among the richest mechanics in New York, had he only continued in the principles he brought with him from England." I said, "I believed he was right;" for, says I, "William, you will remember often when you got engaged in a dispute, your bellows and hammer lay still, and your fire went out, while mine was flying like the clapper of a grist-mill." He smiled, and said, "I was correct." I asked, "Where he found those who were most ready to help, now that he could not help himself,—among his free-thinking friends, or among the church-going folks?" He said, "Last winter he was some time confined to bed by sickness, and was often visited by ladies and gentlemen from the Methodist and other churches, and by the humane societies." They told him (it is his own words), "though they were opposed to his principles, yet it was their duty not to see him want;" and added, "that they were very kind to him; but very few of his free-thinking brethren ever came near him." "Now, William," says I, "twenty-five years ago you branded all these church-going people as a set of unqualified hypocrites; but you have lived to experience the benefits of their principles and practice; they, at least, in this way follow the example of the Master they profess to serve, for he always was found in the hovels of the poor, and by the sick-bed of the wretched. Did you ever see Miss Fanny Wright brave the winter's blast and enter the abodes of misery, like those ladies you speak of? Did you ever hear of a Deist founding a hospital? Did you ever hear of a Deist giving thirty thousand dollars to a blind institution, as was lately done by a rich professor in Boston?" He acknowledged he had not, and that religion was the best thing for this world, and would do no harm in the next. He said he had gone wrong; but now it was too late to retract.

William is honest, sober, and kind to man and beast; industrious, too, he was thirty-eight years ago, till he changed his coat; then he spent a large portion of his time in reasoning, disputing, and spreading abroad his new light. He is courteous, and always was charitable when he had wherewithal to give. These, and other good qualities still in his possession, he learned from the Bible in his youth; and though he has long since thrown away the book, he yet continues to practise many of its most beautiful precepts.

Those monsters who reigned with Robespierre, and cemented the pavements in Paris with the blood of *women*, were not Christians; they, to be sure, were born under a most Christian, or a most Catholic majesty, and might have had the sign of the cross at baptism; but with regard to its principles and practice they were as ignorant as the beasts that perish; they were professed free-thinkers, philanthropists—so full of love for all mankind, that they thought it was doing the Goddess of Liberty service to cut half the throats of the present generation, so that they might transmit the same privilege to the generations to come.

CHAPTER XV.

CORRESPONDENCE BETWEEN THOMAS PAINE AND WILLIAM CARVER.

MANY of my readers will laugh at the unconnected nature of my little book; but I hope the interest is not lessened by it.

I will now fill a chapter with a correspondence between Thomas Paine and William Carver; for in a short time the men to whom Mr. Paine was personally known will have vanished from the earth; and what follows will furnish a valuable document for future historians, and will be read with interest, and no doubt with benefit, by many of the present generation who knew him not. I understand the writer is still an inhabitant of this city, and is considered a man of truth and honorable dealing with his neighbors; and though he continues an admirer of Paine's principles, he has always condemned his practice.

Extracted from Cheetham's Life of Paine, p. 253, *published in* 1809.

No. I.

New York, November 21*st*, 1806

CITIZEN FRIEND—I take this opportunity to inform you that I am in want of money, and should think it as a favor if you would settle your account; you must consider that I have a large family, and nothing to support them with but my labor. I have made calculation of my expenses on your account the last time that you was at my house, and find they amount to one hundred and fifty or sixty dollars; your stay was twenty-two weeks, and Mrs. Palmer twelve weeks' board on your account. I expect, therefore, you will have the goodness to pay me; for you must recollect you was with me almost the whole of the winter before last, for which you only gave me four guineas. If I, like yourself, had an independent fortune, I should not then require one cent of you; but real necessity, and justice to my family, thus prompt me to urge payment from you.

Yours, in friendship,

WILLIAM CARVER.

Mr. Thomas Paine.

No. II.

MR. CARVER—I received your letter of the 21st inst., and as there are several mistakes in it, I sit down to correct them. You say to me in your letter,—"You must recollect you was with me almost the whole of the winter before last, for which you only gave me four guineas." This is a misstatement in every part of it. I paid you four dollars per week for the time I was at your house. I told you so when I gave you the money, which was in the shop. I had lodged and boarded at Mr. Glen's in Water street, before I came to your house. I paid him five dollars per week; but I had a good room with a fireplace, and liquor found for dinner and supper. At your house, I had not the same convenience of a room, and I found my own liquor, which I bought of John Fellows: so that you were paid to the full worth of what I had. As I paid by the week, it does not signify how long or short the time was; but certainly it was not "*almost the whole of the winter.*" I had burnt out my wood at Mr. Glen's, and did not choose to buy any new stock, because I wanted to go to New Rochelle to get Purdy off the farm; I therefore came to your house in the mean time. How does it happen that those who receive do not remember so well as those who pay?

You say in your letter,—"You have made a calculation of your expenses on my account the last time I was at your house, and find that they amount to one hundred and fifty or sixty dollars; that I was twenty-two weeks, and Mrs. Palmer twelve weeks on my account." I know not how you calculate, nor who helps you, but I know what the price of boarding is. The time I was at your house consists of two parts. First, from the time I came from New Rochelle till I was taken ill; and from thence till I came away, Nov. 3; I know not exactly the time I came from New Rochelle, but I can know by writing to Mr. Shute. I know it was some time before the eclipse, which was the 16th June. The time I was taken ill I can know by referring to my will, which is in the hands of a friend.

You seem not to know any thing about the price of boarding. John Fellows took board and lodging for me and Mrs. Palmer at Winship's, Corlær's Hook. Winship asked seven dollars per week for me and her.

The room I was to have was a handsome, spacious room, and Mrs. Palmer had none, nor a fire to come to when the weather grew cold. As to myself, I suffered a great deal from the cold. There ought to have been a fire in the parlor.

The things which Mrs. Palmer did for me were those which belonged to the house to do—making the bed and sweeping the room; and when it happened Mrs. Palmer was not there, which often happened, I had a great deal of trouble to get it done. The black woman said she should not do any thing but what Mrs. Carver told her to do; and I had sometimes to call John from his work to do the servant-woman's work, and your wife knew it. Sometimes the room became so dirty that people that came to see me took notice of it, and wondered I staid in such a place. I am at a loss to understand you when you say, "I have made a calculation of my expenditures *on your account*, and find they amount to one hundred and fifty or sixty dollars. Why did you not send me the particulars of that expenditure, that I might know if those particulars were true or false? The expense, however, that you were at on my account, was the addition of one more to your family than you had before I came, and no more, except for the time Mrs. Palmer was there, which *was not twelve weeks;* and your wife often called her down to cut out and make things for herself and children. I had tea with brown sugar, and every thing else in common with the fare of the kitchen; so that, unless I ate more than anybody else, I was of no more expense than anybody else. What liquor I had, I sent out for myself. On what ground, then, is your calculation founded? I suppose the case is, that you have been a good deal cheated, and your wife and son try to make you believe that the expense has been incurred upon my account.

I had written thus far on the Sunday evening, when Mr. Butler called to see me, and I read it to him, and also your letter; and I did the same to John Fellows, who came afterwards. Anybody seeing your letter, and knowing no further, would suppose that I kept you out of a great deal of property, and would not settle the account. Whereas the case is, that I told you the last time you came for money, and I gave you ten dollars, that I did not choose to pay any more till the account was settled; you ought, therefore, to have come for that purpose, instead of writing the letter you did, which contains no account at all. I did not like the treatment I received at your house; in no case was it friendly, and in many cases not civil, especially from your wife. She did not send me my tea or coffee till everybody else was served, and many times it was not fit to drink. As to yourself, you ought not to have left me the night I was struck with the apoplexy. I find you came up in the night and opened the little cupboard, and took my watch; did you take any thing else?

I shall desire John Fellows and Mr. Morton to call on you and settle the account, and then I desire that all communications between you and me may cease. Butler called on me last evening, Tuesday, and told me your goings on at Martin's on the Sunday night. I did not think, Carver, you were such an unprincipled, false-hearted man as I find you to be; but am glad I have found it out time enough to dispossess you of all trust I reposed in you when I made my will, and of every thing else to which your name is there mentioned.

THOMAS PAINE.

No. III.

MR. THOMAS PAINE—I received your letter, dated the 25th ult., in answer to mine, dated November 21; and, after minutely examining its contents, I found that you had taken the pitiful subterfuge of lying for your defence. You say that you paid me four dollars per week for your board and lodging during the time that you were with me prior to the first of June last, which was the day that I went up by your order to bring you to New York, from New Rochelle. It is fortunate for me that I have a living evidence that saw you give me four guineas, and no more, in my shop, at your departure at that time; but you said you would have given me more, but that you had no more with you at present. You say, also, that you found your own liquors during the time you boarded with me; but you should have said, "I found only a small part of the liquor I drank during my stay with you; this part I purchased of John Fellows, which was a demijohn of brandy, containing four gallons, and this did not serve me three weeks." This can be proved, and I mean not to say any thing that I cannot prove; for I hold truth as a precious jewel. It is a well-known fact that you drank one quart of brandy per day at my expense, during the different times you have boarded with me, the demijohn above mentioned excepted, and the last fourteen weeks you were sick. Is not this a supply of liquor for dinner and supper? As for what you paid Mr. Glen, or any other person, that is nothing to me I am not paid, and found you room and firing besides. You say, as you paid by the week, it matters not how long your stay was. I accede to your remark, that the time of your stay at my house would have been of no matter, if I had been paid by the week; but the fact is otherwise. I have not been paid at all, or at least, but a very small part: prove that I have, if you can, and then I shall be viewed by my fellow-citizens in that contemptible light that they will view you in, after the publication of this my letter to you. You ask me the question, "How is it that those who receive do not remember as well as those that pay?" My answer is, I do remember, and shall give you credit for every farthing I have received, and no more. I will ask you, what consolation you derive to your mind in departing from truth, and endeavoring to evade paying a just and lawful debt? I shall pass over a great part of your letter with silent contempt, and oppose your false remarks with plain truths. As the public will see your letter as well as mine, they will be able to judge of your conduct and mine for themselves. You say that I seem not to know any thing about the price of boarding in the city; but I know the price is from three dollars to five, and from that to ten, with an additional charge if the boarder should be sick for three months or upwards. I shall show you how I calculate my expenditures by the bill that will be rendered to you; and I believe it will be an important lesson to those that may undertake to board you hereafter. I have no person to help me to calculate or write; but fortunately took the advice of a friend, and got him to keep the account of all the times you staid with me. You assert that your being at my house only added one more to the family; I shall prove that it added to the number of three. You know very well when you came I told you I must hire a servant-girl if you stayed with me. This I did for five months, at five dollars per month and her board. This I would not have done unless you had given me ground to believe you would have paid me. After you, departure she was discharged. Now, sir, how will you go to prove that yourself, and Mrs. Palmer, and the servant-girl, are one? In order to do this you must write a new system of mathematics. You complain that I left your room the night that you pretend to have been seized with the apoplexy; but I had often seen you in those fits before, and particularly after drinking a large portion of ardent spirits—those fits having frequently subjected you to falling. You remember you had one of them at Lovett's Hotel, and fell from the top of the stairs to the bottom. You likewise know I have frequently had to lift you from the floor to the bed. You must also remember that you and myself went to spend the evening at a certain gentleman's house, whose peculiar situation in life forbids me to make mention of his name; but I had to go to apologize for your conduct; you had two of those falling fits in Broadway before I could get you home.

You tell me that I came up stairs in the night and opened the cupboard and took your watch; this is one more of your lies—for I took it during the time your room was full of different descriptions of persons, called from a porter-house and the street at the eleventh hour of the night, to carry you up stairs. After you had fallen over the banisters, and the cupboard-door was open, the watch lay exposed. I told you the next morning I put your watch in my desk, and you said I had done right. Why did you not complain before? I believe that I should do the same again, or any other person in my situation; for had the watch been lost, you would have thought that I, or some one of my family, had got it. I believe it will not be in your power to make one of my fellow-citizens believe that, at this period of my life, I should turn rogue for an old silver watch.

You go on and say, "Did you take any thing else?" Have you assumed the character of a father confessor, as well as a son of Bacchus? Did you lose any thing? Why did you not speak out? You have been so long accustomed to lying, one more will not choke you. Now, sir, I have to inform you I lost a silver spoon that was taken to your room and never returned. Did you take that away with you? If not, I can prove that you took something else of my property without my consent. You likewise gave a French boy that you imported to this country, or was imported on your account, a nice pocket-bottle that was neither yours nor mine, it being the property of a friend, and has since been called for. I lent the bottle to you at the time you was sick with what you call apoplexy, but what myself and others know to be nothing more than falling drunken fits. I have often wondered that a French woman, and three children, should leave

France and all their connections to follow Thomas Paine to America. Suppose I were to go to my native country, England, and take another man's wife, and three children of his, and leave my wife and family in this country, what would be the natural conclusion in the minds of the people, but that there was some criminal connection between the woman and myself? You have often told me that the French woman alluded to has never received one letter from her husband during the four years she has been in this country. How comes this to pass? Perhaps you can explain the matter. I believe you have broken up the domestic tranquillity of several families with whom you have resided; and I can speak by experience as to my own. I remember you undertook to fall out with my former wife—and one of the foolish epithets you attempted to stigmatize her with was, that she originally was only in the character of a servant. Was this a judicious remark of the "Author of the Rights of Man?" I well remember the reply she made to you, which was, that you had not much to boast of on that ground, as yourself had been a servant to the British government. And now again you try to break up our tranquillity by insinuating that my wife and son have deprived me of my property. I call this pitiful employment for a man who calls himself a philanthropist. When you tell me that Mrs. Palmer did the work belonging to my family, you know the assertion to be false, which can be proved by her and others that resided in the house. You have written well on just and righteous principles, and dealt them out to others, but totally deny them in practice yourself; and, for my part, I believe you never possessed them. An old acquaintance of yours and mine called on me a few days ago. I asked him if he had not been to see you. His answer was, he had not, neither did he want to see you. He said he believed that you had a very good head, but a very bad heart. I believe he gave a true description of your character in a few words. It has been my opinion for some time past, and many more of those you think are your friends, that all you have written has been to acquire fame, and not the love of principle; and one reason that led us to think as we do is, that all your works are stuffed with egotism. You say, further, that you were not treated friendly during your stay with me, and hardly civilly. Have you lost all principles of gratitude, as well as those of justice and honesty, or did you never possess one virtue?

From the first time I saw you in this country to the last time of your departure from my house, my conscience bears me testimony that I treated you as a friend and a brother, without any hope of extra reward, only the payment of my just demand. I often told many of my friends had you come to this country without one cent of property, then, as long as I had one shilling, you should have a part. I declare when I first saw you here I knew nothing of your possessions, or that you were worth four hundred sterling per year. I, sir, am not like yourself. I do not bow down to a little paltry gold, at the sacrifice of just principles. I, sir, am poor, with an independent mind, which, perhaps, renders me more comfort than your independent fortune renders you. You tell me further, that I shall be excluded from any thing and every thing contained in your will. All this I totally disregard. I believe if it was in your power, you would go further, and say you would prevent my obtaining the just and lawful debt you contracted with me; for, when a man is vile enough to deny a debt, he is not honest enough to pay without being compelled. I have lived fifty years on the bounty and good providence of my Creator, and I do not doubt the goodness of his will concerning me. I likewise have to inform you that I totally disregard the powers of your mind and pen; for, should you, by your conduct, permit this letter to appear in public, in vain may you attempt to print or publish any thing afterwards. Do you look back to my past conduct respecting you, and try if you cannot raise one grain of gratitude in your heart towards me for all the kind acts of benevolence I bestowed on you. I showed your letter, at the time I received it, to an intelligent friend; he said it was a characteristic of the vileness of your natural disposition, and ought to damn the reputation of any man. You tell me that I should have come to you, and not written the letter. I did so three times; and the last you gave me the ten dollars, and told me you were going to have a stove in a separate room, and then you would pay me. One month has passed, and I wanted the money, but still found you with the family that you resided with; and delicacy prevented me from asking you for pay of board and lodging. You never told me to fetch the account, as you say you did. When I called the last time but one, you told me to come on the Sunday following, and you would pay or settle with me; I came according to order, but found you particularly engaged with the French woman and her two boys: whether the boys are yours, I leave you to judge; but the oldest son, of the woman, an intelligent youth, I suppose about fourteen years of age, has frequently told me and others, that you were the complete ruin of their family, and that he despised you; and said that your character at present was not so well known in America as in France.

You frequently boast of what you have done for the woman above alluded to; that she and her family have cost you two thousand dollars—and since you came the last time to New York you have been bountiful to her, and given her one hundred dollars at a time. This may be all right. She may have rendered you former and present secret services, such as are not in my power to perform; but, at the same time, I think it would be just in you to pay your debts. I know that the poor black woman at New Rochelle that you hired as a servant, who, I believe, paid every attention to you in her power, had to sue you for her wages before you would pay her, and Mr. Shute had to become your security.

A respectable gentleman from New Rochelle called to see me a few days past, and said that everybody was tired of you there, and no one would undertake to board and lodge you. I thought this was the case, as I found you at a tavern in a most miserable situation. You appeared as if you had not been shaved for a fortnight, and as to a shirt, it could not be said that you had one on; it was only the remains of one, and this likewise appeared not to have been off your back for a fortnight, and was nearly the color of tanned leather; and you had the most disagreeable smell possible, just like that of our poor beggars in England. Do you not recollect the pains I took to clean you? That I got a tub of warm water and soap, and washed you from head to foot, and this I had to do three times before I could get you clean. I likewise shaved you and cut your nails, that were like bird's claws. I remember a remark that I made to you at that time, which was, that you put me in mind of Nebuchadnezzar, who is said to have been in this situation. Many of your toe-nails exceeded half an inch in length, and others had grown round your toes, and nearly as far under as they extended on the top. Have you forgotten the pains I took with you when you lay sick, wallowing in your own filth? I remember that I got Mr. Hooton (a friend of mine, and whom I believe to be one of the best-hearted men in the world) to assist me in removing and cleaning you. He told me he wondered how I could do it; for his part, he would not like to do the same again for ten dollars. I told him you were a fellow-being, and that it was our duty to assist each other in distress. Have you forgotten my care of you during the winter you stayed with me? How I put you in bed every night, with a warm brick at your feet, and treated you like an infant one month old? Have you forgotten, likewise, how you destroyed my bed and bedding by fire, and also a great-coat that was worth ten dollars? I have shown the remnant of the coat to a tailor, who says that cloth of that quality could not be bought for six dollars per yard. You never said that you were sorry for the misfortune, or said that you would recompense me for it. I could say a great deal more, but I should tire your and the public's patience. After all this, and ten times as much more, you say you were not treated friendly or civilly. Have I not reason to exclaim, and say—O the ingratitude of your obdurate heart!

You complain of the room you were in; but you know it was the only one I had to spare—it is plenty large enough for one person to sleep in. Your physicians, and many others, requested you to remove to a more airy situation, but I believe the only reason why you would not comply with the request was, that you expected to have more to pay, and not to be so well attended; you might think nobody would keep a fire, as I did, in the kitchen, till eleven or twelve o'clock at night, to warm things for your comfort, or take you out of bed two or three times a day, by a blanket, as I and my apprentice did for a month: for my part, I did so till it brought on a pain in my side, that prevented me from sleeping after I got to bed myself.

I remember, during one of your stays at my house, you were sued in the justices' court by a poor man, for the board and lodging of the French woman, to the amount of about thirty dollars; but, as the man had no proof, and only depended on your word, he was nonsuited, and a cost of forty-two shillings thrown upon him. This highly gratified your unfeeling heart. I believe you had promised payment, as you said you would give the French woman money to go and pay it with. I know it is customary in England, that when any gentleman keeps a lady, he pays her board and lodging. You complain that you suffered with the cold, and that there ought to have been a fire in the parlor. But the fact is, that I expended so much money on your account, and received so little, that I could not go to any further expense, and if I had, I should not have got you away. A friend of yours that knew my situation, told you that you ought to buy a load of wood to burn in the parlor; your answer was, that you should not stay above a week or two, and did not want to have the wood to remove. This certainly would have been a hard case for you, to have left me a few sticks of wood.

Now, sir, I think I have drawn a complete portrait of your character; yet, to enter upon every minutia would be to give a history of your life, and to develop the fallacious mask of hypocrisy and deception, under which you have acted in your political as well as moral capacity. There may be many grammatical errors in this letter. To you I have no apologies to make; but I hope the candid and impartial public will not view them "with a critic's eye."

WILLIAM CARVER.

Thomas Paine, New York
Dec. 2, 1806.

CHAPTER XVI.

DEATH OF THOMAS PAINE.—FREE-THINKING

It is not true, as has been reported, that Mr. Paine recanted his free-thinking principles on his death-bed. His physician—a man of good standing and respectability—informed me, that in the same hour that Mr. Paine died he was in the room. Mr. Paine's complaint was excruciating, and ever as the convulsions returned, he would exclaim—"Lord, help! Lord, help! Lord Jesus, help!" he had then a few minutes' respite from the pains. The doctor stood by his bed: says he, "Mr. Paine, you have published to the world, and we all know your sentiments on that subject; I ask you now, as a man who will be in eternity before one hour, am I to understand you as really calling on the Lord Jesus for help?" He thought for about one minute, and then replied—"*I don't wish to believe on that man!*" These were his last words, for in twenty minutes thereafter he died. It is a fact, that he applied (*officially*) to the Society of Friends to have his body buried in their ground; and when notified of their refusal, seemed much hurt.

> "Men may live fools, but fools they cannot die."
>
> YOUNG.

Mr. Paine, with all his failings, was a man of strong mind. I remember (and I have heard him state the fact), when Louis XVI. was condemned by the Convention to suffer death, each member, on voting, was obliged to state his reasons; when it came to Mr. Paine, he voted against his death; and, among others, gave the following very sound reason:—"As I think," says he, "gentlemen, we are not making war on the person of the king, as a man—we are contending for principle. Unfortunately for Louis, he was born a king—he could not help it—it was not his fault. Let us spare his life—give him a sum of money to live on, and banish him to America—there he can do no harm." I thought this the best speech he ever made since the day he wrote the book on "Common Sense."

About January, 1830, there appeared in the Commercial Advertiser a piece taken from Blackwood's Magazine, of November 1829, an anecdote of Thomas Paine:* how it found its way into Blackwood, I know not: but the incidents are true to a letter. I was in Scotland some years ago; and, if I remember right, my brother, who now lives in the neighborhood of Edinburgh, was so pleased with the story, that he made me leave it with him in writing. I suspect this accounts for it. Be this as it may, this, the history of myself and William, has brought all the free-thinkers between Passamaquoddy and Baltimore on my back. I have received as many books, pamphlets, newspapers, and letters, as did our good friend General M'Clure, when he proposed, in the august assembly of this State, to take all the collars from the dogs, and tie them round the necks of the bachelors. (By-the-by, I think

* See page 104.

the General was more than half right in that affair; for in a country like this, where we have more victuals than we can eat, and more trees growing than there are men to cut them down, I think no bachelor above twenty-five ought to be tolerated.) I have deferred answering any of them till they were done, thinking I might then make a kind of wholesale job, and make one letter do for them all. I find no fault with these gentlemen how free they think, or how deep they think, or how long they think; but I think they have taken a liberty of thinking about me, and putting their thoughts in black and white, to such a length, that neither common decency nor common sense will warrant. And first, a curious fellow in Providence—*Subaltern* by name—calls me an old *dotard Scotchman*, and says as much as I won't let Mr. Paine slumber in the grave of the *venerated dead.* (Mark this, gentlemen! *venerated dead!*) Now, what he means by dotard, I know not; but suppose it may be one of his crank Yankee words for *drunkard;* but if this is his meaning, I can only tell him it's not true, for I never was drunk in my life—but a Scotchman I am, and I glory in the name. I would rather be a Scotch mechanic, possessing the comforting principles of their simple and sedate family fireside religion, than be Emperor of all the Russias, with his crown, lands, and royalty; for I think (and I have as good a right to be a free-thinker as any of them) that the national, moral character of the Scotch will stand an unanswerable argument against all the sophistry of Deism, as long as wood grows and water runs. He next blames me about disturbing Mr. Paine's grave. Why, I thought that every free-thinker, in America at least, knew that Mr. Paine, like his old friend Mahomet, had no grave under the sun. He once had a grave; but his warm disciple, the rapacious Cobbett, had his dry bones scratched out of the ground, and carried with him to England. This is fact; and if fame speaks true, he had them made into jacket-buttons, and sold to the radicals, at a very high price, thus supporting the principle of making the most of his friends everywhere. On his late visit of love to this country, he sold his little *black pigs* to all the good democrats who would buy them for five pounds currency apiece, when, at the same time, they could have bought better pigs from the Dutch farmers at Bergen for one dollar. Another of these thinking gentlemen calls me an old nail-maker—that's not true, for all the nails I ever made were new when I had finished them. Another tells me to let the subject rest, for I have not got the brains to pursue it. Now, this is an honest fellow, and speaks the *truth*. Another says, it's not true when I assert that the common people in Ireland don't read the Bible. Says he, "They do read the Bible, but it is not the Bible of the *fanatics* and *missionaries*—it is the Bible of *the Fathers*." Now, I never had the pleasure to see this same Bible of his Fathers; but I have been thinking if it is not a better specimen of domestic manufacture than many of the sons, it must be a pretty rough sort of an article. Another says, "I got Dr. Brownlee, or one of the *holy Vandals* who want to stop the mail on Sunday, to write Cardeus, Index,* &c. Now, this is not true; for neither man,

* These names refer to communications made from time to time to

woman, nor child, either composed, wrote, read, or saw a word of any of these pieces, till I put them in the hands of the printer. Besides, I never saw a Vandal in America since the year 1813 or 1814, when they burned up all the bonnie books and pictures at Washington. Again, there is not a doctor of law, of physic, or divinity, in the city, who saw as much of Thomas Paine as I did; and therefore I think they are not so competent to write about him; besides, truth is so easily told, that the veriest fool can give a straight story, where no *twistification* is necessary. But the last, though not the least in importance, puts the following plain questions:—1st, Did you not *fail* in 1813? 2d, Having become rich, is it consistent with your Bible to refuse paying your honest debts? 3d, Where did you get the money to pay for the Quaker Meeting-house? And then he tells me to pull the beam out of my own eye, as *my Bible directs*, &c. Now, as I believe this is an honest inquirer after truth, and preaches sound Bible doctrine, I will answer him in words of truth and soberness. I will answer the last question first. I got the money to pay for the Quaker Meeting-house (as you call it) from Mr. Robert Lenox, in Broadway. 2d, I am not rich in money, though I account myself the richest man in America, as I would not change situation even with your friend Andrew himself; for no growling, hungry democrat can squeeze me out of my living, and he, honest man,

newspapers and other public journals. I gave the substance of the history of William and myself under the signature of "Cardeus;" and the correspondence between Paine and Carver under the signature of "Index."

has to please all the sovereign people, and millions of them are most sovereign and consummate fools. To return. I did pay my *honest debts.* When I failed in the Jerseys, property that cost me above twelve thousand dollars, was sold by the sheriff for about two thousand eight hundred. I returned to New York without a dollar. Mr. G. H. (of the house of H. B. & B.), a man of feeling, loaned me five hundred dollars. I repaid this money, and settled with all my lawful creditors to their satisfaction. To some I paid the whole original bill; to some seventy-five cents on the dollar, and some few fifty; but the last sums were their own proposals. There is one exception in the person of a very respectable and wealthy merchant in South street, who always refused to receive any part of a considerable sum I owed him when I failed, till, as he expressed himself, I was more able to spare it. The heavy purchase of the meeting-house, and above four thousand dollars' assessments since, has put it out of my power to pay him any thing as yet; but I account myself no less his debtor. Any decent persons who wish to satisfy themselves of the truth of this assertion, and will call at the store, I will show them receipts to the amount of nearly three thousand dollars for debts I owed before I obtained the benefit of the Insolvent Law.

Now, my honest-intending, free-thinking friends, I hope you are satisfied on this point. When you put the questions, I sincerely think that you supposed the censures implied in them were true; and as you thought I had set up for a preacher of righteousness, you had a most undoubted right to say, "Physician, heal thyself." I agree with you, that I know members of churches rolling in wealth, while the widows and orphans they have defrauded are begging. But our Bible countenances no such deeds of darkness; it says a day is coming when these deeds will be brought to light, and punished. An angel of light is no less an angel because the devil steals his cloak when he wants to deceive. If the Mechanics' Bank was not a sound one, and ten dollar bills equal in value to ten hard dollars, the counterfeiting fraternity would never forge them. Who ever thought of counterfeiting a Marble or Exchange Bank* bill?

The substance of these remarks on free-thinking, and my replies to their attacks, which I had made through one of the New York newspapers, provoked the ire of Miss Fanny Wright and her cousins. In their profound wisdom they deigned not or could not, or in their sovereign contempt they would not, answer them. But a plot, as deep and dark as ever sprung from the kitchen of hell, was planned, matured, and partly put in motion, with a view to hurt my reputation. The first act in the play commenced with the following copy of a letter, dated at

"*Philadelphia, Dec.* 8, 1829.

"MR. GRANT THORBURN,

"SIR—The directors of the American Sunday School Union have observed some notices in the New York papers, under your signature, relative to the effects of infidelity upon those who have embraced its cheerless doctrines. They conceive that views of the kind such as you have advanced, are precisely those needed at

* Two unauthorized banks.

present to check the irreligious spirit which is prevalent among us. Practical narratives of the *effects* of such sentiments upon the characters and destinies of individuals, are calculated to arrest the attention of the reader much more than a course of abstract reasoning.

"Actuated by these views of the subject, the Sunday School Union propose to publish in a tract the narrative which you have caused to be printed in the papers of New York; that is, if the directors succeed in making an arrangement upon the subject with you. They propose that you should rewrite the whole, improving it by alteration and addition, as you may think proper. It would be well if you could add a few anecdotes similar to that published in the 'Evening Post' of Tuesday last; and matter enough should be furnished to fill about twelve duodecimo pages.

"The Sunday School Union do not expect that you will take this trouble without compensation, and they are willing to make you a payment of one hundred dollars, if your manuscript shall suit their purpose.

"If you decline this proposal, you will please to communicate that decision to me as soon as you conveniently can. If you accept it, be good enough, without delay, to commence preparing the copy for the printer; for we should like to put it into his hands in the course of eight or ten days, if possible. Let your letter inclose the manuscript; and signify to us how you should like to have the money transmitted.

"I am, sir, with much respect, yours, &c.

"ROBERT BAIRD,

"*Agent of Sunday School Union.*"

It never entered my head that this letter was a forgery. I therefore answered it in substance, that I did not write for money—that I had no time to make and revise manuscripts—that if they thought the pieces referred to worth any thing, they might crop, prune, alter, or amend them as they pleased; and thought they were too flush of money to offer one hundred dollars for an article of so small value, &c. In a few days Mr. Baird called at my store, and showed me the answer I had written him, and said he knew not what it meant. I produced the letter with his signature, which he read with attention, and pronounced it a *forgery* in toto: but added, it was an excellent imitation. This letter I now have in my possession. It bears the Philadelphia post-mark, Dec. 3, 1829.

Now, these kind-hearted philanthropists had thought to bring me into a ludicrous mess by drawing on the American Sunday School Union for one hundred dollars; but the bait was lost. I had no thought that Miss Fanny or her friends were the authors of this piece of *beautiful simplicity*. Men who were continually talking about the *immutability of truth*, and the *eternal fitness of things*, I thought would not have seen fit to practise such a small piece of deception.

The second act (viz. the C—— affair) was only a link of the same chain. This also fell short of its aim: it gave me a lesson, however, on my own folly and ignorance, that will not soon be forgotten. Some of the foregoing pieces were copied into many of the periodicals in America, and a few into those of Europe. I began to think I was something, when, in reality, I was lighter than *nothing* and *vanity*.

CHAPTER XVII.

MR. AND MRS. E.......—A PLANT REMOVED.—MY OPINION OF THEATRES.—OF RELIGIOUS HYPOCRISY.—A BOOKSELLER, AND THE SON OF A BOOKSELLER.

Some years ago, being a passenger on board of the steamboat North America, we stopped at West Point. The annual examination of the cadets had just closed. ——, the secretary of war at that time, had been presiding, and, in consequence of an invitation from the corporation of Newburg, came on board of our boat, on his way to visit that ancient borough. He and his lady were escorted to the wharf by all the officers and professors of that station, with a company of cadets, and a fine band of music. On our way going up, I was introduced to them by a gentleman, one of our passengers, and enjoyed a pleasant conversation with him till we arrived at Newburg. There, on the wharf, ready to receive him, were assembled the corporation, and most of the respectable men of the town: a procession was formed. I was invited to join; and we were thus escorted, with a band of music, to the Orange Hotel, and were marshalled into the large room, where the glass and the toasts went round. I was called on, and gave the health of the secretary of war—hoping he would never need to test the practical part of his office. From my plain dress he supposed I belonged to the Friends, and remarked, he presumed, by profession, I was opposed to war. I answered, "I am not a follower of Fox; but I hold it is better to receive a blow on one cheek, and then turn the other, than to have one's head blown off altogether by a cannon or pistol ball." This produced a hearty laugh, in which he joined, and so that matter ended.

Mrs. E. is a handsome woman, and has been much spoken against. However, of her character I pretend not to judge; but from her manners and conversation, the short time we were in company, I formed a very favorable opinion. If the proposition be true, that the face is the index of the mind, sure am I that nothing unholy or impure can dwell in hers. I have thought it most likely that some of those brainless, senseless, penniless, blustering young officers, whose company her husband, from the nature of his office, could not altogether avoid, may have boasted of favors which they never received; and so, with the fiend-like malice of hell, conspired to deface one of the most beautiful objects in all the creation of God. Just like the old devil, their master, who could not rest when he saw the beautiful, youthful, and happy simplicity of our grandmother Eve, but must needs come with his lies and serpent-like tricks, and was never satisfied till he got the gates of the garden of Eden shut in her face.

One morning, about three years ago, there came into our premises a young man, leading on his arm a very pretty girl. They stopped about an hour; she seemed very fond of flowers, and particularly fixed her laughing eyes on a beautiful japonica. He appeared much inclined to indulge her taste, and would have bought it, but the price was five dollars. Her l knew—him I knew not. He appeared to me, however, to be one of those Broadway clerks who, instead of going to church, ride out of a Sunday, and spend their week's wages; by which means they have no money to spare either to treat their sweetheart or to pay their washerwoman. Be this as it may, that evening, between eight and nine o'clock (the time of shutting our gates), the plant disappeared. My suspicions fell on the young man as above. I resolved next morning on going immediately to the house of the young lady with pretext of giving her some advice about the plants I knew she had in the yard, hoping I would find my own gracing the company. At once my mind took a different turn. I thought with myself thus: these young people seemed very fond of one another—pity that I should spoil so much happiness for the sake of a paltry five-dollar bill. Should I find the plant, it will expose him, and, no doubt, spoil the marriage—for her father is a sterling, honest Dutchman. Now, thought I, should they get married, she may save him from the paws of the devil, from whom many a simple bachelor has been snatched ere this by the helping hand of a good wife; besides, should the old gentleman approve the match, no doubt he will empty one of the black leather bags to set them a-housekeeping, and she having the money, will be able to indulge her fine taste for plants; so, by this means, I may help to count some of the dollars, and thus recover more than I have lost. On thus reflecting, I very quietly gave up the pursuit. To make a long story short, in a few weeks after this they were married, by the consent of all parties; but whether my surmises were right or wrong founded, gave me no further concern—as from the delicate hand of the pretty daughter I came in for a share of the old gentleman's dollars, sufficient to make up the previous loss, and pay a reasonable per centage besides.

Now the same cords of love that impelled him to follow, still lead him along with her to the house of God. Each beautiful Sabbath morning they pass my door on their way to church; she still hangs on his arm, and looks in his face as fondly as she did on that morning when they first entered my garden. I can read, in their animated conversation, and the frequent turn of the head to look on each other's face, as they pass along, that they are happy in each other—and may they long continue so!

It is many years since this thing took place; but I never look on them without a feeling of gratitude to that kind, directing Providence, which turned the course of my thoughts, and prevented me from precipitately running into a project which might have destroyed so much happiness, and ruined him, soul and body—for I think his wife was the means of his reformation.

I have some peculiar notions on theatres, which I think it well to put in print. When Mr. ——, of the London theatre, arrived in our city, as is the custom of most strangers, he called at our store. In compliance with an invitation, I spent an evening with him at his lodgings, and found him to be a man of sound sense, a believer in revealed religion, and in the doctrine of a Particular Providence. Our conversation, of course, turned on theatrical subjects. He was surprised when he learned I had never seen a play. I said, for aught that I knew, plays might be good enough in themselves, but as I always went to bed at exactly ten o'clock, I could not forego the pleasure of lying down on my comfortable bed, after being tired with the labors of the day, for all the plays in the world; besides, from the general character of the actors, and of those who frequented the house, I could never think that the theatre was a school for morality. I observed, that wherever I had seen a play-house erected, there sprung up immediately around it a porter-house, a gambling-house, an oyster-house, and a house that perhaps was worse than any of them; and that the frequenters of the former were generally the supporters of the latter. I told him that one night, about thirty years ago, a fire broke out in the house next door to the theatre in Chatham street. It was play-night, and most of the audience emptied themselves into the street. The fire was soon extinguished; the mob returned into the house, making a great crowd. I thought now was a good opportunity to see the inside of a play-house, and how matters were managed there; so in I crowded among the rest. As soon as order was restored, a fellow came out, dressed like an English wagoner: he had a whip in his hand, and walked round the stage singing a song; he gave a smart crack with the whip—the people clapped their hands, and roared out *encore! encore!* Thinks I to myself, either the people must be fools, or I very dull of apprehension, as I neither saw nor heard any thing to raise a smile. Seeing nothing on the stage to draw my attention, I turned my face to the boxes; but here a sight met my eyes which spoke louder than the thunder of Witherspoon's eloquence, or the still small voice of Miller's strong arguments against the immorality of the stage. It was the fashion of that day for the ladies to wear their frocks cut pretty low in the neck. Well, there sat mothers—ladies who moved in circles very respectable—members of churches, and grandmothers withal. There they sat, surrounded by daughters and granddaughters, from twelve to twenty-four, in all the immodesty of naked truth. Thinks I, for the soul of them they dare not appear in church so. However, I supposed this might be the meaning of the words I saw on a large green blanket they had hung up over the stage—"*Holding the mirror up to nature.*" He remarked, with a smile, that there was too much truth in what I had said.

When I have leisure, and observe any thing very smart or very ludicrous, I generally write it down.

In the forenoon of one August day there came into the store a genuine Mansfield Yankee. He stood leaning on the counter near ten minutes without speaking. "Well, sir," said I, "what is wanting?"

"Nothing particular," said he; "only I am the son of B—— D——, who kept a book-store in Water street, thirty-three years ago, and with whom you were well acquainted."

"You look like him," said I; "and how do you live?"

"By serving the *Lord*," said he, "as well as I knows how."

"Then," says I, "you are a preacher?"

"No; I teach the languages."

I thought it must be the dead languages, for he

looked as dead as a snail; and I knew by the "cut of his jib," and the stock he sprung from, that he was preparing to open his battery on charity; so, thinks I, I will have the first shot. "And why are you not teaching now?" said I.

"My health will not admit; it was too sedentary," replied he.

"Well," said I, "go and hoe corn—that's a healthy trade."

"It *blisters* my hands," replied he.

"When first I began to handle the hammer," said I, "my hands blistered too; but I wrought the blister down, and wrought till my hands grew as hard as a horn; and though I have wrought, on an average, from six in the morning till nine at night for fifty years past, yet my hands have not blistered since: besides, you say you serve the *Lord* as well as you know how. But," says I, "you must be first *diligent in business*, and then fervent in spirit, if you mean to serve Him; and Paul also comes in, closing the matter at once: he says, 'the man that won't work should not eat.' Now," says I, "when a widow with two children comes begging, right or wrong, I help her; but a bachelor of thirty, sound in leg and limbs, let him work or die." I turned to speak to a customer—he was off—I saw no more of him.

This young fellow is a chip of the old block; the father did little else for twenty-five years than go from house to house, talking largely on the theory of religion; with regard to the *practice* of the thing, he knew nothing about it. You might find him in almost every house and family belonging to the Brick Church and

Wall street congregation, talking to the children and the servants on religion—laying down in plain colors and ambiguous terms, to the master and mistress of the house, the vast difference there did exist between Antinomianism and Hopkinsianism—between Arminianism and Socinianism, &c., &c., in great swelling words, and words of profound nonsense. The man and wife sat with eyes staring and jaws extended, swallowing every word as gospel itself; wondering at the head that could contain more than was to be found in the whole of Boston's "Body of Divinity." In this way he would sit till dinner was announced. He was invited, of course. At four P. M. he would resume the application, and, if listened to, would sit till tea, or adjourn to some other house and act the same farce, till he made sure of his tea. In this way he took the care of all the families in both churches on his generous shoulders, while his own wife and children might have gone to ruin for him. Now this man (and there are many such), though every day he was quoting Scripture by the yard, was worse than an infidel, inasmuch as he provided not for those of his own house. He had a store of books, procured from his honest and sincere brethren of the church (who thought him a very dungeon of divinity); but you might have called at his store one hundred times in a week, you would never find him there. He gave notes, too, and got some of his honest, unsuspecting brethren in the church to endorse them. He thought no more of the matter. When his friend got notice, *that the holder looked to him for payment*, he waits on brother D. S.: "How is this, brother?"

"O, my dear sir, I never thought a word about the note—thought it not due for a month to come yet—never gave a note before," &c. This was all his friend got for $150; and though this fellow pretended ignorance, yet there was not a Yankee between Eastport and Gravesend who knew the meaning of a note better than himself.

Now this is no painted character, but a true facsimile of C. D., bookseller in Water street, near Fletcher, about thirty-three years gone by. I had a substantial remembrance from himself; and at this day I could direct your attention to *twa score and twa* just exactly such mortals—men who do more harm to the cause they profess to support than all the infidels who have lived since the days of Herod the tetrarch.

CHAPTER XVIII.

ACQUAINTANCE WITH WILLIAM COBBETT.—SUCCESS OF EMIGRANT SCOTCHMEN.—REMARKS ON FORMS OF GOVERNMENT.—ON EMIGRATION IN GENERAL.—AN ANECDOTE.—"APARTMENTS TO LET."

WHEN William Cobbett kept seed-store in New York, in May, 1818, the following address appeared in the "Evening Post:"

"*Willian Cobbett's Address to the Public.*

"I have received from my own farm, in Hampshire, a quantity of the seed of Ruta Baga, or Russia Turnip, of which I shall sell all that I do not want for my own use at the price of one dollar for a pound weight. It will be put up in pound parcels, and sold by my man in his wagon, in the Fly Market, New York, every Saturday, between an early hour in the morning and two o'clock in the afternoon: I shall put my name on the parcels.

"A storekeeper who has been selling Russia turnip-seed in New York, having a fine large turnip as a specimen, bought, I am informed, of my man, and says it was raised from his seed. This may probably not be recognizable in a court of law; but it may be worth the consideration of this storekeeper, whether it be not recognizable in a court of conscience. Mr. Thorburn has advertised that his Russia turnip-seed is as good as mine; I am very glad of it, for in that case it is a great deal better than seedsmen in England sell, except by mere accident. I am exceedingly glad that America contains a seedsman who is scrupulous about what he sells; though in that respect she possesses, what I believe my native country—dear old England—never possessed, viz., an honest seedsman.

"Dated at Hyde Park, L. I., 16th June, 1818.

(Signed) "WILLIAM COBBETT."

Next day I carried the following answer to the "Evening Post," and offered to pay for its insertion: Coleman refused. However, it was published in another paper.

"MR. PRINTER,

"SIR,—Now that Bonaparte and William Cobbett have gone into dignified retirement—the one to catch shrimps in Saint Helena, the other to raise Ruta Baga turnips on Long Island—I presume you are not so pressed with important matter but that, if inclined, you can spare me part of a column of your paper to state the following facts. Perhaps, too, when you consider the mighty inequality of the parties—one, a small seedsman; the other, a powerful author, whose porcupine quill, dipped in republican gall, has shook the monarch's throne—pity may induce you to give me a chance to rub off the dust thrown on my coat by an advertisement in your paper of yesterday, signed 'William Cobbett;' in which, if I understand his meaning, he says I sold Russia turnip-seed, and told people it was raised from his turnips, or was his seed; and talks about the courts of law and courts of conscience, &c.

The following is the truth:—Coming up Wall street, about the 2d or 3d of last April, I was overtaken by the young man who attends the business of Mr. Cobbett's Register office in this city. He stated that Mr. Cobbett was anxious to get some one to sell his Russia turnip-seed, and that at his office there was some of the turnips, to which, if I would send, he would give me one. I thanked him, and said I would sell the seed for Mr. Cobbett, he allowing me good commissions—sent to the office (not to the wagon), got the turnip, placed it on the counter, and to all inquiries said it was of Cobbett's turnips, and that I would warrant my Russia turnip-seed to be as good as his; as mine was not got from a seed-shop, but was brought over by a gentleman who, like Mr. Cobbett, came off as fast as his feet could carry him, and who got his seed, not from a seedsman, but from a friend in old England, just as Mr. Cobbett got his. I also told my customers that I was surprised, when he, Mr. Cobbett, knew that the people in this country were so wise and enlightened, how he thought he would make them believe he was the first to introduce that turnip, when we had it in our Fly Market every spring these twenty years past; that ten years ago I had sold the seeds that produced the same roots of turnip; that we always knew it by the name of Russia, or Swedish, or Ruta Baga; and that the bulb was always yellow. There is not an old farmer on Long Island but remembers raising that selfsame turnip when Mr. Cobbett was writing long letters in his 'dear old England.'

"In the year 1796 a large field of these turnips was raised by Wm. Prost, on that piece of ground now occupied by the Navy Yard, at the city of Washington. If Mr. Cobbett will turn to page 545 of 'Porcupine's Gazette,' published at that time by Mr. Wm. Cobbett, printer, in Philadelphia, perhaps he will find an account of said field. At No. 43 Beekman street, in New York, lives a gentleman who assisted in pulling the Russia turnips from said field in 1796. Had Mr. Cobbett been the first to introduce this fine vegetable into America, he deserved, as Mr. Windham said on another occasion, 'a statue of gold.'* To conclude, it is not the least of the wonders of the nineteenth century to see William Cobbett and Grant Thorburn scolding one another in the Fly Market, and quarrelling about who sells the best Ruta Baga seed at one dollar per pound.

(Signed) "GRANT THORBURN."

Next morning after this advertisement appeared I received a polite letter of apology, with an invitation to call and see him. I went, and spent half a day very agreeably, in getting the history of his life, &c. He asked how I, a nailmaker, come to be so extensive in the seed business. I answered, I landed in this country with only three cents in my pockets: while making nails, it was as much as I could do to earn

* Some time about the year 1800, Dr. Rush, of Philadelphia, obtained a verdict of some thousand dollars against Cobbett, for defamation of character; he then sold out, and went home. He applied to parliament for a sinecure, or share of the secret-service money. Mr. Windham, in his speech on that occasion, remarked, that for the services Cobbett had rendered to the cause of kings by his writing in America, he deserved a statue of gold.

seventy-five cents per day. Two dollars I paid for my board, twenty-five cents for washing, and twenty-five cents to spend, making sure to lay up two dollars per week. Now, says I, mark the difference. Some of my fellow-passengers received twelve dollars per week; on Sundays they went to the country, got in company, spent their week's wages, contracted loose habits, and went to ruin. I went to church; put two cents in the plate; if the preacher was lively, I heard him—if he was sleepy, I slept also; at any rate, I saved my money, rested my body, rose on Monday morning refreshed for work: while they spent their money, fatigued their body, and on Monday rose with the headache, unable to work. Now, says I, you see it was by keeping the Lord's day that I came to be a seedsman; and added, whatever religion might do for us in the next world, it was the most profitable concern a man could follow in this. He looked earnestly in my face, and said he believed I was right. I made these observations to him, as I suspected that he was a free-thinker.

I think, also, that I owe some of my success to the circumstance of my being a Scotchman. Among the emigrants who arrive at New York from all parts of the world, I observe there are none who so soon establish themselves in respectable business as the poor Scotch mechanic—he who has only his clothes and tool-chest, and five shillings in his pocket: those who *bring money*, and commence business, generally lose it. There are but few among the English, Irish, French, Dutch, or Germans, who get along so well, as far as I have noticed. The uniform and first means of the

Scotchman's rise in the world, lies in the habit they had contracted in their own country of going to church on Sabbath, while the majority of other emigrants walk out in companies, and more or less spend their money; but, no matter from what principle, the Scotchman goes to church—there he can't spend his money. Thus he soon acquires the means to put himself in business. His national pride prompts him to aspire; and while he is seen plodding along on the easy and humble tenor of his way, his heart is planning and swelling in schemes of honorable ambition, till soon he raises himself amongst the first. This day there is not a merchant in New York who was in business when I first saw it. Robert Lenox was the last.

If it is merely for the pleasure of living under a republican form of government, I would not advise any man who is comfortably settled in a situation or business, whereby he makes a living, to throw away certainty for hope; you will find *political rascals* as plenty in a republic as in a monarchy, and perhaps more, as they have more scope for intrigue. You also will find common sense as much insulted by a set of fellows talking about equal rights, while they give right to nobody—about the public good, while they are filling their pockets with the public money—against family pride and kingcraft, and as soon as they make money enough out of the people to set up a two or four wheel carriage, dress up an imported flunkie footman, or Virginia negro, with a green coat, red collar, black hat, and gold belt, daub something on his carriage-doors by way of arms, being the likeness of nothing in heaven above or on the earth beneath;

thus imitating, as near as he can, nobility and royalty; and this is his *republican simplicity!* Talking about disinterested regard for the public good, while it is only to bring down every one to his level, that he may rise on their ruin. And then there are the elections, which never stop. Kept in continual motion by a set of political puppets behind the curtains, descending to means low, dirty, and dishonorable, where no honorable man can follow; so that there is some danger of the government being left to the management of men who are the offscourings of all things. If our elections came only once in six years, I should almost think our government was perfect. But it is not the difference between having a king and a president that makes America more desirable to live in than perhaps any other country under the sun; but we have a large and a fruitful land—a vast deal more land than we have people to eat the fruits thereof. In Europe, they have more people than land to feed them on. The climate does so much for man in America, he has but little to do for himself; in Europe, the whole population are in continual anxiety about crops and weather; our chief anxiety is, how to get clear of our produce: we have no corn-laws, no poor-rates, and no church establishments, that bone of contention which has separated the brethren in Europe for the last thousand years. A man of family will confer a larger and more lasting benefit on his posterity by placing his children in America, than were he to buy a throne for each of them in Europe.

The following anecdote is indicative of the feelings of most young men, after they have resided a year or two in this country, and get weaned, or speaned as we say in Scotland. About twenty years ago, two brothers, farmers' servants from Lanarkshire, arrived at Philadelphia; they both got service with one of those substantial farmers (lords of the soil) within four or five miles of town, whose tables are daily loaded with necessaries and luxuries, and where the farmer and his white servants eat at the same table. The one was named *Sandy*, and the other *Jock*. One morning, after they had been about eighteen months in their place, as they were dressing, Jock says, "Ah! Sandy, I had an awful dream last night." "And what did you dream, man?" says Sandy. "Aye, but it was an awful dream," says Jock. "And what did you dream?" says Sandy; "did you dream you had broken your leg?" "Far waur than that," says Jock. "And what was it, man? did you dream your mither was deed?" "Waur than that yet." "And what was it ye dreamed, man?" says Sandy; "did ye dream ye was in the bad place?" "It was waur than that yet," says Jock. "And what was it, man?" says Sandy. "Oh! I dreamed I was at home again," says Jock.

It is very rare that I have seen a *woman*, whatever may have been her sphere of life in Britain, provided she was rising of forty years before she left her home, that ever got reconciled to or was happy in America. The husband, led abroad in society by his business, soon makes new friends: the children soon make new associates, and form new attachments; but the mother finds every thing strange. The modes and manners of housekeeping are strange to her; there is even a sort of vocabulary, as it were, belonging to the domestic affairs of every country, that a woman brought up in another country never can learn; and though her husband and children are all happy around her, though she can buy apples of the best flavor here as cheap as she can buy potatoes in her own country, and though she has every thing in abundance around her, yet she longs for the conversation and company of those who were the companions of her youth. Nothing to her like London, like Edinburgh, like Dublin, or even like her *hut* on the barren side of some hill in Scotland.

Some years ago, there came to New York from London a smart bachelor, aged about twenty-eight. He had a high opinion of himself, and the place he came from. Wishing to hire a room for an office on the ground floor, he noticed a card in a window, "*Apartments to let*," was waited on and shown the premises by the tradesman's daughter who owned the house. She was a beautiful, modest, sensible girl; he was pleased with the apartment, but more so with the young lady; as he afterwards said, there was a music in her voice which made him ask questions. Having been told the price, says he, "Is the damsel to be let with the apartment?" (at the same time making a polite attempt to take hold of her hand). She made a step backwards, and looking him full in the face, replied, "Sir, the damsel is to be *let alone*." He hired the room, took possession next day, but the apt reply kept sounding in his ears, "Sir, the damsel is to be *let alone*." He never left his office satisfied without having a word or a look from her; he soon became her professed admirer, and before twelve months she became his wife. The countenance and respectability of her relations have given him a standing in society; he is attentive to business, and every thing seems thriving and happy about them.

CHAPTER XIX.

A FEW REFLECTIONS FROM SIXTY YEARS' OBSERVATIONS IN AMERICA.—PARTICULAR PROVIDENCE SHOWN IN THE NATIONAL AFFAIRS OF AMERICA.—CONCLUDING INSTANCE OF SAME TO MYSELF.

MEN, *Fiddlers*, and *Trollopes*, who travel forty days in America, fifteen of which are generally spent in the death of sleep, ought not to be branded as *impostors*. The public, if they think at all, are not to expect any correct information concerning a people, their country, and their manners, from either fiddlers or mountebanks, who may happen to spend a few strolling days in the line of their profession in that country. If they do expect so great a miracle, then they richly deserve to be imposed on. But no; they are not imposed on: they buy these as they do any other work of fiction, to see who among all those hundred-and-one book-makers can tell the most plausible lie. Therefore the writers and printers are not *impostors;* for the people desire to have it so.

I am satisfied the book bearing the name of Mrs. Trollope was never written by an English lady. A lady implies every thing that is mild, pleasant, beautiful, engaging, modest, and discreet. I remember, seventy years ago, in Scotland, to say that a woman was a soldier's trollope, implied every thing that was bad, hateful, and disgusting. Besides, no modest and discreet woman will be found travelling *alone* through seas and floods, in ships and boats, with mates, cooks, and captains, except she were completely unsexed. Besides, the book professes to be an *exposé* of the "Domestic Manners of the Americans." Now, sure am I that no woman, having the feelings of a woman, would ever expose, if she could, the failings and frailties of her sisters, and in such language, too, as that book contains—more like the licentious slang of some minor theatre, or the polluted breath of some London fishwife. If it has been written by a woman, thank God we have no such women in America.

There is, perhaps, no country on earth where ladies are so highly respected and thought of as they are in America (I speak from sixty years' observation). Had the writer of *Trollope* really been a lady of feeling, she would have rejoiced to find that there was at least *one* country under the sun where *woman* holds the exact place in society which nature and the God of nature has assigned her,—that of being the companion and helpmate of man, not his slave. From these reflections, my own mind is satisfied that *Trollope* is no woman, or, if she be, she must be one who wears the breeches. The very fact of her travelling with Miss F. Wright ought to expel her from women's company.

It is really provoking to hear European writers comparing themselves with themselves, and exalting themselves by themselves, and impeaching the Americans for want of *refinement*. Its like C****** teaching honor, or the devil preaching truth. The real standard of refinement all over the world can only be estimated by the place which woman holds in society, and by the usage she receives from those lords of the creation, falsely so called. Mrs. Trollope has the ignorance to compare the modest, beautiful, sprightly, and sensible ladies in America, with the poor, debased daughters of Eve in Europe. I know that God has made many of their women as angels for beauty, but the men have transformed them into devils. Among your singers and players are some of the handsomest women in the world; but the European savage—man, has debased them beneath the brutes that perish. In Africa they are the beasts of burden and laboring slaves of the man; in Asia they are the *soulless* automatons of his pleasures, and the laboring slaves of his profits; and in proportion as they excel in *beauty*, in the same proportion are they transferred from one heartless tyrant to another, and with more unconcern than they would part with an ass or a colt from the stall. But in Europe their degradation is yet keener and deeper, for there they receive just education enough to show them their high origin, and the place in society which by right is their own; thus making them see and feel more acutely the abject state into which they are plunged by the cruelty of man. Many of them, young, lovely, and sensitive creatures, are shut up in monasteries (and this, too, by those who gave them birth), or compelled to be buckled to some old *worn-down, rich, titled debauchee*, whereby all the sweet sensibilities of their nature are destroyed, and all the useful purposes for which the God of nature made them are lost to the world. In comparison with this, the burning of a Hindoo widow, or a Jewess of old placing the son of her youth in the red-hot arms of Moloch, *is like tender mercies.* Even in our own day, we have seen in France

—that country of chivalry, refinement, and gallantry—the young, the learned, the high-born and accomplished females, led out by ruffians whose hands yet smoked with the blood of a sister—we have seen them tied in groups, as is done by the wild savage in our western wilderness—we have seen their beautiful heads roll in the basket of the guillotine, till the arms of the executioner grew faint—we have seen *men* (falsely called) in Europe stand by with indifference and see the beautiful Mary of Scotland murdered by a fire-cat of a sister, and, in our day, the fascinating Marie Antoinette of France, by the ruffianly Sans-culottes. Were such brutalities attempted in America on woman, every rifle from Eastport to the Rocky Mountains would be raised in her defence: and yet these men have the very great *modesty* to talk to the Americans about *refinement.*

In Europe, too, where dwell the most Catholic Majesties, the most Christian Majesties, the Kings by the grace of God, the Defenders of the Faith, the Heads of the Church, and the Lords Spiritual, even there these men of refinement will take the most comely of their women, strip them of their chief ornament, modesty, then tear off rag after rag, till scarcely a fig-leaf is left; then they place them on a large table, which they call a theatre, and sometimes on a rope, and there they make them dance to the sound of an Irish fiddle, or a pair of Scotch bagpipes; and this is what they call, in Paris, in London, in Dublin, and in Edinburgh, *worshipping the fair sex.** Now a body

* I would here inform Messrs. Fiddler, Trollope, and Co., and all other forty-day travellers, who may wish to make a book, that from

would really suppose that this is all right, for it is all done just under the noses of those holy men aforesaid. They also have dancing bears, and live elephants, and monkeys, which they make to dance about just as they make their ladies do; and it's all done for money: indeed, they will do any thing in Europe for money. Some sell their bodies to the doctors while they live, and some sell their souls to the devil when they die; and all for money.

Another source of misery to the ladies in Europe, and which sours all the sweet charities of their lives, is their family distinctions, their bloods, and their titles. Thousands of them are there sacrificed, like Jephtha's daughter; hence the forced marriages, the unhappy marriages, the runaway marriages, the elopements, and, finally, their crim. con. trials,—names, the meaning of which is unknown to the ladies in America.

In America, when a young woman comes to her eighteenth year she is of age, and can marry the man of her choice, despite of cold-blooded parents, or self-interested guardians. There are no laws to obstruct the freedom of marriages in America (as far as ever I could learn), no licenses, no proclamations at the desk, or advertisements on the church-door. Any man and woman, of any age or condition, can go to the mayor, magistrate, minister, or justice of the peace, taking with them two witnesses to prove that they are both

what I have seen, I am confident there is not a lady in America, having a drop of American blood in her veins, but rather than expose her person, as is done by the women in Europe, to the brutal gaze of those noble blackguards, she would take a prayer-book in one hand, and a wooden cross in the other, and walk into the flames of martyrdom.

single people, and they get married without further ceremony. Now, Mrs. Trollope would call this an instance of the loose state of morals in America; but experience shows it has quite a different effect. In Europe, some popish priest or bishop gives them a license to become man and wife in a *political sense*, and some Beelzebub or Lucifer gives them a license to keep as many *masters* and *mistresses* as they please. The marriage is merely to enable the first son of the next generation to hold the estate; but with regard to love or natural affection, they know just as little as the Esquimaux in his cabin of ice: and yet these tramplers on every thing that is pure, holy, and becoming in life, have the impudence to preach modesty and refinement to the Americans.

The laws are *severe* against *bigamy*, and are seldom infringed except by foreigners, who have left wives in Europe. In fact, the Americans know little, not even by name, of the many vices that are rife in old countries.

In Europe, the ladies among the higher castes are waited on by white slaves—in America, by black: among the inferiors in Europe, the women are the slaves of the men—in America, the men are the WILLING slaves of the women: in short, domestic economy in America is comprehended in two words—the man provides, and his wife takes care of what he provides.

With regard to *governments*, it matters little to me whether the *head* is called a king or a president, provided they are a terror to evil-doers, and a praise to them that do well. Even in hell they have a *king*, to keep order in that pit; and among the powers of the air, they can't get along without having a *prince.* All nature obeys the law of its Maker, men and devils only excepted; and they require a strong arm to keep them in order.

In America, I would prefer living under a republican government, but not in Britain. I think now that they have got their parliament so far reformed, they have as much liberty as they can fairly stagger under. If they get along, quietly and easily, to cancel their sinecures as the present incumbents die, and also, by degrees, in lessening their church burdens, and keep themselves from going to war, they will do very well. The experiment of having religion supported in a country without the interference of government, has been tried in America for the last fifty years, and with the most complete success. I verily believe there is more pure and undefiled religion amongst the Episcopal churches in the State of New York alone, than is to be found in the same church all over England. Such a thing as a horse-racing, cock-fighting, fox-hunting, tavern-keeping parson, is not known in America. Were they so to appear, the people would just withdraw their support, and the priests drop into oblivion. There is no priestcraft in America: where civil government is kept out of the church, priestcraft cannot exist. Before the revolution in America, the Episcopals lorded it over God's heritage—now every tub stands on its own bottom.

Those simple dreamers, who, for the last fifty years, have been turning the world upside down, and writing so many fine-spun *theories* on government, always assume the *false* position at the outset, that man is a *perfect being*. Mr. Thomas Paine wrote and spoke so much and so long about the perfectibility of human nature, that he became a perfect beast himself. Were it not for insulting the dignity of the *British nation*, in the persons of some of its *members* in *Parliament*, I could give the history of two or three of them—men whose heads are so long, that they themselves really think they can govern the universe, and yet they never learned to govern their own tongues, to govern their own wives, to govern their own hearts, sons, servants, or affairs. The fact is, they are so filled with a *disinterested ambition* to *rule*, that, were it possible, they would take the reins from the hands of the Governor of the world.

These men, like all other *madmen*, are continually striving to destroy the very means in which is involved their life and safety. Were it not for the arm of a strong government, when O'Connell, Hunt, and Co. collect such a mass of folly and wickedness around them in the fields, as sometimes is done, one word from a bravo in the crowd, and the leaders (like the keeper of some wild beasts let loose) are torn in pieces. We saw it done repeatedly in France; and human nature is the same, under the same circumstances, everywhere.

In America, we have *too much* liberty. The imported patriot, as ignorant as a goose, and as *poor* as Job's hen-turkey, has as good a vote for the men who tax, assess, and take from me my property, as I have myself. This is giving him who has nothing, LIBERTY to be sure, but it is to take from me what is not his.

Often these men have not been three weeks in the country, but as they always *vote* for *our side*, we have some easy modes of creeping through our naturalization laws. From this, and many more defects I could name, we need never expect to see a government without faults.

Democracy and Republicanism sound fine in theory; and were men what God made them, it would work well in practice; and herein lies the mighty odds—God made man upright, but he sought out many *inventions*—God made him wise, and he made himself a *fool*. In Europe many are civilized—some about half—and a number are still in a state of nature. Take a few from every country, town and village, and perhaps you cannot select three from each hundred that are men of sound sense—seventy-five are fools, and twenty-two are rogues; therefore, the more men that are engaged in a matter, the greater is the quantity of human folly and wickedness collected. Besides, I never knew a genuine *bawling republican* in my life (and I have seen many) but he was a most consummate tyrant, as far as his little brief authority went. Some years ago I knew one of these thorough-going *imported* republicans in New York; the "Rights of Man" was continually in his mouth, and the horse-whip in his hand. He was a cabinet-maker by trade; and one day the police justice cancelled the indentures of *seven* of his apprentices, on account of barbarous and cruel usage.

I don't think that a nation in Europe could exist twenty years under a republican form of government; they are not so well informed as the people in America generally are; besides, from their youth the Americans are accustomed to something like this form of self-government, by selecting persons to fill many of their offices, as road-masters, poor-masters, militia-officers, &c., &c. It is not so much the form of our government that makes the people so happy in America, as the fact that we are not saddled with any of the customs of the dark ages, which yet hang about the necks of the good folks of Britain. In America, every man that professes religion attends to the religion of his own house; and if twenty heads of houses conclude to build a church, and engage a minister to lead their devotions on Sabbath, the government has no concern in the matter. In Europe, they hire men at a high price to become a head for their church, but in America *Christ* is the only head of the church that they will acknowledge, and they own no Lord but the *Lord Jehovah*.* We have no poors' rate, and no noble blood. This noble blood

* Many years ago (if fame speaks true) none were admitted into the House of Parliament but members, ladies, and the servants of noblemen. Rev. Dr. M'Intosh, of Edinburgh, being in London while the House was sitting, and probably not knowing the regulation, and having a desire to see how matters were conducted, presented himself at the door. From something about his dress, or probably from the very circumstance of his wanting admittance, they supposed he must be a nobleman's servant. There were two keepers—the first accosts him—"What lord do you belong to?" Instantly replies the doctor, "To the *Lord Jehovah*." "The *Lord Jehovah!*" echoes the keeper, looking inquiringly in the face of his fellow; "the Lord Jehovah! why, I never heard of that lord: I am sure," raising his voice, "he is not in all the *Court Calendar*. Where lays the estate?" "In the northern hemisphere," replies the doctor, gravely. As they knew as little about the hemisphere as they did about the Lord: "O," says keeper No. 2, "let him pass; it must be some poor Scotch lord, I suppose."

spoils a great many happy marriages in Europe; but in America nature displays her most perfect works. We have no standing army, because we don't need one; in Europe, the people must be kept in order by the point of the bayonet; but in America the people have common sense enough to keep themselves in order. Our government is the cheapest; and were it not that our elections are so frequent, I should think it was the best in the world. It's really amusing to hear, when you go to London or Edinburgh, how ignorant the people are with regard to every thing appertaining to America; and yet every week they have a *new book of travels* from some strolling Fiddler, Hall, Hamilton, or Trollope. These Fiddlers, however, are not fools; they know that a wise man cannot live in a country unless the majority of the people are fools. It is for this reason that a *Scotchman* cannot get along in Connecticut among the *cunning Yankees*, because they understand how to *hold* as well as he does how to *pull*.

I was in Scotland some thirty years ago; had with me my son, a lad about ten; stopped to see a lady at the seat of Lord A——, near Edinburgh; was introduced as Mr. Thorburn, from America—and this is his son, a *young Yankee* (the lad was both white and ruddy). The good lady stoops; lays her arm round his neck, her hand on his left shoulder, and looking him full in the face, exclaims, "*The Losh preserve us, but he's as white as our ain folk!*" Observe, this was at a lord's house, in 1818—not among the *mobites.* It is funny to hear their wise men speak, and their wise women write, about the Americans, as if they were nothing but a set of simple men, the sons of silly women. They speak about our generals and colonels being cow-keepers, and horse-keepers, and bar-keepers, &c.; they speak about our captains and our militia as being shoemakers and tailors, having guns without locks; they speak about our *commodores* as being packers of *codfish*, and our ambassadors as being printers or doctors, and pettifogging lawyers. All this may be true; but, then, when they come in contact with them, they find themselves most commonly outgeneralled. Washington and Hamilton generalled them out of a whole continent—General Jackson packed up their generals in rum hogsheads—the shoemakers and tailors, having guns without locks, *locked* up Burgoyne, Cornwallis, &c.—the packers of codfish caught a whole fleet on the lakes at one haul—and Franklin, the printer, Adams, Jay, Lawrence, and other pettifogging lawyers, outwitted and supplanted their diplomatists, in 1776, at almost every court in Christendom.

With regard to the navy in America, there is no doubt but man to man, and gun to gun, they will be able to defend themselves against any nation under the sun. The late war gave a lesson to these men, whose principle of right consisted in making the weak submit to the strong, which they will not soon forget; but as now they know where each other's strength lies, they will find it their interest to cultivate one another's friendship. Their fleets *combined* will be able to protect the world from oppressors.

In reading the history of America for the last fifty years, it often occurs to my mind, that Providence has taken the affairs of the country into his own immediate direction. I think we can't look back on the late war without being convinced that the Governor of the world turned the mistakes and blunders of our own governors into public blessings, and in a way and manner, too, contrary to our own plans and most sanguine calculations. For instance, when the war of 1812 broke out, our governors thought they had only to send a few men into Canada, carrying a pole with a striped handkerchief at its top, and that all the whole country would join them. But after losing millions of money and thousands of men, they found themselves completely discomfited, foiled, and laughed at. And it was right it should be so. It was both unjust and impolitic;—unjust because the Canadians were our brethren, and never had done us any harm. If their masters, three thousand miles away, had robbed our ships, it was not their fault—they could not help it; it was impolitic, because, had our government issued a proclamation, telling them we were brethren of the same soil, we had no quarrel with them, and if they would let us alone we would let them alone—had this been done, I verily believe that ere this time Canada would have now formed another State in the Union.

But look at the *ocean*, that highway of *nations;* there we had been robbed and plundered because we wanted the means of defence. These leviathans of the deep, with their mouths of one hundred fires, told us to stand by or they would sink us in the mighty waters. On these waters, though our cause was just, we thought we could do nothing. But there we looked on, while the Lord wrought gloriously for America—where we looked for disgrace, he gave us honor and for defeat he gave us victory; till at length the skill of the officers, and the strength of the six American *fir-built frigates*, was proclaimed from the Park and Tower *guns of London.*

Look also at New Orleans; their ships darkened our rivers; their men were numerous as the locusts in Egypt; their officers and soldiers were all mighty men of war, having just conquered the conqueror of the world, and laid his *invincibles* low, even in the dust. But here these noble fellows, whose swords had just let loose the heart's blood of Bonaparte's *lancers*, were cut down like grass in the field, and scattered abroad like chaff before the wind, by the unerring aim of the American rifle. They were the *invaders*, the Americans were the *defenders;* but in Canada the Americans were the invaders, and were discomfited.

All these things are arguments with me in favor of the doctrine of a Particular Providence, in regard to nations. As respects myself, in addition to what has been already stated, I beg to give another instance. I could have put on record some scores of such instances, any one of which might suffice to convince a reasonable person of the *consoling doctrine* of the *ministry* of *angels*, or a class of beings, though invisible to us, by far superior in power and intelligence, and who stand ready, at the nod of their Master, to execute his will in a moment, even to the utmost boundaries of space: but here our feeble mind is lost. On what other principles are we to account for the curious incidents which frequently happen to every observing man, viz., of *thinking* or *speaking* about a person whom, perhaps, we have not seen for years, and he will immediately appear; and sometimes going through scenes in your sleep in which you will be a prominent actor next day? These things must be whispered on our senses, or impressed into our souls, by some being to us invisible. Heaven, earth, and sea are full of wonders and mysteries, of which those wise men (self-styled philosophers) never dreamed.

In April, then, we received a letter from Mr. C., ordering about $250 worth of seeds and trees, and stating that B. & Co. would pay our bill. Before complying with the order we showed the letter to B. & Co.; they stated, had the amount not exceeded $100 they would have paid it, but being already considerable in advance, they were not inclined to go further; but added, they considered him a good man, and thought we should be safe in trusting him to that amount. My son being anxious to fill the order, I consented; the goods and invoice were forwarded, but receiving no answer, after six weeks we wrote to him again, requesting him to send us a draft on P. W. & Co.; still no answer came. One day, during the cholera, about the beginning of September, I picked up a piece of paper from the floor, which, from some words on it, brought the matter to my mind. I told my son I was getting anxious about the matter of C., and was resolved to stir in the business; my son thought we had better let it rest till after the cholera, as it was probable Mr. C. might be out of town, &c. However, the thing kept harassing my mind, so I determined to see the Messrs. B., and consult with them before the day closed. I called at their office about fifteen minutes past four P. M., presuming they would have returned from dinner: I waited some time, and they not returning, I went home, drank my tea, and resolved to call again, if spared, next morning—but something in my mind kept prompting me on; so, having finished tea, I returned to the office and found Mr. B. alone. I showed him Mr. C.'s letter, and asked his advice. He advised me to draw on C. at ten days' sight, in favor of R. C., to give the draft to him (Mr. B.), and he would give it to C. to forward. I came home, told my son, bid him go to tea, and draw the drafts as soon as he came back. He smiled, and said he could not see what made me so pushing in this business all at once. Says I, "I can't either; but something hurries me on, that I can't rest satisfied till I push it as fast as I can." The draft was drawn that night. Next morning I gave it to B., with an *earnest request* that he would give it to Mr. C. to forward by that day's mail. About a month after, Mr. B. came into our store, and told us a long story about the failure of Mr. P., and how much they had lost by him, but added, your *draft is paid*, and paid, too the very day before he failed. Next day Mr. C. stepped in and told us the same story, adding, "You are a lucky fellow, Thorburn, for had not the draft gone on that very day, I don't think you would have got one cent." Now, in reviewing this matter, I can't help being assured, in my own mind, that there was some invisible influence that urged me on in a manner, for which I could not account, to bestir myself in this business on that very day; and I also think I can see the hand of Providence in inclining the hearts of both Messrs. B. and C. to transact their parts of the business on that same day, with more promptness, perhaps, than if their own interests had been at stake.

I might fill a much larger book than this with remarkable instances, but I will conclude with only one more. After having made and lost two fortunes in the course of my life, I find myself, in old age, without much of this world's goods, but with a thankful and a cheerful heart. God has provided for me in the following manner.

I sailed from Leith, in Scotland, 13th of April, 1794, in the good ship "Providence," a name propitious, bound for New York. Among the passengers was a lady, having with her, in charge, four or five young children. The father had gone before, to prepare for them a habitation, no small undertaking when three months was a tolerable passage. Among the children was a boy, seemingly of four years' growth. He was lively and playful, always on deck. His mother was in continual fear on his account. I told her, as I had nothing to do, I would take care of the boy. This to her was a great relief; so, comparatively speaking, I carried this boy in my arms over the waves of the Atlantic.

Now this boy is Collector of the Port of New York. In the arrangements of Providence, he is the man, and I am the child; he, in turn, carries me in his arms. Or in plain Scotch, he gives me an office in the department, whereby I earn enough to keep soul and body together. The sovereign people need not infer from this that I spend Uncle Sam's money for naught. The office must be filled by some one, and, though seventy-nine, I can perform the duties of my department as well as when in my twenty-ninth year. I never eat the bread of idleness, nor will I while I can grasp a hammer, or blow the bellows.

I have made these remarks without the knowledge of any of the parties referred to. It is to cancel a debt of gratitude due the Giver of all good, and to men; his instruments; and to remind my neighbors that a deed done with a good intent seldom goes unrewarded, even in this life. "Cast thy bread upon the waters, thou shalt find it after many days." In my case the promise is fulfilled to the letter. In 1794 I cast my bread on the waters of the Atlantic Ocean; in 1851 I found it floating on the shores of the Hudson River.

APPENDIX.

A FLOWER EXTRACTED.

[*From the New York Commercial Advertiser, May 19th*, 1829.]

The following characteristic communication is too good to be delayed for a single day, and we make room for it without hesitation:

To the Editors of the Commercial Advertiser.

I really believe that you gentlemen printers save more money to the good people of this city, by the cautions you give, and the exposures you make of the practice and tricks of thieves, than all the paltry sum of ten dollars which you usually ask, to pay for paper, ink, and carrying. Since last fall, when you gave an account of the fellow who stole the gold fish, we have not been sensible of a single depredation: but one morning last week, about six A. M., a figure strolled into our yard, his feet being half covered with a pair of sea-green morocco slippers; his stockings, which had *once* been white, rolled down to his ankles, and displayed part of a leg, which, from appearance, had not been anointed with soap since the 4th of July last; his cassimere pantaloons of the same color as the

Scotch snuff that is made in Chatham street, and ornamented at the top by a bunch of seals as large as a *mock* orange, and as yellow as if they had really been made from gold found in North Carolina; around his neck, too, he wore an iron chain, appended to something at the end which was meant as an apology for a watch, but from the spider-like appearance of his *spine*, I thought it might be intended as a preventer (as the sailors say), to keep the extremities from separating from the trunk; or, like the men of Jersey, who with an ox-chain fasten the small, to keep them from running away with the large wheels of their wagon. His face was pretty enough, and on the whole he might pass for a very handsome fellow; but in the vacant stare of his eye, you might easily perceive that Madam Nature, getting tired with laboring all day to form a handsome person, at last being vexed with the job, had rolled him from her work-bench, forgetting to put brains in his head. Thinking he wanted the capacity to contemplate the beauties of nature aright, and therefore must have some other object in view by so early a visit, I told Argus to look out. In a few minutes he reported a hyacinth flower broken off, and deposited in the steeple crown of his hat. On examining the spot I found a red *Groot voorst* (probably so named after one of the ponderous beauties of Amsterdam) had just been cropped off by the ground. I arose in anger, and was just going to upbraid him, when three decent young lads, and their pretty young lasses, entered the gate. Thinks I to myself, I won't discompose them, and, bad as he was, expose him to the ridicule of the ladies; so I asked him to step into the store. Says I,

"Sir, you have not paid for the flowers in your hat." Says he, "I intend to pay." "Then," says I, "we're agreed at once, for I intend you shall pay. The price, cut to order, is twenty-five cents; but as you helped yourself without leave, I will only charge Wall street commissions; so you may give me fifty cents, and be off. Having got the *mōney* in my *hand*, I began to deliver an extempore lecture on the baseness of such conduct, comparing it with the ox in the meadow, who, having not sense to discern these beautiful works of the Creator, tramples them in the mire with his cloven feet; but, being conscience-struck, he shuffled himself out of the gate, up into Broadway, as fast as his long legs and green sluffs could carry him.

P. S.—Stepping into the green-house the other day, I observed a decent-looking woman holding up, admiring, and smiling at a pretty rose-bud she had just plucked from a bush. As she did not attempt concealment, I was sure it was not done in evil design, or with *malice prepense* (as they say at the Hall of Justice). Says I, "Madam, I daresay you thought no harm when you broke off that rose?" Says she, "I thought where there were so many to pluck off, one would not be missed." "But," says I, "ma'am, had you thought for a moment that if every lady who visits this place was to carry away a rose, or break off a branch, in a short time *we* should have nothing left to look at but bare poles and brickbats." She looked so, and said she was sorry, and I really believe she was sorry; so I cut a slip or two of geranium, and a sprig of myrtle, to tie to the rose, and so made a bouquet complete. She went home more repenting than if I had scolded as loud as Mrs. Socrates of old, when she emptied the salt-water bath on the bald head of her husband.

LIVERWORT.

[*From the New York Commercial Advertiser*, 17*th August*, 1829.]

We cannot deny the use of our columns to our friend Grant Thorburn for the following characteristic letter in defence of his favorite plant. If our "Subscriber" who ridiculed it on Saturday has any music in his soul, he will laugh; and if he has any magnanimity, he will "give it up." His closing allusion is very good; but we suspect Mr. Thorburn went to church so many times yesterday, that he had not time to refer to the text of his authority. It was not the King of Assyria who preferred "the rivers of Damascus" to "all the waters of Israel," but Naaman, an officer of the King of Syria.

"*Liverwort again.*—I met a grave-digger the other day, and asked him how was trade. He said it had not been so dull before in the month of August since the year 1816—and were it not that a few young ladies get every week squeezed to death by their *corsets*, he did not believe he would make salt to his *kail*.* That year there were so many black spots on the sun that the cucumbers were frozen to death in July, and seed became so scarce that the Yankees were obliged to invent a machine whereby they made seed from the wood of the whitewood-tree, and peddled it round the continent for the moderate price of one dollar per

* Scotch soup.

ounce. Now, I am thinking, Mr. Stone, that this same *subscriber* of yours must be an undertaker, or grave-digger, whose business of late has been so much curtailed by the introduction of *liverwort* and *mustard-seed* (the character of the latter is so firmly fixed he dare not say a word against it), that having nothing better to kill his dull time, he sits down to vent his spite on the poor liverwort. I think, too, Mr. Printer, he gives you a pretty good knock on the head in the outset of the letter, when he says, he is *provoked* to see you puffing up an herb which has no *medical qualities*. In all the vegetable kingdom, a plant or herb has not yet been discovered that God made without possessing *medical properties*. Your subscriber next comes down on the poor sober-sided Shaking Quakers—a set of the best mechanics and honestest fellows I ever met with—and were it not that they hold the doctrine of that consummate blockhead, Malthus, I would call them among the best members of society too. He therefore almost commands you not to come out with your white paper and black *printer's-devil* advertisements, thus aiding and abetting these monstrous Shakers to deceive the public. I really wonder what makes the man so angry. He asks you, too, if you have any interest in the *apothecaries' stores?* I think I sell more of that weed (without medical properties) than any apothecary in town, and therefore think he strikes me over your tall head. But if he is really in search of truth, and will call at the meeting-house in Liberty street, I will give him the names of some gentlemen, probably of his own acquaintance, in whose renovated countenances he may read the medical properties of this herb. Every improvement in science or mechanics has been met by the opposition of the ignorant or interested. When the bright eye of Clinton first sketched the lines of a canal through a thousand hills and dales, a host of fellows, who could not see an inch before their nose, wrote volumes to prove that he was born blind. If this same liverwort grew only on the banks of the Ganges, it would be a sovereign remedy; but as it is to be found in abundance on the banks of the Hackensack River, in New Jersey, we are to be told it is the only herb that ever God Almighty made which has no *medical properties.* This thing will sound strange in the hall of Princeton College. It reminds me of the great King of Assyria, who would not believe the prophet when he told him to wash away his leprosy in that clear running brook close by—but he must needs go to one of the great rivers in Damascus wherein to bathe his royal brown hide. To be serious, this herb is doing much good in pulmonary complaints—it is a pity to knock it in the head at once anonymously.

"Yours, &c.,

"Grant Thorburn."

[*From the New York Commercial Advertiser*, 15*th August*, 1829.]

Messrs. Editors—It is provoking to read in your paper, occasionally, an editorial puff of some herb which has no *medical properties.* Eighteen months ago there was a cure (related by the newspapers) produced by liverwort. The article became immediately very common, and everybody who had a liver complaint or affection of the lungs drank freely and continually of the decoction, till every one was satisfied that the liverwort was an inert article. Now you are trying to get it up into use again. The leaf has three lobes, which gave name to the plant, as the liver has three lobes likewise: this is the origin; but many suppose it derived its name from its virtues in diseases of the liver. I was knowing to the following fact:—A child had the quinsy very bad—so bad that there was danger of suffocation. The doctor prescribed an emetic and a blister-plaster; but an old woman came in, and said that the swallow was affected, and the best thing was a poultice made of a swallow's nest. This took with the father and mother, and the doctor's medicine was laid aside. The nest procured consisted of excrement and clay, and was applied for two days, when the child died. So with the liverwort. Have you an interest in the apothecaries' stores which induces you to recommend it so highly? I presume not; therefore do not deceive the public with the advertisement of the Shakers, which was got up to produce a sale of the article.

One of our religious papers recommended and wrote columns, and printed hundreds of certificates of drunkards who were cured by Chambers' remedy. A year afterwards the same editor stated he had been deceived, for every one of whom he had published a cure were still drunkards. So it is with all these quackeries. I fear the day will never come when the community will not be stuffed with nostrums got up merely to make money.

A SUBSCRIBER.

ROMANCE IN REAL LIFE.

[*From the New York Commercial Advertiser of September 12th*, 1833.]

Having spent an hour in company with this young lady, on the day of her arrival in New York, and being privy to some of the facts, I think they are worth preserving.

> "From Susquehannah's utmost springs,
> Where savage tribes pursue their game,
> His blanket tied with yellow strings,
> A shepherd of the forest came."—FRENEAU.

On Sunday evening last we were fortuitously witnesses of an incident equally interesting and painful. Many people have denounced Shakspeare's Othello as too unnatural for probability. It can hardly be credited that such a fair, beautiful, and accomplished woman as Desdemona is represented to have been, could have deliberately wedded such a blackamoor as Othello; but if we ever entertained any incredulity upon the subject, it has all been dissipated by the occurrence of which we are to speak.

About two years ago, an Indian of the Chippewa nation—formerly said to have been a man of some rank in his tribe, but now a missionary of the Methodist church among his red brethren—was sent to England to obtain pecuniary aid for the Indian mission cause in Upper Canada. What was his native cognomen—whether it was the "Red Lightning," or the "Storm King," or "Walk-in-the-Water,"—we know not; but in plain English he is known as Peter Jones. An

Indian is a rare spectacle in England. Poets and romancers have alike invested the primitive sons of the American forest with noble and exalted characteristics, which are seldom discernible to the duller perceptions of plain matter-of-fact people; and which English eyes could alone discover in the hero of the present story. But no matter: Mr. Peter Jones was not only a missionary from the wilderness, and, as we doubt not, a pious and useful man among his own people, but he was a *bona fide* Indian, and he was of course made a *lion* of in London. He was feasted by the rich and the great. Carriages and servants in livery awaited his pleasure, and bright eyes sparkled when he was named. He was looked upon as a great chief—a prince—an Indian king; and many romantic young ladies, who had never passed beyond the sound of Bow-bells, dreamed of the charms of solitude amid the great wilds—"the antres vast and deserts wild" of the great West; of the roaring of mighty cataracts, and the bounding of buffaloes over the illimitable prairies; of noble chieftains, leading armies of plumed and lofty warriors, dusky as the proud forms of giants in twilight; of forays and stag-hunts, and bows and arrows, and the wild notes of the piercing war-whoop, in those halcyon days when, unsophisticated by contact with the pale face,

"Wild in woods the noble savage ran;"

and all that sort of thing, as Mathews would most unpoetically have wound off such a flourishing sentence. But it was so:

"In crowds the ladies to his levees ran—
All wished to gaze upon the tawny man;

> Happy were those who saw his stately stride—
> Thrice happy those who tripped it at his side."

Among others who perchance may have thought of "kings barbaric, pearls and gold," was the charming daughter of a gentleman of Lambeth, of wealth and respectability. But she thought not of wedding an Indian, even though he were a great chief, or half a king—not she! But Peter Jones saw, or thought he saw—for the Indian Cupids are not blind—that the young lady had a susceptible heart. Availing himself, therefore, of a ride with the fair creature, he said something to her which she chose not to understand—but told it to her mother. Peter Jones sought other opportunities of saying similar things, which the damsel could not comprehend—*before him*—but she continued to repeat them to her mother. He sought an interview with her; it was refused. He repeated the request; it was still refused, but in a less positive manner. Finally, an interview was granted him with the mother, and the result was, that before Peter Jones embarked on his return to his native woods, it was agreed that they might breathe their thoughts to each other on paper across the great waters: thus was another point gained. And, in the end, to make a long story short, a meeting was agreed upon, to take place the present season in this city, with a view of marriage. The idea is very unpleasant, with us, of such ill-sorted mixtures of colors; but prejudices against red and dusky skins are not so strong in Europe as they are here. They do not believe, in England, that

> "These brown tribes who snuff the desert air,
> Are cousins-german to the wolf and bear."

The proud Britons, moreover, were red men when conquered by Julius Cæsar. What harm in their becoming so again? But must we hasten our story.

On Tuesday morning of last week, a beautiful young lady, with fairy form—"grace in her step, and heaven in her eye"—stepped on shore from the elegant packet-ship United States. She was attended by two clerical friends of high respectability, who, by-the-way, were no friends of her romantic enterprise. She waited with impatience for her princely lover to the end of the week, but he came not. Still she doubted not his faith, and, as the result proved, she had no need to doubt; for on Sunday morning Peter Jones arrived, and presented himself at the side of his mistress! The meeting was affectionate, though becoming. The day was spent by them together, in the interchange of conversation, thoughts, and emotions, which we will leave to those better skilled in the romance of love than ourselves to imagine.

Though a Chippewa, Peter Jones is nevertheless a man of business, and has a just notion of the value and importance of time. He may also have heard of the adage, "there's many a slip," &c.; or, perchance, of the other, "a bird in the hand," &c. But no matter. He took part, with much propriety, in the religious exercises of the John street church, where he happened to be present, which services were ended at nine o'clock by an impressive recitation of the Lord's Prayer in the Chippewa dialect. Stepping into the house of a friend near by, we remarked an unusual ingathering of clergymen, and divers ladies and gentlemen. We asked a reverend friend if there was to be another religious meeting? "No," he replied; "but a wedding!" "A wedding!" we exclaimed with surprise. "Pray, who are the happy couple?" "Peter Jones, the Indian missionary," he replied, "and a sweet girl from England!"

It was then evident to our previously unsuspecting eyes, that an unwonted degree of anxious and curious interest pervaded the countenances of the assembling group. In a short time, chairs were placed in a suspicious position at the head of the drawing-room, their backs to the pier-table. A movement was next perceptible at the door, which instantly drew all eyes to the spot, and who should enter but the same tall Indian, whom we had so recently seen in the pulpit, bearing upon his arm the light, fragile, and delicate form of the young lady before mentioned—her eye dropping modestly upon the carpet, and her face fair as the lily. Thereupon up rose a distinguished clergyman, and the parties were addressed upon the subject of the divine institution of marriage; its propriety, convenience, and necessity, to the welfare of society and human happiness. This brief and pertinent address being ended, the reverend gentleman stated the purpose for which the couple had presented themselves, and demanded if any person or persons present could show cause why the proposed union should not take place. If so, they were requested to make their objections then, or forever after hold their peace. A solemn pause ensued. Nothing could be heard but a few smothered sighs. There they stood, objects of deep and universal interest—we may add, of commiseration. Our emotions were tumultuous and painful. A stronger contrast was never seen. She, all in white, and adorned with the sweetest simplicity; her face as white as the gloves and dress she wore, rendering her ebon tresses, placed *à la Madonna* on her fair forehead, still darker; he, in rather common attire, a tall, dark, high-boned, muscular Indian: she, a little, delicate European lady; he, a hardy, iron-framed son of the forest: she, accustomed to every luxury and indulgence, well educated, accomplished, and well-beloved at home, possessing a handsome income, leaving her comforts, the charms of civilized and cultivated society, and sacrificing them all for the cause she had espoused—here she stood, about to make a self-immolation; and, far away from country and kindred, and all the endearments of a fond father's house, resign herself into the arms of a man of the woods, who could not appreciate the sacrifice! A sweeter bride we never saw. We almost grew wild! We thought of Othello—of Hyperion and the satyr, or the bright-eyed Hindoo and the funeral pile! She looked like a drooping flower by the side of a rugged hemlock! We longed to interpose and rescue her; but it was none of our business. She was in that situation by choice, and she was among her friends. The ceremonies went on: she promised to "love, honor, and obey" the Chippewa; and, all tremulous as she stood, we heard the Indian and herself pronounced man and wife! It was the first time we ever heard the words "man and wife" sound hatefully. All, however, knelt down, and united with the clergyman in prayers for a blessing on *her*, that she might be sustained in her undertaking, and have health and strength to endure her destined hardships and privations. The room resounded with the deep-toned, heartfelt, and tearful response—Amen! The audience then rose, and after attempting, with moistened eyes, to extend their congratulations to the "happy pair," slowly and pensively retired. The sweet creature is now on her way to the wilds of Upper Canada—the Indian's bride!

Such is the history of a case of manifest and palpable delusion. Peter Jones cannot say, with Othello, that "she loved him for the *dangers* he had passed." The young lady was not blinded by the trappings of military costume, or the glare of martial glory. But she is a very pious girl, whose whole heart and soul have been devoted to the cause of heathen missions; and she has thus thrown herself into the cause, and resolved to love the Indian for the work in which he is engaged. For our own part, we must say, that we wish he had never crossed the Niagara. But the die is cast, and the late comely and accomplished Miss F——, of London, is now the wife of Mr. Peter Jones, of the Chippewas; but that she is deluded, and knows nothing of the life she is to encounter, there can be no doubt. As evidence of this, she has brought out the furniture for an elegant household establishment: rich China vases for an Indian lodge, and Turkey carpets to spread on the morasses of the Canadian forests! Instead of a mansion she will find a wigwam, and the manufacture of brooms and baskets instead of embroidery.

In justice to the spectators of the scene, however, it is proper to state, that a few of her real friends in this city—those into whose immediate society she was cast—labored diligently to open her eyes to the real state of the case, and the life of hardship and trial which she is inevitably destined to lead. Poor girl! We wish she was by her father's ingle in Lambeth, and Peter Jones preaching to the Chippewas, with the prettiest squaw among them for his wife!

HINTS TO MARRIED MEN AND BACHELORS.

Having seen the building of almost every house in this great metropolis, I think I must have been dull, indeed, not to have learned something of the men and their manners for the last half century. I think, also, it is the duty of every man, woman, and bachelor, who know any thing whereby they may benefit their neighbors, to tell it.

A young attorney among my friends, in copying an instrument, began, "Know *one woman* by these presents," &c. His partner, in passing, glanced at the apparent mistake. "Stop, sir, you should say, 'know all men.'" "Oh, never mind," replied the junior; "if one woman knows, all men will soon know." So, as I speak to one woman, I hope all men who hear may attend.

Life and health being continued, I purpose to send forth, in the Home Journal, a weekly bulletin on the domestic economy of kitchen, parlor, store, and housekeeping, being the results of fifty-four years' experience in that department.

As I sat in my tent-door on Washington's birthday, I thought of the four celebrations I had witnessed while he lived in our midst. With the pleasures of memory,

I retraced the years of twenty-two to twenty-five, and thought to myself that if I were to live my life over again, I would just manage my treaty of peace, amity, and concord, with the lassies, after the same mode and form which I pursued fifty-five years ago. Therefore, my young friends, I will just describe the process, and say unto you, Go and do likewise. When I emerged from the cottage wherein I first drew breath (in Scotland), I looked on the daughters of men, and saw that they were fair. I resolved that as soon as I could earn one shilling sterling per day I would enter on a life copartnership with one of these native beauties. What God makes beautiful, it is for man to admire; and perceiving by statistical tables, that God sent annually into the world an equal proportion of men and women, I therefore thought it must be His law, that every man should have his mate at once, leaving future provision and consequences to Him who hangs creation on his arm, and feeds her at his board. It is fifty-four years since I ratified that treaty of peace, amity, and equal rights, and never for one moment did I regret the contract; nor did I ever lack a loaf in the pantry, or a dollar in my purse. If God sent another mouth, he always sent food to fill it. With regard to courtship, it is the easiest thing in the world. Love is the language of nature. The veriest fool, if he can't pronounce, can speak it with his eyes, and women are nice interpreters. When first thinking of these affairs, I resolved in my own mind never to spend an hour in private conversation with any young woman till I had determined on taking to myself a wife; and also, never to spend an hour with any woman except she was the one whom, above all others in the world, I wished to make my wife. On this principle I practised and prospered. There is nothing to be gained by hanging around a sensible woman for months, repeating opera gossip or play-house nonsense. You mistake the sex if you hope to win their favor by this means. While you think they are smiling at your small wit, they are only laughing at your great folly. I have sojourned with ladies who had more sense in their little finger, than you could squeeze from a dozen of such heads as you may see daily leaning on the door-posts and lintels of the Astor *for support.*

If you wish to gain the affections of a virtuous woman, you must speak to her the words of truth and soberness. If you wish to make her your wife, tell her so; if you don't, you have no business in her company. Ladies often suffer martyrdom when, from politeness and pity, they are compelled to sit for hours, hearing (not listening to) the small talk of some biped whom Madam Nature had been toiling on all day to form his handsome person, but, having tired of the job by sundown, had rolled him from her workbench, forgetting to put brains in his head. As I said before, Mr. Bachelor, if you don't want that lady to become your wife, you have no business in her company. You, perhaps, keep at a distance a worthy, modest, but bashful young man, who would gladly give a dollar per minute, for the next half hour, could he only occupy the place on the sofa which you now fill with your useless identity. If you wish that lady to become your partner for life, tell her so, like a man of sense. She don't want a monkey without nerve, muscle, sinew, or brain in his frame, and whose most prominent point of distinction is a wild-goat's beard, projecting from the nether circle of his under lip; she wants a strong arm to lean on for support and protection; she needs a man of mind, who will lead, guide, cherish, and protect her on their life-journey, till the end.

I need not say what the woman should be; for, as I think, she is the most perfect subject in all creation's work, in all creation's plan; as Burns speaks of Nature:

> "Her 'prentice hand she tried on man,
> And then she made the lassies, O!"

Having just learned that Mary and you are agreed on the preliminaries of a matrimonial treaty, I will only remark, in conclusion, and by way of encouragement, that if you behave to your partner like a man of sense, while you walk together by the way, the honeymoon will never wane, but shine brighter and brighter, till you put up at the last inn by the wayside—the grave.

MR. MARRIED-MAN:—Having heard of your marriage, I send you, with my congratulations, a few hints, which, if followed, will keep the chain of matrimonial felicity ever bright and burnished. Devote your leisure hours to the company of your wife; leave politics to politicians; they will make as many Presidents, at one sitting, as will serve you for a lifetime. If your circumstances are easy, and you are fond of out-door amusement, let your wife be your constant companion. It is unkind, unmanly, and impolite to leave her pining alone at home, while you are abroad enjoying yourself.

To him whose lot it is to earn his bread by the sweat of his brow, I would say, when the labor of the day is done, spend the evening at home with your wife; or, if no cares prevent, walk together in one of the beautiful parks, or accompany your wife to a public lecture. Thus will you learn something, and make the evening seem short. If your wife is engaged in repairing your garments or in smoothing your linen, then sit by the table, and read to her the news of the day. If the children are to be cared for, stay at home and do your part. If one is fretful, take it on your knee, and sing to it; if the other stirs in the cradle, put your foot on the rocker. This will lighten the cares of your partner, and cause a smile upon the face of her whom you so fondly admire. I speak from fifty-four years of experience.

I have a word to say to you young men of moderate circumstances. You expect to, and no doubt many will, become merchant princes of the next generation. I advise you to take a wife, as the first and best step in commencing business. If yours is a retail business, have your dwelling under the same roof, if possible; and if there is a room at the back of the store, so much the better. Have the door which opens into the store made of glass, so that when you are out on business, your wife can sit and sew by said window, and see what is going on in the store at the same time. Never leave your store except on business which no one but yourself can perform. Horse, foot, and poney races, fishing, fowling, and sailing, will never pay your rent; and while you are hooking fish from the river, the boy in the store is hooking money from the till. Besides should you meet with an accident, which often occurs on these occasions, your first exclamation would be, "What business had I there?"

As profit, pleasure, and small capital never long agree, our fish-catching merchant, in a few months, shuts up two hours earlier than usual. Says Dick, "What's the matter?" "Hush!" says Tom; "the sheriff is taking an inventory." He now discovers, when too late, that the cheapest fish are caught in Fulton Market with a silver hook.

When you are out on business, hurry home as fast as possible. I lost thirty dollars one day, about fifty years ago, by standing five minutes in the street, rehearsing the items of Bonaparte and his battle of Wagram. When I came home, I said, "Good wife, has any one inquired for me?" "Mr. Brown," she said, "called to pay his bill. Some explanation is wanted, and he says he will call at two o'clock this afternoon." He started for Canada that night, and I never saw him more. I wished Napoleon and Wagram in Hackensack swamp.

Again: As you are only beginning the world, abstain from purchasing costly furniture, and fly, as you would from the plague, all temptations to purchase *plate.* Perhaps your wife will attend a tea-water party at the house of a lady friend, whose husband is an old-established merchant. On the table is a silver tea-pot, a silver milk-pot, sugar-bowl, and tongs. At nine o'clock you accompany your wife home. (This little incident occurred about fifty years ago, when we had no Italian fiddlers, rope-dancers, men and women singers, live elephants, and monkeys, to keep people out of bed all night.) On the way home, your wife looks sad, and never opens her mouth. Arrived at home, she takes her stand before the looking-glass while untying her hat. Her late pretty face is now as long as a May-pole. You are distressed on her account. In the most soothing manner possible, you inquire what is the matter with your dear. For a minute or so she will not speak, and, perhaps, begins to cry. Now be cool; take it easy, and acquit yourself like a man. These tears are the grape-shot which the ladies always carry in the magazines of their sparkling eyes, with which they mow down their opponents as fast as did the Invincibles of Bonaparte on the plains of Austerlitz. We have whole-hog, half-alligator, and half-horse men in Tennessee and Kentucky, who will stand before Colt's six-barrel revolvers, without flinching; but there are not ten men between Plymouth Rock and the shores of the Pacific who can stand the shot from a woman's eye.

As I hinted above, keep cool; move your chair closer to hers; cover your face and cry a little, by way of sympathy. As soon as she hears you sigh, her tender heart will relent, and become your comforter. Now you will hear that this *much ado about nothing* was only a storm in a tea-pot—this hateful tea-pot, this sugar-bowl, and this milk-pot. "I am sure, Mr. Snodgrass, you can afford me a silver tea-pot as well as Mr. So-and-so can his wife." Now another crystal drop is rolling from her pretty eyes; but don't look; you will be shot. For her sake, for your own sake, and for the sake of the next generation, don't give up the ship. Draw closer your chair; commence a mild and soothing speech, sprinkled with some of the elegant sentiments and metaphors with which you were wont to address your lady-love before marriage. Commence the exordium somewhat after this fashion:—"You know, my dear, that Mr. So-and-so has been long established in a sure and profitable business; has made a fortune, and is now on the point of retiring; whereas we are only beginning with a small capital. I can't conduct my business without borrowing money from the bank. When I borrow one hundred dollars from the bank, I pay seven dollars a year as interest. Were we to get a silver tea-pot, sugar-bowl, milk-pot, and tongs, they would cost over three hundred dollars. The interest on this sum is twenty-one dollars a year. This would buy you a good winter and a good summer hat; and I would much rather look on your lovely face, under a pretty hat, than to see you pouring tea from a silver tea-pot, to wet the mouths of some one who might go home and laugh at what they would call our extravagances." If she has the right feelings within her, she will wipe her weeping eyes, and, with a smile, acknowledge the justness of your speech. It is thus that a woman should be led; she was never made to be driven.

We left the happy pair complacently smiling on each other as the storm in a tea-pot began to subside. In fact, there had been no storm; there was only a small dark spot on the matrimonial horizon, about as large as a man's hand, such as the servant of Elijah the Prophet espied from the top of Mount Carmel. She smiled, seeing she had a companion who would pity her weakness, bear with her infirmities and inexperience, be a light to her feet, and a lamp in her path. He smiled when he looked on the beautiful, delicate, laughing little mortal whom heaven had given him, and he vowed in his heart that he would nourish and cherish her all the days of his life.

In process of time, two small children were climbing upon the sofa, and sitting around the table—one a boy, two years old; the other a girl, twenty months younger. We were literally next-door neighbors, and on such sociable terms, the knocker on the door was never used on entering either dwelling. Our wives, too, being women of like passions, were knit together in bonds of sisterly love.

I stepped into my neighbor's house at three o'clock in the afternoon. At a considerable distance from the fire, at the southwest side of the table, sat Mrs. Snodgrass, with her little girl on her lap; on the northeast side of the table sat Mr. S., feeding the little boy. I said, "Neighbors, you look like a family party. The storm in the tea-pot has blown over!" We had a hearty laugh about the old tea-pot. Their circumstances were prosperous and thriving. They saw their children's children, and at last were gathered to their fathers, like a shock of corn fully ripe. He died first, and two years thereafter she was laid by his side. They sleep in St. Paul's church-yard.

Another cotemporary was Cornelius Snyder, a rich and prosperous merchant, who always felt poor. When the profits and loss of the last voyage were balanced, he always looked miserable if he had not made over five thousand dollars clear profit when he had confidently expected ten thousand. The days which he should have been enjoying with the wife of his youth, were spent over the day-book and ledger. He thus passed the years of discretion (in fact, he never had any discretion, or he would have sooner ordered that "pearl of great price" in the merchant's invoice—a pretty little wife). But hereby hangs a tale which, in spite of discretion, I must relate, by way of digression; and I fear the whole chapter will be nothing more than a string of abstract, incoherent, and unconnected ideas, which come floating on the brain as the smoke rises curling from my pipe. The brightest of repartee and the flattest of nonsense alike provoke a hearty laugh; and as I write to make the lassies laugh, they will not too critically scrutinize the incongruities contained in the tales of their grandfather.

I lived in Virginia during the winter of 1848. At an evening party in Richmond, there were twelve mothers, twelve daughters, and a tolerable sprinkling of fathers, sons, widows, and widowers present, with Laurie Todd in their midst; and you may be sure we had some fun. Conversing with an ancient lady, she remarked that her grandfather came from Scotland when young, and settled in Virginia. He became a merchant and planter, and grew rich. His agent in Glasgow was Alexander McAlpin, to whom he consigned two or three cargoes of tobacco every year, and received in return cash, dry goods, hardware, etc. He had flocks and herds, men-servants and maid-servants, horses and mules; but one thing he yet lacked—he had no pretty wife to sing with him when he came home at night, fatigued with counting money, and satiated with worldly pelf, for he had more of that than heart could wish. So, after a while, he concluded to take a wife—as soon as he could catch one. But here was the rub. His time was so occupied with his business that he could not find time to look about him for a wife; and, worse than all, he was a bashful man. When he saw a maiden of twenty advancing in his path, he would cross the street, fearful of being killed by a shot from her sparkling eyes. But a remedy was at hand, however. He had often heard his parents speak much in praise of the bonny lassies who play among the heather on the hill-tops in Scotland. A bright idea struck him. When he was leaving the office, his clerk was copying a duplicate order for sundries to be sent as part of the return cargo. He thought to himself that he would order a young lassie for a wife, as the last item on the list. The article was ordered accordingly. At the same time he wrote a private letter of instructions to his agent, Mr. McAlpin, giving a minute description of the article wanted, as to age, height, health, etc. In short, she must be a bonny Scotch lassie; to be sent on the return of his own ship; her name to be on the manifest, bill of lading, etc. He promised, on arriving, to have her stored in the house of a respectable widow whom he named, and, if agreeable to the parties concerned, he would make her his wife in thirty days after her arrival. If not, and she wished to return, he would pay expenses, loss of time, etc.

When Sandy McAlpin had finished reading the letter of instructions, he slowly removed his spectacles, muttered to himself, "The lad (his correspondent, who was thirty years old) is *daft;* he tells me to send him a wife, as if she was a barrel o' *sa't* herrings; *gude kens* the *fash* (trouble) I was at to get a wife for mysel'. I'll see what the gude wife says" (a bright idea).

Next day Mrs. McAlpin sat in council with Mrs. A. and B. Invitations were sent to ten matrons, whose daughters were in and out of their teens, to assemble at Mrs. McAlpin's tea-board. Each matron was requested to bring with her a daughter who was not "o'er young to marry yet." All being present an hour before tea, Mr. McAlpin read the letter, and made an explanation. They then sat down to tea. After tea each lass gave in her ultimatum, when it was found that only three were willing to accept the offer. These three agreed to draw lots to decide the preference. Mary Robinson drew the longest straw, and was hailed as the bonny bride.

In ten days thereafter they set sail for America. They entered Chesapeake Bay after a voyage of twelve weeks, and in two days more they were in James River. When Mr. Crawford, our hero, heard of the arrival of the ship, he, with four servants, repaired to the wharf. Mary was standing on the quarter-deck, admiring Nature's wildest grandeur. She had recovered from her sea-sickness when four days out. The healthful breezes of the broad Atlantic had imprinted on her pretty face a beautiful freshness. There she stood, her cheek tinged with the roses of Sharon, and her bonny brow white as the lily of the valley. Crawford sprang on deck, and was introduced by the captain. He looked on Mary with love and admiration; her soft hand lay in his; he was *shot!*

They all descended from the ship, and repaired to

the mansion of the widow aforesaid. On the thirtieth day of probation the lovers were united in the holy bonds of wedlock. In conclusion, the sprightly, though venerable widow, remarked, that a happier couple were never linked together.

We return to friend Snyder. His father came from Hesse, being one of those mercenaries whom George the Third sent forth to extinguish the flames of liberty, which threatened to burn up every hut, tree, and shrub in this country. After having dodged the grape-shot and musket-balls of the Yankees, he gave the British army the slip when about to embark, set up a small tavern, denominated a grog-shop in these days, married a Yankee lass, became rich, died, and was buried, leaving one son and two daughters to divide the spoils.

But, before we commence with the son, perhaps it will be better to finish the remark about Pocahontas, with whom we parted on the banks of the James River. I think it was in November that I traced the Chesapeake Bay, and sailed on the James River. Every foot of that country is rich in historical fame, or sacred to Revolutionary tradition. There stood Yorktown; there stood the American, French, and English redoubts; and there stood Lord Cornwallis when he surrendered his sword to Washington. (George the Third made Lord Cornwallis, but no power, save the hand of Omnipotence, could form a WASHINGTON.) There, also, stood the wigwam of Pocahontas. Near by is a large round stone, scooped out so as to hold about a gallon of water, in which Pocahontas used to lave her face and wring her flowing tresses. There is the cleft of the rock under which she disrobed, when bathing her slender limbs in the still waters of James River. She was a queen of nature's own making. The name of her father was Powhattan, a celebrated Indian warrior. She was born in the year 1595. She discovered the warmest friendship for the English when she was only ten years old, and was afterwards useful to the first settlers. A remarkable instance of this attachment was displayed in 1607, when Captain John Smith was taken prisoner. He was brought before her father, that he might put him to death. As the savage lifted his club to dash out his brains, Pocahontas threw herself upon Smith's body, and prevailed on her father to spare his life. Captain Smith was permitted to return to Jamestown, from whence he sent presents to Powhattan and his lovely daughter.

From this time Pocahontas frequently visited the settlements of the whites, to whom she furnished provisions at times when they were much needed. In 1609 Powhattan invited Smith to pay him a visit, promising him a supply of provisions, but designing to destroy both him and all his people. Pocahontas becoming informed of the plot, ventured through the forest at midnight to disclose it to Smith. For three or four years she continued to assist these settlers in their distresses, and to save them from the effects of her father's animosity. During this period, Smith had been driven, by faction, to England, and the rapacity of his successors plunged the settlement into an Indian war. An attack was made on one of the forts by the Indians, under Powhattan, when the commander and thirty men were slaughtered, only one person, a boy, surviving, and he was saved by Pocahontas.

About this time she left her father's house on a visit to a neighboring chief, when she fell in with Mr. Thomas Rolfe, an Englishman of respectable character. He became attached to her, and offered her his hand. It was accepted, and the consent of her father being obtained, they were married. In 1616, she embarked, with her husband and several Indians of both sexes, for England, where she was baptized by the name of Rebecca, a sweet name, and one to be held in everlasting remembrance. (See Genesis, 24th chapter.) She became a subject of curiosity to all classes. During her stay in London, she advanced greatly in the knowledge of the English language, and her conversation was much sought at court. Her residence among civilized men, however, was destined to be short. While about to embark from Gravesend with her husband and an infant son, to revisit her native land, she died, at the age of twenty-two years, leaving one son, who was educated by his uncle in London, and afterwards became a wealthy and distinguished character in Virginia. His descendants still reside in that State, numerous, rich, and respectable. While sojourning there, I was introduced to one of them, who was every inch a gentleman.

When ascending the river, I was the only passenger; our skipper was the second edition of Captain Baltus (see Paulding's Dutchman's Fireside). Tide or wind being ahead, he would quietly drop anchor, smoke his pipe, and ruminate, until luck changed. Having drawn my attention to the location of the wigwam of

Pocahontas, about a mile ahead, I was much gratified, on nearing the spot, to see the anchor plunge into the river. The captain went with me to the spot. While there, with my hand in her wash-bowl, I beheld, in my mind's eye, this tall, straight, slender Indian maiden, with a towel on her arm, her slender foot and tiny moccasin scarcely leaving an imprint in the sand, as she passed from the basin to the river. There can be no mistake in the locality of her dwelling. Posts are set up, from time to time, by those who cherish her memory, to mark the spot; and as the wash-basin forms part of the rock, it will remain while woods grow and waters run.

We return to our friend Snyder. After his father's death he went largely into the shipping line, and prospered. At the age of forty-eight he resolved that, as he had no partner in his office, he would have one at his table. He married a handsome young woman, whose parents were poor, but respectable. He was old enough to have been her father. He had a very small portion of the milk of human kindness; so they lived ten years in splendid misery, when he died, leaving his wife and a son seven years old to wind up the affairs of his large establishment. Being thus in the power of strangers, the task of closing a concern of such magnitude was far beyond her capabilities. She was cheated by some and robbed by others. Finally, the balance left was not sufficient for the support of the widow and her son. I knew many who were "merchant princes" fifty years ago, whose families were ruined in a similar way.

If you expect to be a merchant (being now only a

clerk, with five hundred dollars a year), get married. Choose a partner who is willing to live according to your income—one whose mother has taught her to work, wash, mend stockings, make pies and cake, and knows how to put an apple in a dumpling. Let her be handsome, and one whom you can love above all others in the world. You will then want no other companion. You will then live happier and cheaper than you now do, paying board, washing, and mending, besides every now and then having a piece lost. Your washer-woman is poor, and can't make good the loss you sustain.

As you now live, perhaps you don't save fifty out of the five hundred dollars per annum. You leave your office at seven or eight o'clock in the evening, and stroll up Broadway, where you fall in with one or two companions. You step into Niblo's, and call for three glasses of ice-cream (three shillings); another companion then joins you; you call for a cigar, and four are handed (one shilling). Here, then, are four shillings gone for what most people would consider nonsense. Only think, four loaves of bread blown away in tobacco smoke. These four loaves would supply the table with bread for yourself, wife, and child, from Monday morning to Saturday night. You say you *wish* to marry, but can't support a wife. Get such a one as I have described; she will more than support herself. You now pay more for cigars than it cost me to keep my wife fifty years ago. Your income is five hundred, while mine was only three hundred dollars. My expenses after marriage were less than they were before; besides, the prattle of her little Yankee tongue and the light of her countenance were, *to me*, worth a hundred dollars a month. But we return to Niblo's.

The cigars being lit, you adjourn to the street, and "where shall we go?" is the question. "To the theatre," say all. There you pay fifty or seventy-five cents for admission. The play over, the porter and oyster house come next in rotation. Half boozy, you stagger on your way to your boarding-house, or to sleep in the store. In the morning you are aroused; having slept only three hours, you get up with a headache and all the torments of a person not blessed. Verily, the way of the transgressor is hard.

During a sojourn of fifty-seven years in New York, I have trod the streets at every hour of the day and night, in search of doctors and nurses; and I have seen, at daybreak, between Liberty street and the Park, as many as six of the "guardians of the night" make a peaceable entry into a store, by means of the key, while the master is playing whist with his neighbor in ——— Place, and his clerks playing funny tricks in an adjoining street, with money purloined from the till the day previous. Thus, the candle being lit at both ends, will soon bring the concern to a close.

In choosing a wife, let her be of a family not vain of their name or connections, but remarkable for their simplicity of manners and integrity of life. Never fix your eyes on a celebrated beauty. She is apt to be too proud of her pretty face, and afraid of soiling her delicate hands. The woman who washes her own silver spoons, China cups and platters, and performs other light services in the family, is always the most healthy, the most happy, and the most contented; for thus her mind is occupied, and she gains the approba tion of her husband and of her own conscience. The woman who leaves her family four or five hours every day, running from shop to shop, and making calls, is always unhappy, for conscience says, "You have sown the wind, and you shall reap the whirlwind."

Beauty is very desirable in the choice of a wife. You will be proud of your handsome wife when you introduce her to a friend; but by all means find out, if you can, if she is vain of her beauty. If you find she is daily washing her already pretty face with milk of roses and patent cosmetics—that she is daily pouring Cologne-water and Macassar-oil on her already glossy hair—if this is the case, it is rather an alarming symptom. A handsome woman never looks so pretty as when she don't know it. I dare say some of the young lassies will laugh at a man near fourscore talking about *pretty faces;* but I was once as young as any of them, and in the pleasures of memory I live my life over again; and though I now and then look through spectacles, yet I would rather gaze an hour on a handsome picture, than to squint at a homespun piece of work for a minute.

Good-nature is another necessary virtue in a wife. This, though, is not so very essential, as a man must be a consummate blockhead indeed if he can't lead (not drive) a woman by fair words. A good manager is another indispensable qualification. After marriage, if a woman does not pride herself on her knowledge of family affairs and laying out money to the best advantage, let her be ever so sweet-tempered, gracefully made, or elegantly accomplished, she is no wife for a man of business. When people are harnessed in the yoke matrimonial, they must draw together. It is a man's duty to give to his wife; it is the wife's duty to use it with the most scrupulous economy.

THE NIGHT FUNERAL OF A SLAVE.

Travelling recently on business in the interior of Georgia, I reached, just at sunset, the mansion of the proprietor through whose estate for the last half hour of my journey I had pursued my way. My tired companion pricked his ears, and, with a low neigh, indicated his pleasure, as I turned up the broad avenue leading to the house. Calling to a black boy in view, I bade him inquire of his owner if I could be accommodated with lodgings for the night.

My request brought the proprietor himself to the door, and from thence to the gate, when, after a scrutinizing glance at my person and equipments, he inquired my name, business, and destination. I promptly responded to his questions, and he invited me to alight and enter the house, in the true spirit of Southern hospitality.

He was apparently thirty years of age, and evidently a man of education and refinement. I soon observed an air of gloomy abstraction about him. He said but little, and even that little seemed the result of an effort to obviate the seeming want of civility to a stranger. At supper, the mistress of the mansion appeared and did the honors of the table in her particular department. She was exceedingly lady-like and beautiful, as Southern women generally are. She retired immediately after supper, and a servant, handing some splendid Havanas on a silver tray, we had just seated ourselves comfortably before a blazing fire of oak-wood, when a servant appeared at the door of the parlor, and uttered in a subdued, but distinct tone, the, to me, startling words:

"Master, de coffin hab come."

"Very well," was the reply, and the servant disappeared.

My host remarked my look of surprise, and replied to it as follows:

"I have been sad," said he, "to-day; I have had a greater misfortune than any I have experienced since I lost my father. I lost this morning the truest and the most reliable friend I had in the world—one whom I have been accustomed to honor and respect since my earliest recollection. He was the playmate of my father's youth, and the Mentor of mine.

"A faithful servant, an honest man, and a sincere Christian, I stood by his bedside to-day, with his hand clasped in mine. I heard the last words he uttered—they were, 'Master, meet me in heaven.'"

His voice faltered a moment, and he continued, after a pause, and with increased excitement: "His loss is a melancholy one to me. If I left my home, I said to him:

"'John, see that all things are taken care of;' and I knew that my wife and child, property, and all, were as safe as though guarded by a hundred soldiers. I never spoke a harsh word to him in my life, for he never merited one. I have a hundred others, many of them faithful and true, but his loss is irreparable."

I came from a section of the Union where slavery does not exist; and brought with me many of the prejudices which so generally prevail in the free States in regard to this institution. I had already seen much to soften these; but the observation of years would have failed to give me so clear an insight into the relation between master and servant, as this simple incident. It was not the haughty planter, the lordly tyrant, talking of his dead slâve, as of his dead horse; but the kind-hearted gentleman, lamenting the loss and eulogizing the virtues of his good old *friend.*

After an interval of silence, mine host resumed: "There are," said he, "many of the old man's relatives and friends, who would wish to attend his funeral. To afford them an opportunity, several plantations have been notified that he will be buried to-night; some, I presume, have already arrived, and desiring to see that all things are properly prepared for his interment, I trust you will excuse my absence for a few moments."

"Most certainly, sir," I added; "but if there is no impropriety, I would be pleased to accompany you."

"There is none," he replied; and I followed him to one of a long row of cabins, situated at the distance of some three hundred yards from the mansion: the house was crowded with negroes, who all arose on our entrance, and many of them exchanged greetings with mine host, in tones that convinced me they felt that he was an object of sympathy from them; the corpse was deposited in the coffin, attired in a shroud of the finest cotton materials, and the coffin itself painted black.

The master stopped at his head, and laying his hand upon the cold brow of his faithful bondsman, gazed long and intently upon the features with which he had been so long familiar, and which he now looked upon for the last time on earth; raising his eyes at length, and glancing at the serious countenances now bent upon his, he said solemnly and with much feeling:

"He was a faithful servant and a true Christian. If you follow his example, and live as he lived, none of you need fear when your time comes to lie there."

A patriarch, with the snows of eighty winters on his head, answered—

"Master, it is true, and we will try to live like him."

There was a murmur of general assent; and after giving some instruction relative to the burial, we returned to the dwelling.

About nine o'clock a servant brought word they were ready to move.

Mine host remarked to me, that by stepping into the piazza, I would probably witness a novel scene—the procession had moved, and its route led within a few rods of the mansion; there were 150 negroes, arranged four deep, and following a wagon, in which was placed the coffin, down the entire length of the lane, at intervals of a few feet on either side, were carried torches of the rosin-pine, or candle-wood. About the centre was stationed the black preacher, a man of gigantic frame and stentorian lungs, who gave out from memory the words of a hymn suitable to the occasion.

The Southern negroes are proverbial for the melody and compass of their voices, and I thought that hymn, mellowed by distance, the most solemn, and yet the sweetest music, that ever fell on my ear; the stillness of the night, and the strength of their voices, enabled me to distinguish their sound at the distance of half a mile. It was to me a strange and solemn scene, and no incident in my life has impressed me with more powerful emotions, than the night funeral of the poor negro.

RIGHTS OF WOMEN.

At the corner of Beekman and Nassau streets I met an acquaintance, a bachelor of fifty-six. Thirty years ago I advised him to form a life-partnership, for bed and for board, with one of the bonnie lassies whom he used to stand staring at as he saw them enter the Brick Church at the ringing of the bell; at that time he said he would, but did it not; now he says it is too late.

"I say so too. Now what have you done," says I, "to any good purpose in the world? Your bank stock, your fancy and humbug stock, will soon go to heirs you know not who, and your name will soon perish out of the city; while I will never die—with my children, my grandchildren, and GREAT-grandchildren, the name of Thorburn will live in this Model Republic as long as wood grows and water runs."

"Have you great-grandchildren?" he inquired.

"I have," says I, "and the oldest is no chicken

either, for she opens and shuts the door when I call to see her; and the greeting of Great-Grand-Pa, and the parting kiss from her pouting lips, gives pleasure more sublime than you or John Jacob ever felt when counting your bank shares, or summing up your railroad stock."

"Stop, Grant," he exclaimed, "you'll compel me to marry in spite of my teeth."

And he was compelled to marry in spite of his teeth, in three months thereafter; for, meeting at a tea-party (bachelors are always invited by widows and matrons) a blithesome spinster of twenty-eight summers, who took his fancy, he resolved to make her his own; and so well did he run the parallels, and so close did he lay the siege, that she surrendered at discretion in less than two months; and, as she remarked afterwards, she only said YES to get quit of his teazing.

But we return to our friend. On the corner of Beekman street this conversation was held, three weeks previous to his introduction at the tea-party.

Having now got a wife and a house of his own, he left his card. It was four o'clock P. M. when I called; they had just finished dinner, and sat, having the table between them, cracking nuts and cracking jokes. He seldom turned his eyes from admiring her handsome countenance, and she seemed highly pleased with her new husband, her new house, her new sofas, carpets, chairs, glasses, &c., and, above all, with her own new life; pleasure sparkled in her eyes, and with the exuberance of her spirits, her deportment had more of eighteen than twenty-eight years.

"My worthy friend," said I, "I should think from

appearances, that one day spent in this house is better than a thousand spent in the solitary haunts of a bachelor."

"Yes," he replied, "and I only wish I had taken your advice twenty years ago."

They seem as happy now as in the full of the honeymoon. A boy and girl make glad their hearts. While the son deposits the checks, the daughter escorts the mother on all shopping excursions.

But we return, for I had almost forgotten the rights of the Ladies. For the last sixty years the world has been turned upside down by a set of vain philosophers—miserable fools and silly dreamers—writing volumes of theories (which will never work in practice), whose leaves, if cut in strips, would circumnavigate the globe; and all this about the *Rights of Man*. Not a word about the *Rights of Women!* These champions of Freedom would not even allow the ladies of Paris to choose the color of their own night-caps, for they cut off the head of the Queen, and the heads of thousands of the prettiest women in France, merely because they thought a white night-cap better became them than a red one; and this was French gallantry, this was French liberty of speech, thought, and action. How profound the wisdom of those vain philosophers! they wisely surmised that if the head of a woman was once severed from her shoulders, she never would wear a white or Royalist cap any more.

N. B. I never knew a genuine red republican, either in Europe or America, but he was a genuine tyrant over his wife, children, servants, and apprentices.

Next came Thomas Paine, with a huge compound of

abstract ideas, entitled "Rights of Man." While thus employed, however, he found time to court and marry a respectable young woman. Three years afterwards she obtained a divorce from him for cruel usage. Ladies, this was the author of the "Rights of Man," the author of "Common Sense," and the author of the "Age of Reason," while he was the most unreasonable mortal I ever conversed with.

But to bring the matter home to our own doors and to our own firesides. Here I might fill a volume were I to give the names of a set of matrimonial jugglers whom I have known in the city for fifty-seven years past. They were married to some of the finest specimens of women the world could produce; they swore at the altar to nourish and to cherish these weaker vessels all the days of their lives. But, within six months after marriage, should his delicate partner happen to be indisposed, away he goes to some ward-meeting, or card-meeting, or club-meeting, or may be he takes some country cousin and away they hie to Niblo's, the Lyceum, the Opera, or Castle Garden;—she sits by the window, her pale cheek resting on her delicate hand—the tears, like drops of pearl, are trembling in her beautiful eyes, while her husband and cousin descend the front steps with loud peals of laughter, every one of which strikes on her heart like the sharp point of the cold steel in the hand of an assassin. Perhaps she sees no more of him till eight o'clock next morning, when he asks if his coffee is ready.

Now, Mr. Whisker-face, or Mr. Goat's-beard, is it thus that you nourish and cherish your wife? she don't treat you so. This conduct in a young husband is mean, unmanly, and despicable in the extreme. It is cruel to leave her moping alone, while you are abroad finding your own pleasure. But you say you left her in the hands of a good nurse. No doubt you did, but to a young wife there is no nurse like a kind husband. Had you stayed at home, mixed the medicine, carried the cup to her lips (from your hand the bitter drug would taste sweet), then sat down beside her, and as close as you please too, and if you had told her *one-half* of the fine stories you were wont to relate three weeks before marriage, she would have been perfectly well before the going down of another sun. This is *woman's right*, and you are sworn to respect it; in her presence maintain the same modest deportment, the same gentle address, and the same winning glance from your eye which you were wont to assume in the days of courtship; if you do this her love will never fail, and she will say that she is the happiest woman in the world; thus the honeymoon will never wane, but shine brighter and brighter, till you put up together at the last Inn by the wayside—the grave. I speak from fifty-four years' experience, and can add that I never saw an unhappy marriage out of five score but that the man was either a *rogue* or a *fool*.

There is another class of land-pirates who prey on the rights of women. New York, and Broadway in particular, is completely infested by them in pleasant weather, for these fowls of fine feathers can't breast a storm; you may see them on the steps of the Astor, and every other hotel where drone bees do congregate. There they stand, planted like the Mandarins in the show-window of a tea-shop. If you have time and patience to stand by St. Paul's, you may count some scores of these automatons, passing and repassing fifty times, between Leonard and Rector streets, in the course of three hours. They generally hook arms, and as they grin, and talk, and look in one another's faces, their motion has much of the swagger of the Siamese twins. You may know them by the cut of their jibs; they have beards like the goats on the mountains of St. Gothard; their slender waists (I am now speaking of *two-legged animals* who call themselves men) are squeezed up with whalebone, cord, and buckram; they resemble a group of spiders suspended between heaven and the great deep from the branch of a peach-tree. They also wear suspenders, which are intended to act as preventers (as the sailors say), to stop the extremities from parting with the trunk. Now these simple sons of silly women do nothing but hunt among the weaker sex, seeking whom they may devour. They are of their father the devil, for he was the first lying dandy that ever deceived a woman. The weaker sister having *lost caste*, is driven from society to the highways and hedgeways for food and shelter; trodden under foot by the scorn of man, a by-word and hissing to her more fortunate sisters, and laughed at by the perjured wretch who wrought her destruction,—while he, provided his brown hide is covered with black superfine, is admitted into the *best society*. Best society, indeed! It is only a few years ago that Munroe Edwards counted one in this *best society*. Edwards was a forger, a swindler, and a cheat, and closed his life in the states-prison; but the black-hearted villain who robs a confiding maiden of her fair fame and spotless character, is a villain of a deeper dye; and this villain is a magnate in the best society! He eats their dinners, he drinks their wine, struts on their carpets, lolls on their sofas, and salutes the fair lips of their daughters. Ladies, these things are done in every grove, and under every green tree, in the *best society.* But it ought not to be so.

I was led to these reflections by a visit to the penitentiary; many, very many of the female prisoners were models of beauty in face and person; God made them angels, man made them devils. They walked in pairs with other outcasts from society, under the rod and correction of a savage-looking mortal, a "Lord of the Creation."

> "Man's inhumanity to man
> Makes countless thousands mourn."—BURNS.

It is an opinion current with all red republicans, that all kings, princes, and potentates are born natural fools; and seeing that we are all born sovereigns in this model republic, and as Webster affirms in his dictionary, that a king and a sovereign are the same in law, it follows, of course, that we are only a nation of most sovereign, consummate fools. Were it not so, why is it that we act just the opposite from every principle of common honesty and common sense? When a beggar removes a pair of pants from the door of a store, to protect his hind quarters from the piercing winds of a winter morning, or to hide them from the prying gaze of a vulgar throng, he is sent to the penitentiary at once; but the men who steal hundreds of thousands of the people's money at the Custom-house,

Post-office, Banks, and Insurance companies, are seldom brought to trial, and having enough of the people's money in hand, they dress like gentlemen, and all the exclusives and upper-tens will lift the hat and grasp his hand in Broadway, invite him to dinner, and play cards with him till three o'clock A. M. on Sabbath morning.

The small respect that is paid to the Rights of Women is another instance of the folly of the sovereign people. Thomas Jefferson (and he was the greatest sovereign among all the sovereign people), in his Notes on Virginia, avers that "man is made with strength of body and powers of mind to direct and protect his weaker companion, the woman;" but, instead of directing and protecting, he too often employs the cunning, subtle, devil-like powers of his mind, and the brute strength of his body, to work her destruction. But I cannot better describe this operation than by quoting from Mrs. L. Maria Child's "Letters from New York." Mrs. Child is a lady of modest worth, and an eloquent writer. Had she been born in Europe, she would have been a paragon here:

> "For many a flower is born to blush unseen,
> And waste its sweetness on the desert air."

Mrs. Child was paying a visit to the penitentiary, when the editor of the "Weekly Rake" (a scurrilous paper) was brought in to do penance for his evil deeds. She asks—"Why should the 'Weekly Rake' be shut up, when daily rakes walk Broadway in fine broadcloth and silk velvet?" She adds—"More than half of the inmates of the penitentiary were women; and, of course, a large proportion of them were taken up as 'street-walkers.' The men who made them such—who, perchance, caused the love of a human heart to be its ruin, and changed tenderness into sensuality and crime—these men live in 'ceiled houses' on Broadway, and sit in council in the City Hall, and pass regulations to clear the streets they have filled with sin. Do you suppose their poor victims do not feel the injustice of society thus regulated?"

Yes, my dear Mrs. Child, they do feel it; and, as it is held in our model republic to be just, right, and lawful for *men* to kill tyrants now and then, provided they may thereby recover their just and natural rights, so we need not feel surprised when we hear, now and then, that one of these pirates is shot by the hand of a woman in Leonard or any other street; nor did I wonder the other day, when one of these injured sisters dragged the usurper of her rights from the steps of the Astor, and made him strut through the mud like a crow in the gutter. Served him right. He had broken his oath and his promise, and had robbed her of all that is dear to a woman. *If the ladies only knew their power*, and were rightly to improve it for their own advantage, they could twist the whole male generation, like a thread of tow, around their fingers.

There seems to be something wrong in society with regard to the rights of women. Why should the woman be driven away into the wilderness, like a scape-goat for the man, and bearing *his sin* on her own head? She is cast out to perish; he, though the *first transgressor*, is caressed and courted by all, as if to sacrifice one of the weaker sex were an honor to the

16

man, whom God and nature has appointed to be her protector. You may see him in Broadway, at mid-day, escorting a female whose character, *as yet*, is unsullied. She meets and receives the salutations of her friends without a blush for being seen in contact with the man who has *worse than murdered* her playfellow. But, should his victim come within a hundred yards, she would fly from her as from the plague.

Now, Miss Mock-Modesty, why shun your poor, young, and blasted friend, when you are not ashamed, in the face of the sun, in the public street, to be seen hanging on the arm of her destroyer? This thing ought not to be so. You say that this is the fashion; and so is it the fashion in Turkey for a man to have six wives.

I have a remedy to propose; and as this is the age of improvement, the age of experiment, and the march of intellect, I think the project is deserving of being tested by experience. I would propose that a new court be established, under the name and title of the "*Court of Conscience.*" Let this court consist of three matrons, not under forty and not over fifty years, *widows*, otherwise their husbands—who perhaps in their *daft* days were weekly or daily rakes, and themselves being in the same condemnation—might bias their better judgment, and thereby the perjured villian might escape, unwhipt of justice. These three matrons, each being a judge; also, twelve matrons of a younger growth, by way of a jury, all of them to hold their office during life. Thus, when one dies, her successor is initiated into the routine of business without for one moment clogging or stopping the wheels of government. This perpetual motion, or *rotation in office* (which Mr. Jefferson recommended in his inaugural speech in 1801), is the canker-worm which is gnawing at the vitals of our model republic. With every new President, new Governor, or new Mayor, from the High Constable down to the deputy clerk of a dirt-cart, they are removed; they had just rightly learned the duties of their office, when the new incumbent had to commence his apprenticeship. Thus they "are ever learning and never come to a knowledge of the truth." Our affairs are solely managed by apprentices. It is a rare case when we have a journeyman; and a master grates on the nerves of our plain, *simple*, high-minded, sovereign people. Thus, we have blundering accounts, defaulters, swindlers, "and every evil work." I verily believe that when our city comes to her latter end, she will die from an attack of this *rotary* fever. But we return to the Court of Conscience.

We said there should be twelve matrons for a permanent jury. Now, presuming said court is properly constituted, let the injured sister appear before them, state her case on oath, and pray judgment against her deceiver. As it is customary in the Senate of the United States to sit with closed doors, so it will be highly decorous in this court that they shut their chamber doors behind them. The man need not be cited before them, for, having perjured himself to the plaintiff already, his word, truth, and honor are totally damned. Well, then, a majority of these matrons finding the complaint well founded, issue their precept to the Recorder of the city, setting forth that they having found Tom, Dick, or Harry guilty of certain high crimes and misdemeanors, have mulcted him to pay over one-third of his estate, real and personal, to Jane Maria, by way of indemnity, and ordering him to seize on his property at once; if he has no property, send him to the State-prison, and give his earnings to the said Jane Maria during her life; at her death, let him out, and perhaps he will learn better manners. There can be no appeal from this to any other court; for, as these lawgivers have refrained from enacting laws for the protection of women's rights, it is but fair play for the women to take the law in their own hands.

That this may be done *instanter*, have a petition made out for Congress, call a meeting for ladies in the Park, let our worthy Mayor be requested to send a posse of old veterans from the police-office (the Mayor, being a man of choice gallantry, will never refuse the ladies' request) to guard the gates, so as to prevent the entrance of dogs, hogs, bachelors, or any of the male creation; have the resolutions and speeches cut and dried, so that when the ladies get on the stage, they have only to read them and let all the wondering multitude say "Aye! Aye!" Thus having done their duty to their *country and themselves*, they can eat their dinner with a merry heart and a quiet conscience, showing an example of modest worth to those would-be lords of creation who hold their meetings there, and who generally break up in a fight between the aldermen and constables, plaintiffs and witnesses, defendants and counsel, peace-keepers and head-breakers, pell-mell, over and under each other; and this they call liberty of speech and freedom of debate.

Having now engrossed the petition with fifty thousand signatures, send it on by a deputation of at least one hundred matrons, selected from among the handsomest in the city. This will look respectable, and give weight to the argument; besides, to look on the faces of so many sparkling beauties, will thaw the hearts of those cold-blooded, back-woods, sling-drinking members, and they will grant the petition, were it for the "half of the kingdom." But peradventure there should be a company of cold, calculating bachelors there, whose influence might frustrate the passage of the bill; let the ladies be in attendance, in case of an emergency, ready to employ the force of their *own arms* (an invincible weapon) on the morning of the day of presenting the petition. After partaking of a substantial breakfast, let one and all of them replenish their reticules with a modicum of nourishing compound-cake, likewise with a vial of *simple* waters, merely to refresh the lips. Thus armed for a siege, repair early to the Capitol, before these drowsy Sampsons have awoke from the lap of Delilah. Fill the gallery, and should any opposition appear on the part of the bachelors, declare your sitting permanent. Thus, by making a prudent use of the power which the God of Nature has given you, soon those lords of the manor will surrender at discretion.

The following is a case in point:

About a century ago it was customary for the wives and daughters of the peers, and other honorable ladies, to sit in the gallery of the House of Lords, listening to or looking at the speakers. The younger members of the House were often detected by their seniors, with their eyes fixed on the gallery, when they should have been looking at the speaker; and winking, nodding, and playing pantomime with their female cousins, when they should have been laying in funds of political economy. The elders, taking offence at this levity (stupid old fools, they played the same tricks at twenty-five), passed a resolution, that hereafter no woman should be admitted to the House or gallery. Next day all the West End was in commotion, ladies in their carriages flying in all directions; shortly before six P. M., the whole posse of noblemen's wives, headed by the Duchess of Devonshire, beset the door, demanding admittance. In obedience to his instructions, the doorkeeper refused. They made a rush, pushed him on one side, while they entered like a flock of pigeons, and filled the whole gallery. When the peers took their seats, they were confounded to see their wives and married daughters, to the number of some hundreds, dressed with all their ornaments, and holding a silent meeting, like a company of Friends. As soon as a quorum arrived, the Speaker took the chair; the sergeant-at-arms was desired to clear the galleries; the ladies dared him to touch them, and claimed their right as peeresses of the realm. The sergeant-at-arms looked to the Speaker for orders. The noblemen began to laugh, the resolution was reconsidered, and laid on the table. The majority were proud of their dames for the noble stand they had taken in defence of their rights.

Now, ladies, here you have both precept and example. If you don't stand up for your rights, it is not my fault.

U. S. Bonded Storehouse, Sept. 20, 1851.

FRIEND WALKER—

Below is another remarkable instance of Providential help in my time of need.

In 1849 and 1850 I kept a seed-store in Charleston, S. C. On a certain day I had a draft payable in the bank at three P. M. I was short twenty dollars at one P. M. The only friend that I could depend on had left town that morning for a week. I was walking behind the counter, ruminating what next to do, when a gentleman, a planter in appearance, stepped in, inquiring for turnip-seed; having paid twenty-five cents, the amount of his purchase, he walked off, leaving the door open. I stepped round the counter to shut the door; I noticed a scrap lying on the floor; I took it up—it was *two ten-dollar bills* on the Bank of Charleston. I stepped out, looked up and down, and stepped to the corner of the first cross street (within three hundred feet of my door)—he was not to be seen. His coat was very noticeable, being an extraordinary light sky-blue; his speech and deportment were pleasing and prepossessing; his features are stamped on my heart. I will know him if we meet in eternity. Observe, it was neither more nor less, it was just the amount I stood in need of. I advertised—it was never claimed. I state a fact, which will be explained on the day when the dead shall rise. You can form your own opinion; for my own part, I sat ruminating for minutes, whether in the body or out of the body I cannot tell.

In 1808 my store and dwelling stood on the corner of Nassau and Liberty streets, next lot was occupied by Edward Watkeys, soap and candle maker; the house and back building were all of wood, filled with rosin, fat, candles, and soap. On the night of the 25th of August, at twelve o'clock, it burst out, from front to rear, in one tremendous blaze. The buildings stood on the south side of mine. A strong south wind blew at the time. My store, and green-house in the yard (all built of wood), were enveloped in flame; ten houses were burned around me; yet, strange to tell, next morning my premises stood entire, having scarcely the mark of fire on any part of my frame buildings; only one hole, about the size of a man's hand, was burned through the shingle roof—*twenty dollars* made good the whole damage. Twenty thousand people were witnesses of this *fact*. So rapid was the fire, that Mrs. Watkeys, her daughter—aged twenty-two years—a colored woman, and her three children, were all burned to death.

On the afternoon, just six hours before commencing of the fire, I had been painting flower-pots with green varnish-paint; on the shelf stood a half gallon of spirits of turpentine, a half gallon of rosin-varnish, and a dozen of flower-pots new painted; they stood on a shelf, side by side, in a loft on the second story, on the south side, adjoining the candle factory; there was only an inch board between this combustible matter and the fire; through this board a hole was burned about twice the size of a man's hand; directly opposite this hole stood the combustible matter above named.

The turpentine spirits filled a strong half-gallon stone jug, corked; the varnish-paint nearly filled a keg six inches deep and seven broad; the *mouth* of this keg was *open* (no covering); next morning, when clearing up, I perceived the keg filled to the brim with black coals, being pieces of the burnt board, which must have dropped into the varnish-pot when they were burning coals. The pot was coated outside with paint and varnish, which had run over when mixing the paint. This paint melted (it stood within eight inches of the burnt board) and ran down on the shelf, which glued the pot to the board as soon as it cooled. The new-painted pots were all fast to the board by the same cause and means. Before removing the pots I brought in a dozen of the neighbors and respectable citizens, who were viewing the ruins, that they might see this great sight—a pot of varnish burned, yet not consumed. I let them remain *fixed* as they stood, one day, to satisfy the curiosity of thousands who called to look.

I was insured in the Eagle Insurance Company: the directors came also to view the scene; among whom were Henry Wyckoff, Henry Rankin, and others, then among our merchant princes, now all numbered with the dead. Twenty dollars repaired the buildings, and $1200 the damage by water, on seeds and fixtures in the store—paid promptly. Mr. Smith Anderson, for many years the President of the North River Bank, and who is yet in our midst, can testify to some of these particulars.

John Edwards, at that time a noted street-preacher, professing the Quaker creed, having visited the premises the day after the fire, stepped in the store; says he,

"Friend Grant, thee ought to go in the street, before all these people, fall on thy knees, and thank God for thy deliverance." Says I, "John, that thing is better done in closet, and the door shut."

The death of five persons, and other attending cir cumstances, brought people from all quarters to visit the spot, for many months after.

Another: About four years ago I had spent my last shilling, and knew not where the next would come from. I was walking up Broadway, between John and Fulton streets, when I saw a half-eagle lying on the pavement: in a second it was in my pocket, my heart light and thankful.

Another,—rather laughable. I stepped in the green-house one morning, about three months ago. I picked up a small pot that might hold a half pint of earth; in the pot was a dear little rose-bush, as your daughter would say—a bud was bursting into flower. I land at Peck Slip, go along Pearl, and up Pine street to the office. When coming through the market I put my hand in my pocket to pay for a peach. I found I had left my purse at home. This gave me no thought,—I could go *tick* for a dinner. I meant the rose-pot as a present to a young man in my office, who is courting a very pretty girl, and I thought it might give him a shove on the track matrimonial. I carried the pot in my hand. In Pearl, between Cedar and Pine streets, a young man came in my front. He appeared, from his superfine pants and neat round jacket, like the *mate* of an Indiaman. "Is that for sale?" "It is." "The price?" "Fifty cents." The plant was in his hand, the money in mine, in a half minute. I smiled when I saw the *dinner-money* in my hand. Next day I brought another plant for my young friend. I firmly believe in the doctrine of a Particular Providence. He numbers the hairs on our head. The fall of a sparrow and the crash of an empire are alike noticed by Him whose eye is everywhere.

Another: It is known to all the inhabitants of the city (comparatively speaking) that seventeen summers the yellow fever prevailed. I never left the city, and nursed among the sick, yet neither I, my wife, nor any of my children ever caught that disease. I had nine in family.

I could fill a small volume with like instances, but the following may suffice.

In 1798 the yellow fever prevailed to a fearful extent in the city; all fled who were able, or who had friends in the country to receive them into their houses.

At that period it was customary for masters of in-door trades, as tailors, shoemakers, bookbinders, &c., to have all their work done under the same roof with their families, and often to board such of the journeymen as were bachelors. In many instances, one or two of these young men, who did not wish to leave the city, would propose to their employer when he was about shutting up the house:—Leave out stuff, we will work, keep bachelor's-hall, and take care of the house. In general, this offer was gladly accepted by the employer. But now came the drawback;—it often happened they were all seized in one night, and being unable to help one another, in some cases their lifeless bodies were found before any one knew of their situation. Many valuable lives were lost by this thoughtless arrangement.

On Sabbath, September 16th, I was sent for by three young men, corner of Pine and Front streets, one in Liberty, near Broadway; and on Monday to three on the corner of Dover and Water streets—four Scotchmen and three Americans, all young and esteemed friends. Not one was able to give a cup of cold water to his brother in distress. I got doctors, but money could not procure a nurse. From the 25th of August previous, I had been among the sick; now my whole time was spent in these three abodes of death. I had now been twelve months married to Rebecca, and the time of her deliverance was at hand. Her mother, who, through fear of death, was all her life subject to bondage, *fled.* Rebecca had no fear; her heart was fixed where fear never enters. At the door of the Methodist Chapel in John street, I engaged an aged widow, and a mother in Israel, as a companion to Rebecca while I was absent among the sick. They slept in one bed below, I up stairs, in another. I was *out* every night in this fatal week, but they knew it not. Had they known it, they would have prevented my going. On Tuesday, the 18th, two died on the corner of Pine and Front streets; next day the third died. I saw his corpse put in the dead-hearse. Now the house was vacant; I locked the door, went home with the key, and in six weeks thereafter the owner called and thanked me.

I stated above I slept up stairs. After seeing the two ladies stowed away snug, kissed *both* good-night, I crept to my own berth, read a chapter, listened; all being quiet, I stepped softly down the *back stairs* on my stocking-soles; got in the same way before they were up in the morning, so they knew it not. Before parting on Friday night I saw symptoms of a crisis. I sat on a chair and communed in my heart—am I doing my duty to my wife? If trouble comes to-night, there is none to call for help, not a neighbor in the block. My wife and the widow think I am in bed. Should they call, and receive no answer, what will be the issue? On the other hand, there lie three dying mortals: without the cup from my hand they must perish. God can time her *hour*, but except by a miracle, they must die. I rose on my feet with excitement. By some optical illusion or delusion, or what, I know not, I saw her Heavenly Father standing in the centre of my bedroom with outstretched arms, ready to receive her. With my arms of faith I raised her from the couch and laid her head on his bosom. "Lord, take care of her," I mentally exclaimed; and rushed down stairs. How well he took care of her you will find in the next page.

That night I spread a mattress on the floor, and slept in the same room with two sick and one *dying* man. I had slept only an hour or two each night that week: this was Friday. I tied a cord round my wrist, with the further end to a chair by the sick man's bed; he pulled the string when wanted. I could not wake by calling. I thought no more of Rebecca (I had left her in good hands) till day broke in the morning. At that hour the eldest patient died (they were three brothers); at six A. M. I saw his corpse in the hearse; the other two recovered. The patient in Liberty street recovered; thus four died of the seven.

At seven A. M. I got home, and found all well; having eat our breakfast with thankful hearts, says I,

"Rebecca, it is four weeks since I grasped the hammer or blew the bellows (then I was a wrought-iron nail-maker): I will go to work to put me in sorts, for I am nearly worn out." I came in to dinner at twelve P. M., Rebecca was smiling, comfortable and happy; she was fixing her ruffles, &c., preparatory for church—this being on Saturday. While at dinner the door was opened without knocking, and in stepped Mrs. Hunter. I started. Says I, "Mrs. H., are you not afraid to come in town, the fever is on the increase; you have been six weeks in the country, and the doctors assert that people from the country are more liable to infection than those living in the infected districts?" She replied, "Whether it's for life or death, I was *compelled* to come in. Thinking of Mrs. Thorburn by day, and *dreaming* about her by night, I have had no peace in my mind for the week past." I said we were glad to see her, and hoped no evil would befall her. And, thank God, no evil did befall her. She stopped two weeks in my house, returned to the country in sound health, and so continued ten years, when she died.

Mrs. Hunter was housekeeper in the family of Charles Dickinson, an officer of the Revolution, and went with the family to the country. Dickinson's house was next to mine, hence the intimacy of Mrs. H. with my wife. My Methodist widow was the mother of children; Mrs. H. was a lively widow of forty, and the mother of three children; thus both qualified to meet the *crisis* at hand. Mrs. H. joined issue at the table, I returned to my anvil, leaving the three matrons in lively conversation. My dwelling was opposite the Post-office, and my workshop in Liberty street, opposite Little

Green. I had not been forty minutes absent from my dwelling when Mrs. H. stepped in my shop door. "Run for the doctor, your wife is in sore trouble." He lived in Park Place; I rang the bell: "Is the doctor home?" Said the servant, "He was buried this morning." I found the door of another, he was in bed, sick: I stood at a door where dwelt a nurse, she had fled. I knocked at the door of my dwelling; "Mrs. H.," says I, "I can get no *help*." "Fear not," she replied, "we *need no help*." We had only one room, six feet by ten, so there was no room for me in that inn on the present occasion. I walked in Nassau street between Liberty and Maiden Lane about half an hour; it was the 22d of September, sun set at six; the clock in the Middle Dutch Church struck the hour; I saw a candle burning in the room; I knocked. "Walk in," said Mrs. H., with a cheerful voice, "all is over, and all is well." I opened the door; in front of the bed, on a small table, covered with a napkin, stood a candle burning; on a snow-white pillow lay the head of Rebecca; on her milk-white arm lay the head of her son. "Come," she exclaimed, with one of her sweetest smiles, "and see what I have brought you." I stood fixed on the threshold for a moment; at one glance I saw that God had ordered all things well; He held her up till my work was done. At six A. M., that morning, I buried my last patient; at six P. M. Rebecca was a mother.

Yours,

GRANT THORBURN.

P. S. These facts are too good to be lost to the world;

if doubted, I can prove every one of them; and, as formerly stated, my present existence is not less wonderful than any there narrated. I owe this debt of gratitude to God and my fellow-men, and I think it is my duty to see it paid before I die.

G. T.

THE END.

GRANT THORBURN

IN HIS

GOLDEN AGE.

The days of our years *are* threescore years and ten; and if by reason of strength *they be* fourscore years, yet *is* their strength labour and sorrow; for it is soon cut off, and we fly away.—PSALM XC. 10.

Containing his last fragments of happy scenes in his life's evening, previous to his sun setting, in which he still recognizes the hand of a kind and faithful Benefactor watching over his path. Hoping these fragments will interest his many kind friends, he indulges the hope that both writer and reader will be benefited; for how truly can he testify that he has been young, but now he's old! "Yet hath he not seen the righteous forsaken, nor his seed begging bread;" for Jehovah Jirah is the safe conductor of his people, through floods and flames, and all distresses, landing them safely upon the eternal Rock of Ages.

NEW YORK, OCTOBER, 1853.

CONTENTS.

NEW YORK: EDWARD WALKER,

114 FULTON-STREET.

A ROMANCE IN THORBURN'S LIFE;

OR, LOVE'S STRATAGEMS AT EIGHTY-ONE.

With certain letters, where more is meant than meets the eye.

MR. PRINTER: On the 25th of August, 1852, a call of business led me to Wolcottsville, Litchfield County, Connecticut. I was yet seven miles short of my destination. With a guide and a light wagon, I went forward. It was dark: we got lost in the woods. Seeing a house by the way-side, says I to the driver, "Hold the reins, and I will inquire." All was dark in the house. I knocked at the door. In about a minute, a window opened in the second story, and a female voice inquired—

"Who's there?"

"A stranger," says I, "lost in the woods. Let me lie on the carpet or sofa; I will pay you for your trouble, and thank you besides."

"I am in bed," she replied.

"Just where all honest folks should be at ten o'clock at night," I replied.

"But I am all alone," she continued.

"So much the better," says I; "I'll keep you company."

"Who are you?"

"Laurie Todd, from New York," I replied.

She smote her hands the one against the other:

"May the Lord preserve me!" she exclaimed. "Stop—I'll place a light in the passage, and unlock the door. You sit in the parlor; I'll be with you in ten minutes."

In five minutes, she entered the parlor, when we first saw one another face to face. I was hungry, and she gave me to eat; thirsty, and she gave me to drink; a stranger, and she took me in. There was neither sleep to our eyes, nor slumber to our eyelids; and ere the morning sun had streaked with gold the eastern sky, we had agreed on the preliminaries of a treaty matrimonial.

Obstacles, apparently insurmountable, soon intervened; but, like other kings, princes, emperors, and potentates, we courted by proxy, by go-betweens, by letters, and dumb signs. By the arrangements of Providence, the mountains were removed, without my intervention. I immediately wrote the following, which may serve as a pattern to others in like case, made and provided.

New York, 30th May, 1853.

Dear Maria: The difficulties are removed. God willing, I will be in thy house on Friday, the 10th, tell thee all about it on Saturday, marry thee on Sunday, and do as the Lord may direct on Monday. Thy *true* Scotchman,

GRANT.

N. B.—Send for your brother, and make proclamation at 9 A. M., in the church, and get married at 9 P. M.

It was done in order. I left Peck Slip for Bridgeport at 10 A. M., on Friday, the 10th of June, by steamboat, railroad, and Yankee wagons. I reached her dwelling at 10 P. M., told her all about it on Saturday, was married and paid the minister at 9 P. M., on Sunday, the 12th, which closed the concern. I left her at 11 A. M., to gather up the corn-stalks and make other arrangements, on Tuesday, the 14th, while I went forward to prepare a roost for my bonny bird. I arrived in New York at 12 P. M., on Wednesday, the 15th, having travelled stem and stern, hither and thither, near seven hundred miles; and hence we may infer that Love walks on the wings of the wind, from eighteen to eighty-one.

My partner is a comely matron of forty (thus meeting me half way), was five years married, two years a widow, no family, two inches taller, and five pounds heavier than I; thus I think I have got the best of the bargain: a lady by birth, education, and refinement; a daughter of the Puritans, with a mind as pure as was the heart of our Mother Eve on the day before Lucifer played the devil with her: in every thing but the *song*, she is a second edition of *Jenny Lind*. I received the following in a letter from her a few days ago. Having described her person, here you see her heart:

DEAR HUSBAND: I send you this copy of a prayer, from the pen of Basil Montague. It is very beautiful; and I trust I can adopt every sentiment in it as my own.

PRAYER.

LORD, bless and preserve that dear person whom thou hast chosen to be my husband! Let his life be long and useful, comfortable and holy; and let me also become a great comfort and blessing to him,—a sharer in all his joys, a refreshment in all his sorrows, a meet helper for him in all the accidents and changes of the world! Make me amiable forever in his eyes, and very dear to him! Unite his heart to mine in the dearest union of love and holiness, and mine to him in all sweetness, charity, and compliance! Keep me from all ungentleness, all discontentedness, and unreasonableness of passion or humor, and make me humble and obedient, useful and observant, that we may delight in each other according

to thy blessed word and ordinance, and both of us may rejoice in thee, having our portion in the love and service of God forever! Amen.
MARIA.

I must confess, Mr. Printer—and I own it before the world—when I read that prayer, I bowed my knee before the Lord, my Maker: I gave thanks for this *unspeakable earthly gift.* The skeptic may sneer, and the fool may laugh—it is but the crackling of thorns under a pot. For a space, I communed with my own heart, and was still. With my mind's eye, I saw this comely matron, of forty summers, in her lonely cottage in Connecticut; one feeble lamp made darkness visible; she kneels by the sofa; her aspirations ascend to Him who hears the cry of the humble,—and for whom is she pleading? It is for her husband,—and who is her husband? He is a small remnant of mortality—her grandfather in years—whom she vows to nourish and cherish all the days of his life.

Some coincidences in this romance are worth noting. On Sabbath, 22d June, 1794, I first entered a place of worship in America. It was the Old Methodist in John-street (the first erected by that Society in America). I entered a pew, and sat by the side of her who became my wife a few months thereafter.

On the 12th June, 1794, at 9 P. M., I first saw the Blue Hills of Jersey, from the ship's deck, fifty miles at sea. At the same hour and day, in 1853, I was married to my third partner, by the Methodist minister at New Hartford, Connecticut, having been proclaimed in the Methodist church at 9 A. M. From this you may observe, it was Methodist first and last, and Methodist all round.
GRANT THORBURN.

JUNE, 1853.

A VISIT TO JENNY LIND.

Hitherto, the time, talents, and conversation of Miss Lind have been so much monopolized by the good, the great, and the noble of the land, that a small mortal like myself could not so much as see the hem of her garment. Hearing, that to escape from the heat, noise, and fashionable crowd of New York, she was removing to the pleasant Heights in Brooklyn, I obtained from Mr. Barnum a letter as follows:

New York, 21st May, 1851.

The bearer, Mr. Thorburn, is a man of the highest respectability, —a funny old Scotchman, and an author, &c. Miss Lind will be pleased to talk with him; he is a very celebrated man, well known to all the literati; he is wealthy, and don't come begging.

(Signed,) P. T. Barnum.

Armed with this missive, I stood by the door of her mansion next morning, at 9 A. M. I rang: the servant appeared.

Says I, "This note is for Miss Lind, from Mr. Barnum."

Says he, "She aint up."

"No matter," says I, "the sun's up; she can read that note in bed. Tell her, if she is willing to see me, I will wait in the parlor till Christmas, if she says so." [I knew she would not say so; it was only a figure of speech, to denote the sincerity of my wish.]

The man looked in my face, without moving: I dare say, he thought I was crazy.

"Go ahead," says I, "and deliver your message."

In two minutes he returned smiling—"Miss Lind says she wont make you wait till Christmas: please sit in the parlor; she will be with you in ten minutes."

I had never seen Miss Lind. The door opened; I advanced; she met me with a quick step, both hands extended. I held her right hand in my left, her left hand in my right. Approximating as near as common sense would permit, and looking in her face—"And this is Jenny Lind," said I, returning the look, and advancing a foot.

"And this is Laurie Todd," said she.

She placed a chair in front of the sofa: she sat on the sofa; I sat on the chair. Thus we looked on one another, face to face; and thus the language of her speaking eyes confirmed the words which dropped from her lips.

She remarked, she read my history (Laurie Todd), about three years ago, in Europe; that she thought the description there given of the baptism of Rebecca was the most interesting scene she ever read in the English books. She continued—

"Can you repeat that scene from memory?"

Says I, "Death only can blot it out."

"Will you oblige me?" she continued.

Says I, "You have seen the painting of the Goddess of Liberty; that is, the costume which adorned the persons of the ladies at that period? Her father had been already dead better than three hundred days; the dress, therefore, was in half mourning. Her hat was a small black beaver, all the fashion at that time; the rim turned up on each side, so as to have the ears visible; the hair was in a broad fold, resting between the shoulders, having the extreme ends fastened with a pin on the crown: hers was very long, and very-flaxen. She was clothed in a white garment, fine, neat, and clean; her neck encircled with a black bracelet, and around her waist was a black ribbon. The train of her garment was hanging on her left arm. The thought, that before another hour the eyes of the whole congregation would be fastened on her alone, brought a faint blush on the cheek. When she walked up the middle aisle and sat down, third pew from the pulpit, I thought I never had beheld any thing half as lovely.

"Lecture being ended, the preacher proclaimed, 'Let the person present herself for baptism.' She walked to the altar, a tall, slim figure, straight as an Indian arrow, with a measured step, like a sentry on duty before the tent of his general. While the minister was binding the vow of God upon her heart, before the whole congregation, she made the responses with the same thoughtful composure, as if none but the eye of Omnipotence was there. While the minister was slowly descending the fifteen steps which led from the pulpit, she was untying the strings which held on her hat. There she stood, her black hat in one hand, a white muslin 'kerchief in the other, her beautiful and neatly-arranged flaxen locks all exposed under a blaze of light. When the minister dropped the water on her white transparent brow, she shut her eyes, and turned her face to Heaven. As the crystal drops rolled down her blushing cheeks, I thought her face shone like an angel, and I swore in my heart, if it so willed Heaven, that nothing but death should part us."

Here Miss Lind stood up with excitement. "Stop, Grant!" she exclaimed, "you ought to have been a painter; you place Rebecca before me!"

"And why not?" said I. "Perhaps her ransomed spirit is hovering over that *splendid Bible* (pointing to the centre-table), and smiling to see two kindred spirits enjoying a foretaste of pleasures so divine."

"I doubt it not," she observed; "for, with Young, your English poet, I believe that 'Friends departed are angels sent from heaven on errands full of love.'"

"And, with Paul," I added, "they are 'ministering angels, sent to minister to the heirs of salvation.'"

Here we entered invisible space, and soared to worlds on high. She repeated, with fine pathos, the beautiful legend current among the peasantry on her native mountains. It concerned a mother, who, at the dead watches in every night, visited the beds of her six motherless babes, covering their little hands, and smoothing their pillow. It is a beautiful illusion.

We spoke of the especial care which God takes of little children; how many instances are recorded in our weekly journals of children being lost in the woods, for days, sometimes for weeks, the weather inclement, the feet naked, the clothes scant, yet found unhurt. They were fed on manna from heaven, and the angel of the covenant muzzled the mouths of the ravenons beasts of prey.

Having read Laurie Todd, she put several explanatory questions about the yellow fever, and other scenes recorded, &c. On these and similar subjects we conversed more than an hour without being interrupted. But the time of my departure was at hand. We rose simultaneously; we held each other's hands; we promised to remember one another at our morning and evening sacrifice, that God would so prepare our hearts that we might meet where the assembly never breaks up, where friendship never ends.

Here the fountain of the great deep was broken up; a big tear o'erflowed its banks; I caught the *infection.* Now, I never saw a tear on a woman's cheek, but I longed to kiss it from its resting-place; that is to say, provided the thing was practicable; and whether or not I reduced this principle into practice on the present occasion, I can't conceive the sovereign people have any right to inquire. Be this as it may, at that time her lips were her own; she had no lord Goldschmidt to dispute an old man's privilege.

NEW YORK, JULY 22, 1852.

A TALE OF A TEA-KETTLE.

On a winter's evening, nearly one hundred years ago, the tea-board was laid out, and the window-curtains closely drawn, in the humble parlor of a small house in the town of Greenock, in the west of Scotland. A tidy, active matron was bustling about, slicing the bread and butter: a blazing fire gleamed and roared in the grate, and curled round the black sides of the kettle which reposed in the midst of it; and the fire crackled and the water boiled with a faintly-heard popling sound, and a stream of white vapor came whizzing out of the spout of the kettle with a shrill, cheery hiss. Now, the matron aforesaid saw nothing particular in all this; kettles had boiled, and fires had burned from the beginning, and would probably do so to the end of the chapter.

As the matron stopped to pour the boiling fluid in the tea-pot, her son James, a boy of twelve summers, sat on a low bench in front of the fire, his elbows resting on each knee, while his hands supported his head, being placed under the chin. The boy was intently gazing at the fire, the kettle, and the steam, swallowing them with his eyes, absorbed in deep thoughts and lost in contemplation. The boy looked at the fire, and the mother looked at the boy.

"Was there ever sic an idle, ne'er-do-weel in this

warld as our Jamie?" was the question which almost unconsciously she proposed to herself.

Mrs. B. stepped in at this moment.

Turning to the visitor, Jamie's mother said, "Mrs. B., did you ever see the likes of our Jamie? Look at him: he'll sit there for hours, staring at the kettle and the steam, till you wad think his een wad come out o' his heed."

And, truth to tell, there was something peculiar in the glance of the boy's eye. There was mind, active, speaking mind looking through it. He seemed as one who gazed upon a wondrous vision, and whose every sense was bound up in the display of gorgeous pageantry floating before him. He had sat watching the escaping steam, until the thin vaporous column had appeared to cast itself upward in fantastic, changing shapes: sometimes the subtle fluid, gathering in force and quantity, would gently raise one side of the lid of the kettle, emit a white puff, and then let the metal fall with a low, clanking sound. There was power and strength in that watery cloud; and as the dreaming boy saw this, an unbidden thought came upon his mind, and he knew that the fierce struggle was symbolical of intellect warring with the elements.

And still he gazed, and saw in his day-dreams ships sailing without wind or sails, and wagons propelled o'er deserts wild by some power unseen to mortal eye.

"Jamie! Jamie!" exclaimed his mother, "sit by to your tea; if I find ye staring at the fire again, ye'll feel the wicht o' my hand."

The boy rose meekly, and did as he was told. His name was James Watt, afterwards Sir James. He was honored by the title of knighthood, being the first who applied the powers of steam to any useful purpose. Steam has made this old world of ours a new one. What does it not do for man? It hurries him across the Atlantic in ten days, and grinds wheat in the grocer's store; yet this triumph of art and science was once the laughing-stock of jeering thousands; and once it was only the waking fantasy of a boy's mind, as he sat, and in seeming idleness, watched a little column of vapor rise from the spout of a tea-kettle.

The above anecdote is literally true. Watt was born in 1736. This incident occurred when he was in his twelfth year. He was the son of a poor tradesman in Greenock (in Scotland), and probably had never read a book, the spelling-book and the Bible excepted.

John Brown, the self-taught preacher, the author of the Bible Dictionary, the Self-interpreting Bible, &c., &c., and whose praise is in all the churches, was the son of a cotter, an orphan in his tenth year, and who probably never saw a book except the Bible, till he entered his eighteenth year; yet, while tending the sheep on the heather hills of Scotland, and without having seen a college, he confounded the learned Doctors in Edinburgh, with High Dutch, and Low Dutch, Greek, Hebrew, and Latin, besides the dead and living languages. His church was near my parish. I often heard him preach. He died in 1787. I was then in my fourteenth year—no judge of preaching—but my father said he was a great preacher; and I thought then, and I think so now, that my father was the best judge of preaching in all Scotland.

Burns, Hogg, and other self-taught Scottish luminaries, whose writings have enlightened and charmed the world, were all the sons of the Scottish peasantry: most of them had come to the years of maturity, before they ever read a book, excepting the Bible, the book which makes men wiser than all their teachers. The sublime, beautiful, and grand descriptions there given of the goodness, power, and majesty of God expand and refine the soul. It gathers light from the throne of the Eternal, and soars in worlds on high.

Now, Mr. Printer, you never read of a self-taught peasant in all the Pope's dominions, from the day of Pope Joan down to the present incumbent, Pope Pius the Ninth. Look at them, as they land on our shores, from France, Spain, Germany, Hungary, Italy, Ireland, and other lands of Popish darkness. Our jails, penitentiaries, State-prisons, and alms-houses are heaped full and running over with them. But this day, comparatively speaking, there is not a Scotchman in one of them. It is the Bible that makes them to differ. I would not exchange being a Scotchman, to be the emperor of all the Russias, with his crowns, lands, and royalties; for I think (and I have as good a right to think as any pope, cardinal, or freethinker in the world) that the national moral character of Scotland will stand an unanswerable argument against all the sophistry of Deism, as long as woods grow and waters run; for Scotland is emphatically the land of Bibles, and there the inhabitants lead quiet and peaceful lives, in all godliness and honesty.

A RARE DOG STORY.

In 1792—I was then in my nineteenth year—and well remember the circumstance:

A gentleman, whose country-seat stood within six miles of my "cottage on the moor," kept a fine mastiff dog. By day, he was chained up near the house; by night, he was loose to range through the garden and inclosures, a terror to evil-doers, but kindly affected to all such as do well. Now, whether it was natural instinct (for wolves are only wild dogs), or whether he had received some real or supposed affront from the sheep fraternity, I never could learn: for though the dog had a language of his own, and in which he conversed very fluently at times, yet I must confess, I could better understand the language of his eyes (dogs have very expressive eyes), than the language of his lips. Be this as it may, one morning he was accused of having murdered two of a neighbor's sheep. His master, unwilling to take up an evil report against his faithful watch-dog, had the trial postponed to Monday next, as they say in court. On the following night, however, another murder was committed. This time the fact was too clear to admit a doubt. Hero was brought in guilty, not by a verdict of his peers, but by a convention of two-legged animals, who were too dull to appreciate his motives, and too blind to sympathize with him under the circumstances; neither had they courtesy to ask, as has been the custom in all civilized communities, ever since the days of Haman, who, himself, was strung up fifty cubits, if he had any objection to make against being hung, but straightway they proceeded to execution. His master, while a tear crossed his eye-ball, says, "John, get a stout piece of rope. Hang Hero behind the barn, so as not to be seen from the house." Having spoke thus, he entered his dwelling. Hero heard his sentence with the same philosophic indifference that I have heard some two-legged animals receive theirs in the Hall of Justice in the Park. He never opened his mouth; but, thinks he, there will be a long respite between the sentence and the hanging-day. So, without speaking a word, he cleared a stone-fence five feet high. O'er hills and dales, o'er fields and floods he flew, as with the wings of the wind. He never drew up till he entered a city of refuge: here the avenger of blood dared not to enter.

You have read in that book, for which all other books were made, a man drew a bow at a *venture:* the unerring eye of Omnipotence became pilot to that shaft; it entered between the joints of his armor, and the proud monarch sunk dead in his chariot. The same unerring eye directed the flight of this dog to the spot, where, after an absence of nearly seven years, he was the means of saving the life of his master, as you will see in the sequel.

It came to pass, when nearly seven years had expired since the fright and flight of Hero (no doubt the poor dog was scared enough, when he heard the order for immediate execution), that his late master was sojourning on the borders of Scotland and England. It was winter, and dark in that climate at 5 P. M. He put up at a tavern by the wayside. As soon as he dismounted, and went in the stable to see that his horse was cared for, he was followed by a large mastiff dog, who, by every means that a dog could invent, endeavored to draw his attention. The gentleman sat down in the hall, the dog by his side, when he began to think there was something strange in the dog's attentions and manner. He put his hand on the head of the dog, and spoke kindly. The dog encouraged, laid his paw on his master's knee, and looked earnestly in his face. Recollections arose in the memory of the master, and he exclaimed, in surprise, "Why, Hero, are you here?" Hero was so pleased at the recognition, that he almost leaped on his master's back. Whether the landlord was informed of the merits of the case, or not, my informant did not say. At any rate, Hero and his master were never separate from that hour. Hero followed his master in the bedroom, when, seeing him about to undress, he seized the skirt of his coat with his teeth, and drew his master towards a closet. On opening the door, he discovered the corpse of a man, suspended against the wall. He saw his danger, and made preparations accordingly. This matter occurred shortly after the return of the army from America, after the war for Independence. Many of the disbanded soldiers took to robbing on the highways, and gentlemen always travelled well armed. He saw that his four pistols were in right trim, piled every thing movable in the room against the door, and sat down to wait the result. At midnight, there was a knock at the door: a vial of medicine which was standing on the mantel-piece was wanted for one of the family, who was taken suddenly ill. Hero growled, as if to say, "There are two of us." Mr. Morton (which was the gentleman's name) informed the assailant he was prepared with fire-arms, and would shoot the first man that entered. Presently, he distinguished the voices of three men, when, after some further parley, an axe was sent for to break in the door. At this critical moment, the sound of carriage-wheels was heard from afar; the robbers paused; Mr. H. thrust his head out of the window, and as the carriage approached, hallooed at the top of his voice. They heard his cries, and stopped, when the robbers fled by the back door. There were four men in the carriage. They secured three women, whom they found in the house, and lodged them in jail. By their information, the men were caught soon after, tried, and hung. The women were banished to Botany Bay for life.

On searching the house, several corpses were found buried in the cellar; and in the rooms many articles identified that belonged to persons who had disappeared, and were never heard of till this occurrence.

Hero went home with his master, and was a happy dog many years thereafter, when he died and was buried. A stone, recording the Providential deliverance, was set up over his bones, and his portrait hung in the hall, with the family escutcheons.

The story was published in the newspapers and periodicals of that day, all over Britain, as a fact beyond controversy.

OCTOBER, 1851.

THE KING AND HIS SCOTCH COOK.

The witty Earl of Rochester being in company with King Charles II., his queen, the chaplain, and some ministers of state, after they had been discoursing on business, the king suddenly exclaimed: "Let our thoughts be unbended from the cares of state, and give us a generous glass of wine, 'that cheereth,' as the Scripture saith, 'God and man.'" The queen, hearing this, modestly said she thought there could be no such text in the Scriptures, and that it was but little else than blasphemy. The king replied that he was not prepared to turn to chapter and verse; but was sure he had met with it in his Scripture reading. The chaplain was applied to, and he was of the queen's opinion. Rochester, suspecting the king to be right, slipped out of the room to inquire for a Bible [a pretty king, by the grace of God, and defender of the faith, and a pretty chaplain to a king, that could not muster a Bible between them] among the servants. None of them could read but David, the Scotch cook; and he, they said, always carried a Bible about him. David being called, recollected both the text and where to find it. Rochester told David to be in waiting, and returned to the king. This text was still the subject of conversation; and Rochester proposed to call in David, who, he said, was well acquainted with the Scriptures. David was called, and being asked the question, produced his Bible and read the text. It was from the parable of the trees of the wood going forth to appoint a king over them,—Judges, 9th chapter, and 13th verse. "And the vine said unto them, Should I leave my wine, which cheereth God and man, and go to be promoted over the trees?" The king smiled, the queen asked pardon, the chaplain blushed. Rochester then asked this doctor of divinity if he could interpret the text, now it was produced. The chaplain was mute. The earl therefore applied to David for the exposition. The cook immediately replied: "How much wine cheereth man—looking Rochester in his eyes—your lordship knoweth [no doubt David had seen him *fou* a dozen times]; and that it cheereth God, I beg leave to say, that under the Old Testament dispensation, there were meat-offerings and drink-offerings: the latter consisted of wine, which was typical of the blood of the Mediator, which, by a metaphor, was said to cheer God, as he was well pleased in the way of salvation that he had appointed, whereby his justice was satisfied, his law fulfilled, his mercy reigned, his grace triumphed, all his perfections harmonized, the sinner was saved, and God in Christ glorified."

The king looked astonished; the queen shed tears; Rochester, after some very severe reflections upon the chaplain, gravely moved that his majesty would be pleased to send the chaplain into the kitchen to turn cook, and that he would make this cook his chaplain. Now, by way of conclusion to this historical fact, I will only remark that this same cook is a true specimen of what the Scottish peasantry are at this present day.

Few of them learn more at school than to read the Bible and write their own name; but the beautiful and sublime language in which the narrative is conveyed, the true and concise descriptions of men and matter, &c., make those whose Bible was their school-book, and who make it their companion by the way, to be wiser than their teachers. Hence, in the heather hills among the shepherds, and in the lowlands among the ploughmen of Scotland, you will find thousands deeply read in almost every science and language. They are the most profound engineers, the most scientific gardeners and botanists, the most learned physicians, surgeons, and anatomists, learned, independent, and conscientious preachers of righteousness; and by them the Gospel is preached to the poor.

Now, Mr. Printer, I challenge all the popes, from the days of Miss Pope Joan the First down to the present incumbent, to produce as many Bibles in any country under the sun, of the same dimensions, as are to be found in Scotland. It is, therefore, a fair inference, that the Bible alone makes them to differ from the restless Frenchman, the ferocious Spaniard, the German serf, the Russian boor, and other white slaves in Europe. The Goddess of Liberty, when sent from above, was nourished and cherished in the Bible shops of America.

The present policy of the crowned heads in Europe, popes, priests, and cardinals, is to blot the name of Republic from the earth. No Bible, no Republic, is their watchword. Hence, when they see a Bible in the hand of a white slave, they tremble on their thrones.

The Church of Rome, always the right-hand agent of tyrants, is now in the full tide of successful experiment to drive the Bible from our schools, colleges, and firesides: this accomplished, the Republic dies.

JANUARY 1, 1853.

FOURTH OF JULY, 1794 AND 1849.

THIS day, Mr. Printer, completes fifty-five celebrations which I have witnessed in America. Being a holiday (pity it is not kept more holy), and not liking your *spells of sunshine* in July quite as well as I do in January, I thought I would sit down in my cool store and note down a few abstract, incoherent, and unconnected ideas that were floating in my brain, as the smoke rose curling from my pipe. By-the-by, Mr. Printer, *them glimpses of sunshine* with which the columns of your paper have been illuminated for some days past, must come from the pen of a *Master of Arts*, not by *diploma* from Princeton in the Jerseys, but from the college of Him who is the author of every good and perfect gift: he ought to be a preacher.

When I look on our country to-day, and compare it with what it was fifty-five years ago (I was then in my twenty-second year), I feel as if I could join the festive throng at the *Pavilion* and sing the one-hundred and third psalm, first part, till sundown. I suppose now, some one of the cod-fish democracy (see his portrait in Hart's bookstore window in King-street, near George), will smile at the words, *our country*. "Why," says he, "Laurie is a true Scotchman, *frae the gude toon o' Edenburg*." Well now, my college-bred friend, I hope you don't infer from this, that if a man is born in a stable, he therefore must of necessity be nothing but a horse; besides, when WASHINGTON was president, I was naturalized, and I have married two American girls, which I think is of itself being naturalized enough, in all conscience; besides, Dr. McFungus, or some such *unsavory* name, half a century ago, delivered an oration in New York, before twelve doctors of law, physic, and divinity, together with some tens of scores of the swinish multitude, wherein he proved to his *own* satisfaction, that by a certain process of evaporation, man changed his system every seven years—therefore, I must have evaporated into thin air fifty years ago.

The celebration of the Fourth in New York, in 1794, was a very meager affair: the population about fifty-five thousand. No uniform military companies had been commissioned at this period, and only three or four different branches of mechanic societies turned out; but I saw on that day what will never be seen again—a company of thirty old men, called *veterans* by way of distinction. They had with them a field-piece and flag, under which they had fought for independence: they wore the old tattered uniform, and some of them the three-cornered cocked hat, which oft they had touched while giving Washington the passing or marching salute. Some of them had been with Washington, in that winter march to or from Valley Forge, when the army being without shoes, the ice and snow were stained by the blood from their wounded feet. Hard was the lot of these honest men. The country was poor, and unable to support those who had lost limbs, health, and property in the service of their country; and, still worse, when in 1801, the pure democracy (with Aaron Burr at their head) got into power, most of these officers and soldiers were turned out, to make room for a host of political favorites who had never done the country a service.

Thank God, the lines are fallen to us in more pleasant times ; and if every man would mind his own business, not interfering in the concerns of his neighbors, we would be the happiest people under the sun. Therefore, Father Garretson and Madam Folsom, you may cook your Irish potatoes by white slaves, and let the South cook their sweet Carolinas by black slaves ; then eat without asking any questions. Thus may brotherly love continue, as your parson prays.

P. S.—Yesterday, while viewing the splendid military array of caps, helmets, plumes, swords, and scimeters, with drums, trumpets, and other well-stringed instruments in all the pride and circumstance of war, I thought of my thirty poor veterans whom I had seen that day fifty-five years ago. No bugle sounded in front, nor tinkling cymbals in their rear : a solitary Ethiopian was pounding on the calf-skin, while another most manfully was squeaking on a fife to the tune of "Yankee Doodle." No matter, the hearts of those patriots leaped with joy ; for they had heard that same drum beat when the charge was led by Washington.

At that time no man read an American book, and no man looked on an American coin. French crowns, Spanish dollars, halves, quarters, and eighths, New York Corporation paper bills, twelve, six, three, two, and one penny, constituted our circulating medium Now we have gold-dust thrown in our eyes, while we are struck to the ground with lumps of pure *yellow*, weighing seven pounds, seven ounces; our copper, silver, and golden eagles are soaring above the clouds; the gold of Ophir is pouring into the lap of the Goddess of Liberty, and American funds are the *safest investment* in the world: we have food for ourselves, and to feed the world, and gather up seven baskets of fragments besides. Therefore, let us be thankful.

CHARLESTON, JULY 5, 1849.

MERCHANTS OF NEW YORK IN 1774–75.

"—— the race of yore—
How they are blotted from the things that be!"

GENTLEMEN: In compliance with the request of your venerable correspondent, "An Old Merchant" (in the Home Journal of the 5th inst.), I inclose the list referred to. I believe it is correct. The other incongruities which he notices in my former epistle, I hope to explain to his satisfaction in my next.

Yours,
GRANT THORBURN.

A LIST OF ALL THE IMPORTING MERCHANTS OF NEW YORK DURING 1774–75—FROM THE CUSTOM-HOUSE BOOKS.

Garnets Abeel, Joseph Blackwell, Samuel James, Robert and George Bonne, Thomas and Walter Buchanan, William Butler, Samuel and John Broome, James Beekman, Joseph Bull, Derick Brinckerhoof, Everet Brancker, Richard Brancker, D. Beekman, Benjamin Booth, Garrett Beekmans, father and son, Henry Brevoort, Gerardus Beekman, Everet Byvanck, Isaac Corsa, Cornelius and Peter Cloper, Peter T. Curtenius, Elias and James Desbrossus, William Downing, Abraham Duryee, Gerardus Dinking, Thomas Ellison, Walter, John, Samuel, James, and Thomas Franklin, Edward Gould, George Folloitt, Gilbert Forbes, E.

Graham, Patrick Gorlet, James Hallet, Nicholas Hofman, Andrew Hammersley, Henry Hydock, Ebenezer Hazard, Jacob Leroy, James Lefferts, Francis Lewis, G. H. Ludlow, W. Ludlow, Isaac Low, Nicholas Low, George Ludlow, Philip Livingston, Edward Laight, Robert Murrey, James Morton, Chas. McEvers, Thomas Moore, Peter Messier, William Nelson, Garret Noel, Jeremiah Platt, Daniel Phœnix, James Parsons, Thomas Pearsall, Lewis Pintard, J. J. Roosevelt, Alexander Robinson & Co., Henry Remsen, Thomas Randall, John Reade, Richard, John, and Samuel Ray, Isaac Sears, Comfort Sands, Christopher Smith, Solomon Simpson, James Seagrove, Oliver Templeton, William W. Stick, Henry Van Vleek, Patrick Vandevoort, Jacob Van Voorhis, Samuel Verplank, Jacobus Van Zant, Anthony Van Dam, John Vanderbelt, Hubert Van Wagner, Henry White, Hugh Wallace, John Watts, Jacob Watson, Alexander Wallace, Richard Yates, Hambelton Young,—103.

All dead—" Man giveth up the ghost, and where is he?" Their sons came to honor, they knew it not; they were brought low, but they perceived it not of them.

Comfort Sands was the last survivor of the above list of Importing Merchants. Mr. Joshua Waddington was the last survivor of the old New York merchants, but his name is not among the list of importers in 1775. Conversing with Mr. Waddington, some twenty years ago, he remarked (if my memory serves me right), that he first saw New York in 1784 or 5; but it matters not when or from whence he came—he was a gentleman in full.

THE FIRST STEAMBOAT.

Cheap Enough.—Soon after the first steamboat was built on Lake Erie, the "Walk in the Water," commanded by Captain Rogers, we took passage in that boat from Buffalo to Detroit. If our recollection is right, the price of passage was then $14, and we heard of no complaint. Now, as we observe by the Detroit Advertiser of the 13th instant, there is a strong opposition between the steamboats running between that city and Buffalo. The "Julia Palmer" left on Tuesday last for Buffalo, with a large number of passengers, charging only twenty-five cents, including berths and board. As a farther inducement for passengers, a band of music was engaged for their amusement. It will be recollected that the distance between Detroit and Buffalo is about three hundred miles.

It may be interesting to some of our subscribers to look back a few years, and see what was said concerning the first successful effort at steam navigation on the Hudson—the commencement of that vast enterprise which has added so largely to the wealth, not only of the United States, but of the whole civilized world. We copy the following from the Picturesque Tourist, a work just published in this city:

Copy of an advertisement taken from the Albany Gazette, dated September, 1807.

The North River steamboat will leave Pauler's Hook ferry (now Jersey City), on Friday, the 4th of September, at 9 in the morning, and arrive at Albany on Saturday, at 9 in the afternoon. Provisions, good berths, and accommodations are provided.

The charge to each passenger is as follows:

To Newburgh, - - -	$3,00.	Time 14 hours.
" Poughkeepsie, - -	4,00.	" 17 "
" Esopus, - - -	5,00.	" 20 "
" Hudson, - - -	5,50.	" 30 "
" Albany, - - -	7,00.	" 36 "

For places apply to Wm. Vandervoort, No. 48 Courtlandt-street, on the corner of Greenwich-street.

September 2, 1807.

Extract from the New York Evening Post, dated Oct. 2, 1807.

Mr. Fulton's new invented steamboat, which is fitted up in a neat style for passengers, and is intended to run from New York to Albany as a packet, left here this morning with ninety passengers, against a strong head wind. Notwithstanding which, it was judged she moved through the water at the rate of six miles an hour.

Extract from the Albany Gazette, dated Oct. 5, 1807.

Friday, Oct. 2, 1807, the steamboat Clermont left New York, at 10 o'clock, A. M., against stormy tide, very rough water, and a violent gale from the North. She made a headway beyond the most sanguine expectations, and without being rocked by the waves.

Arrived at Albany Oct. 4, at 10 o'clock, P. M., being detained by being obliged to come to anchor, owing to a gale, and having one of her paddle-wheels torn away by running foul of a sloop.

NOTE.—It is stated on the authority of Captain E. S. Bunker, that the Clermont, or "experiment boat," as sometimes called, the first steamboat constructed under the direction and superintendence of Robert Fulton, in 1807, was one hundred feet long, twelve feet wide, and seven feet deep. In 1808 she was lengthened to one hundred and fifty feet, widened to eighteen feet, and had her name changed to "North River." The engine was constructed in England, by Watt & Bolton, and brought to New York in December, 1806, by Mr. Fulton. The hull of the boat was constructed by David Brown, an eminent shipbuilder in New York. In August, 1807, the boat was propelled by steam from the East River to the Jersey shore; and on the 2d of October following she started on her first trip to Albany.

Forty years since, Robert Fulton requested of Congress the use of the Hall of the House of Representatives, to deliver an address on the use of steam for propelling boats, but was refused—the assembled wisdom of the nation deeming the idea too absurd for the consideration of reasonable men.

ORIGIN OF THE BATTERY.

"Kapsie Point," pronounced by the old Knickerbockers "Copsy," was the original name of this famous promenade, according to Dunlap and other writers. The old bayside walk, however, was probably where State-street now runs; and the first filling-in was during King William's time, when the half-moon, known as "Leisler's Battery," was constructed. Of this there is the following notice in Sparks' "American Biography:"

"The next act of Leisler was to write a private letter with his own hand to the king, giving him an account of every thing that had been done, describing the present state of affairs and future prospects of the province; stating the repairs he had deemed necessary to commence in the fortification of the city, and detailing the consequent expenditures of the public money that he had found. Among other things, he told the king that, foreseeing the war with France that must ensue from William's accession to the throne of England, he had, for the protection of the army against the enemy's cruisers, erected *a new battery of six guns to the south of the fort.* From that battery, the noble promenade which the city of New York thus incidentally owes to Leisler, derives its name."

FINIS.

www.ingramcontent.com/pod-product-compliance
Lightning Source LLC
LaVergne TN
LVHW020238110826
845151LV00003B/964